The
King
and the
Kingdom of Heaven

THE KING
AND
THE KINGDOM OF HEAVEN

A Study of Matthew

WATCHMAN NEE

Christian Fellowship Publishers, Inc.
New York

ISBN 0-935008-24-1

Available from the Publishers at:

11515 Allecingie Parkway
Richmond, Virginia 23235

TRANSLATOR'S PREFACE

"Rejoice greatly, O daughter of Zion; shout, O daughter of Jerusalem: Behold, thy king cometh unto thee; he is just, and having salvation; lowly, and riding upon an ass, even upon a colt the foal of an ass" (Zech. 9.9 and quoted in Matt. 21.5).

Matthew the first Evangel presents to us Christ as the King, the One who at His first coming some two thousand years ago came incognito in the person of Jesus of Nazareth. The world in general did not and does not know Him, nor will it accept Him; but to those to whom the heavenly Father reveals the Son, this Jesus of Nazareth is the Anointed One of God. And hence the purpose of the King's coming to the world, as is shown by this Evangel, is to gather to himself a people in whom by the Spirit of God He can build a kingdom that is not of this world but which is of heaven.

But Matthew also shows us that the church has been taught to pray, "Thy kingdom come" (6.10), indicating that the King is coming once again! He intends to manifest publicly His kingdom on earth. At the appointed hour the King will indeed return; and then will come true what is told in Revelation, that "the kingdom of the world is become the kingdom of our Lord, and of his Christ: and he shall reign for ever and ever" (11.15).

So that this Evangel perceives the gospel of Jesus Christ in its fullest sense as being the gospel of the King. We will not have a total gospel if we fail to recognize Jesus Christ as King and Lord of our very lives.

Hence in the present volume, Watchman Nee leads us through the Gospel according to Matthew with this one theme in view—Jesus as King. The highlights are found in Matthew chapters 5–7 where the reality (or spiritual principles) of the kingdom of heaven is explained, in chapter 13 where the mysteries (or transient outward appearance) of this same kingdom are interpreted, and in chapters 24–25 where the coming (or final public manifestation) of the heavenly kingdom on earth is expounded.

All who love the appearing of the King of Kings and Lord of Lords are encouraged to read this commentary that they may be better prepared to meet Him. May all be helped by these pages to understand the kingdom of heaven and to place themselves daily under the kingship of Christ Jesus the Lord.

CONTENTS

Translator's Note

During his early ministry in Shanghai, China, Watchman Nee delivered in Chinese a series of detailed Bible readings on Matthew over an extended period of time in the early 1930's. Longhand notes were taken down at the time. These were copied and circulated in mimeograph form but were never published as a book. Today, however, these notes—which have been translated into English for the first time—are now being published and made available in this one volume edition.

In addition, the reader should be aware that in the original Chinese longhand notes the study ended at Matthew 25. Accordingly, the present volume concludes with that chapter.

Scripture quotations are from the
American Standard Version
of the Bible (1901),
unless otherwise indicated.

THE GOSPEL ACCORDING TO MATTHEW

Chapter 1

v.1 "The book of the generation of Jesus Christ, the son of David, the son of Abraham"—The book begins with Jesus Christ, just as the book of Revelation commences with the same Name.

The particular Greek term translated here as "generation" and meaning birth or origin is the Greek word *génesis* and is used only once in the New Testament—here in this verse—and but once in the Old Testament, which according to the Greek translation of the Hebrew Bible known as the Septuagint is found in chapter 5 of Genesis and is in regard to the generation of Adam (when the Lord was on earth, He more than likely read the Septuagint). The one relates to the first Adam, the other relates to the Last Adam. They stand in contrast to each other.

"The Son of David"—The Lord is called by this name nine other times in this book: in 1.20, 9.27, 12.23, 15.22, 20.30–31, 21.9, and 22.42,45.

The period from Adam to the Lord Jesus is altogether 75 generations (see the Gospel according to Luke; Luke records one more name of Cainan as the son of Arphaxad and the father of Shelah).

Why does the book begin not with the son of Adam, of Isaac, or of Jacob, but specifically with the names of David and of Abraham? It indicates that two lines are followed in this book— one is the son of David (the prophetic line), the other is the son of Abraham (the priestly line)—for our Lord is to fulfill both of these functions.

Naturally the son of David is Solomon. To speak of the Lord as the son of David intimates that the Lord is to be as Solomon. In his lifetime Solomon did two things in particular: he uttered words of wisdom and he built the holy temple. But our Lord is greater than Solomon both as a prophet and as a builder. He builds a spiritual temple by sending forth the Holy Spirit.

Now in speaking of the Lord as the son of Abraham the Bible intimates here that He is to be like Isaac. In his own day Isaac also performed two outstanding things, which were his being offered on the altar and his marrying Rebecca who was not a Hebrew. In like manner, our Lord was offered as a sacrifice on the cross and by His death and resurrection He has entered into a marriage union with His church that is formed of the Gentiles as well as the Jews.

The genealogy of a human is usually traced back from the sons to the fathers. But the genealogy of a king comes down from the fathers. Hence in the genealogy given by Luke the pedigree is retraced backward while that given by Matthew proceeds forward from the ancestry.

vv.2–6 The purpose of mentioning these four women is to cause us to see that the Lord has His relationship not only with the Jews but also with the Gentiles (cf. Eph. 3.6).

The Lord Jesus comes not to call the righteous but to be the savior of all mankind.

The Old Testament never registers a woman in any genealogy, especially a foreign woman. Yet the four listed here are not only women but are even Gentile sinners: Tamar was daughter-in-law to Judah and she committed the sin of incest. Rahab was a harlot. Ruth was a Moabitess who belonged to a nation which was forbidden to enter the assembly of the Lord even to the tenth generation (see Deut. 23.3). And Bathsheba's name was not mentioned; instead, she was known as the wife of Uriah the Hittite—showing what kind of woman she was (see 2 Sam. 11.3).

According to the manner of the Bible, the man is always used to signify objective truth whereas the woman is used to signify subjective experience. For example, Solomon and the Shulammite woman in the Song of Solomon.

Although this chapter includes the names of fourteen kings, only David bears the title of "king", for he is a man after God's own heart.

vv.7–9 Compare these verses with 1 Chronicles 3.11–12. The names of Ahaziah (2 Chron. 22.2,9), Joash (2 Chron. 24.24) and Amaziah (2 Chron. 25.14–16,27) are recorded in 1 Chronicles but are missing in Matthew. The reasons are: (1) being born of Jezebel, (2) being wicked, and (3) dying an unnatural death. God will visit the iniquity of the fathers upon the children, even to the third and the fourth generation (see Ex. 20.5). These men are unfit to be kings, therefore Matthew omits their names.

vv.10–12 Again compare with 1 Chronicles 3.15–19. The name of Jehoiakim is missing in Matthew. This is due to the fact that Jehoiakim was made king by Pharaoh of Egypt, not by God. Furthermore, he tried to please the king of Egypt by heavily taxing the people (see 2 Chron. 36.3–4). Hence his name is deleted from the genealogy of the kings.

"Shealtiel begat Zerubbabel"—Shealtiel probably died early, so his brother married his wife in order to raise up seed after him according to the custom of those days; or else Pedaiah might have just let his son Zerubbabel be named after his brother (cf. 1 Chron. 3.17,18).

Also, compare Matthew 1.12 with Jeremiah 22.24–30: "Jechoniah begat Shealtiel"; yet Jeremiah prophesied that this man would be reckoned as childless, "for no more shall a man of his seed prosper, sitting upon the throne of David, and ruling in Judah" (Jer. 22.30). Joseph came from Jechoniah, but our

Lord was not Joseph's son. How marvelous is the way God works!

vv.13–16 In verse 16 the lineage suddenly turns to read: "of Mary, of whom was born Jesus, who is called Christ"—and thus the difficulty mentioned above is wonderfully solved.

v.17 "Forty-two" (3 times 14) is the Biblical number signifying the experiencing of sufferings. It is different from the number "40" in that 40 signifies only trial, without necessarily involving great suffering. After 42 there will be rest. The book of Revelation mentions 42 months; the book of Numbers records 42 stations. The 43rd station will be Canaan, the Promised Land. As soon as the 42nd passes, Christ our Promised Land shall come; and with Him there will be eternal rest.

Three times 14 generations make up 42 generations. Yet counting the enumeration in chapter 1, there are only 41 generations; but because David is counted twice (he concludes the first 14 generations and at the same time he commences the second 14 generations), the number still totals 42.

vv.18–19 "Joseph, . . . being a righteous man"—Righteous in the sense of being just, according to which attitude such a woman as she appeared to be to Joseph must be dealt with; righteous in the sense of being kindly disposed, according to which feeling he did not wish to disgrace her publicly. Hence he was thinking of putting her away privately. And thus the two facets of righteousness were altogether present.

v.20 "But when he thought on these things"—By thinking on these things he gave God opportunity to speak and to guide him.

v.21 "Jesus" in Greek is equivalent to "Joshua" in

Hebrew. It means "Jehovah is salvation" or "Jehovah is the Savior".

v.23 "Immanuel" means "God with us"—Hebrew names which end with "el" contain the name of God in them, such as Daniel, Israel, Eli, and so forth.

King David is a type of the Lord Jesus as King in the following respects: (1) the king set up by God, (2) the warrior-king, and (3) the king rejected by men.

THE GOSPEL ACCORDING TO MATTHEW

Chapter 2

The Conspiracy of Herod, 2.1–12

v.1 Herod was an Idumaean, an Edomite, a descendant of Esau (see Mark. 3.8). He was a Roman tetrarch.

Bethlehem (see Gen. 35.19, 1 Chron. 4.4). Luke 2.1–2 records the first enrollment made. Politically it was done by the order of Caesar, but we are given to see how God had the prophecy of the Scriptures fulfilled, for Joseph resided at that time in Nazareth. "The king's heart is in the hand of Jehovah as the watercourses: he turneth it whithersoever he will" (Prov. 21.1). Had the time of enrollment been a little earlier, the report would have been finished and Joseph and his wife would have returned to Nazareth. Or had the enrollment been taken a little later, Mary might have given birth to the child on the way. But the timing was just perfect.

"Wise men"—The Magi, who belonged to a sacred caste, like the "Sadhu" holy men in India.

"The east"—The Bible does not specify the region of the East. It merely indicates that it was east of Jerusalem, east of Judea.

v.2 "Where is he that is born King of the Jews?"—This may appear to seem as though the Lord Jesus was only for the Jews. Yet the very first people who sought the Lord were Gentiles. And it was through the mouths of the Gentiles that Jesus was entitled the King of the Jews. From this we may conclude that the work to be done by the Lord Jesus is for the Gentiles as well as for the Jews.

"His star"—How did the wise men of the East know about the birth of Christ? The Bible does not explain explicitly; nevertheless, there are certain hints given about it. It will be recalled that God raised up prophets among the Gentiles, Balaam being one of them. He ranked among four of the Old Testament prophets who prophesied most about the Lord Jesus (see Num. 24.17). These prophecies were no doubt quite prevalent in the East. Perhaps these wise men from the East had also read the prophecies of Daniel (see Dan. 9.24–25). During his captivity in Babylon, Daniel spoke of the seventy sevens which were related to the Messiah.

"To worship"—The Greek word denotes an act of reverence whether paid to a creature (see 4.9 mg., 18.26 mg.) or to the Creator (see 4.10 mg.).

v.3 Herod himself might have reason to be troubled, but for all Jerusalem to be troubled with him was rather strange. The period from the time of Malachi to the present moment was approximately 430 years. During this period the Jews suffered greatly. They naturally were expecting the coming of the Messiah. So that when they heard the news of the birth of the King of the Jews, they ought to have been joyous, yet they were troubled instead. This could be for no other reason than that they did not really care for the Savior. (Let Christians who are expecting the second coming of the Lord and the rapture take warning from this.)

In verse 3 Herod is seen as troubled in heart (a motive arises); in verse 7 we learn that he secretly inquired about the time (a plot develops); and by verse 16 we are told that he slew all the male children in Bethlehem and vicinity who were from two years old and under (an action taken).

vv.4–6 The prophecy of the Scripture is one thing, but the revelation of the Holy Spirit is another. There is teaching, and there is revelation. Added to the words of the prophets must be the unveiling of the star in heaven. The knowledge of the Bible needs to be accompanied by the revelation of God.

If people are not hungry, God will not give revelation. The wise men of the East were perhaps those who waited upon and pursued after God. If all we have is only dead knowledge we will be like the Pharisees. Though we may know the word of the Bible, we do not see the light in heaven. The word of the Bible indeed gave them the details about the Savior; but the appearing of the star in heaven caused them to realize the presence of the Savior! Both the star in heaven and the prophecy of Micah (see Micah 5.2) were necessary.

Conditions for receiving God's revelation are (1) wait, and (2) desire.

The unquoted part of Micah 5.2 is, "whose goings forth are from old, from everlasting"; this shows that the One who is to be born in Bethlehem is none other than God. Nevertheless, when our Lord said, "Before Abraham was born, I am" (John 8.58), the Jews took up stones to cast at Him; for they would not acknowledge Him as God.

v.7 "Privily"—Things done secretly are not necessarily wrong, but they can easily drift into darkness. Christians may have privacy but not darkness.

"Learn . . . exactly"—Herod inquired exactly the time the star appeared. By then it was over a year, the evidence of which will be presented below.

v.8 Herod's intention was not to worship but to kill the Christ.

v.9 None of the scribes and Pharisees followed the wise

men in their pursuit of Christ. The wise men sought from the East until their arrival at Bethlehem, yet none others would go from Jerusalem to Bethlehem. This betrays the fact that while the Gentiles sought after the Lord, the Jews rejected Him. We must seek to know the power of God as well as to understand the Scriptures. Andrew Murray once said how pathetic is much knowledge of the Scripture stored in a carnal mind.

"The star, which they saw in the east"—This was the same star which they had seen at first. If we wish to be assured of God's guidance, there should be the appearing of the star the second time after its first emergence. This is a spiritual principle. The second showing of the star verifies the accuracy of its first appearance.

God said to Abram: "Unto the land that I will show thee" (Gen. 12.1). If after the first step was taken there was no confirmation with the second word from God, this first step might be our own error. The revelation that follows a revelation proves the correctness of the earlier step. The verifying of a revelation with another revelation is a divine principle continually to be remembered.

v.10 "And when they saw . . . they rejoiced with exceeding great joy"—Yet all Jerusalem was troubled when they heard the good news. Our attitude towards the Lord reveals the condition of our spiritual life.

Love is the characteristic of Christ. A Christian not only believes but also loves the Lord. He who believes and yet is not inwardly moved by the love of Christ is unfit to be a disciple.

v.11 "The young child"—Not a baby. This indicates that some time had already elapsed.

Due to inconvenient transportation it took time for the wise men to travel from the East to make inquiry at Jerusalem. Herod asked concerning the exact time the star appeared and he subsequently killed all the male childen from two years old and under.

Matthew 2.8 says "young child" whereas Luke 2.12,16 says "babe"; Matthew 2.11 mentions "house" while Luke 2.12,16 mentions "manger"—the young child was no longer a babe and the house was not a manger. All these serve as evidences that when the wise men came to see Jesus it was not at the time He was newly born. The house mentioned here was probably rented by Joseph.

The wise men came to worship Jesus in the house. Such action demonstrated that Jesus is King. In the Gospel according to Mark the birth of Christ is not recorded because there He is presented as the servant. The Gospel according to Luke exhibits the Lord as man, and therefore it narrates fully His birth, His being laid in a manger, and His being visited by commoners— even the shepherds. The Gospel according to John shows forth Christ as God, and for this reason, instead of giving the story of His birth, it declares: "And the Word became flesh" (1.14).

"Gold" signifies divine nature, "frankincense" stands for delight, and "myrrh" is a substance used for the dead.

Isaiah mentions only gold and frankincense (60.6) because this Old Testament prophet speaks of the Lord as King in the millennial kingdom. There is, therefore, no need that myrrh be mentioned, since it is for the dead. But the wise men here also offered myrrh, for on this occasion the Lord is to go through death.

The gold was given to provide traveling expenses to Joseph for fleeing with his family. How marvelous is the work of God!

v.12 Those who have seen the Lord cannot go back to see Herod.

The Escape of Jesus, 2.13–23

v.13 "Until I tell thee"—God leads step by step.

v.14 "By night"—On that very same night.

v.15 God did not perform a miracle to save His Son, instead He required His Son to flee. Not long after His birth our Lord had to flee for His life. He never put up any resistance: "But when they persecute you in this city, flee into the next" (Matt. 10.23), so says the Lord Jesus to the Christians who are to undergo persecution.

"Out of Egypt did I call my son"—God had thus spoken to the children of Israel. When Israel could not stand any more persecution in Egypt, she was to flee. Isaiah 49.3 tells us how the Lord is identified with Israel. It seems as if He is the last Israelite, for He includes all the Israelites in himself. For their wickedness, He is to go to the cross.

vv.16–18 Jeremiah 31.15 is being quoted here.

Rachel was buried at Bethlehem. For her to weep and to cry out from the grave for her children was descriptive of the lamentation for the many children in Bethlehem killed by Herod. Ramah is about two hundred yards from Bethlehem.

v.19 What is man? He is finished after he dies. He who caused other people to die died himself. God performed no miracle to keep His Son from fleeing, He instead called His Son out of Egypt.

v.20 "Into the land of Israel"—The Lord was still an Israelite.

v.21 Joseph obeyed the leading of God. As he obeyed, he would receive the next direction for his steps.

v.22 We need to exercise common sense in the midst of God's guidance. God only charged Joseph to go back to the land of Israel; He had not told him where in the land he should reside. Had Joseph gone to Jerusalem he would have had trouble. His common sense stopped him, thus giving God an opportunity to lead him.

"Galilee"—According to Matthew 4.15, it is called "Galilee of the Gentiles": it was jointly inhabited by Jews and Gentiles.

v.23 "Through the prophets"—Yet none of the prophets in the Bible prophesied that the Messiah would be a Nazarene. "Can any good thing come out of Nazareth?" (John 1.46) Hence calling our Lord a Nazarene simply meant that He was despised and not esteemed. About this fact all the prophets had indeed predicted concerning Him (see Is. 53.2–3, Ps. 22.6).

Addenda to Chapter 2

1. The Old Testament Scriptures are quoted five times in chapters 1 and 2. And they are fulfilled in three different ways:

(a) "That it might be fulfilled" (2.15)—Being of similar situation.

(b) "Then was fulfilled" (2.17)—Being literally fulfilled.

(c) "That should be fulfilled" (2.23 Darby)—Being symbolically fulfilled in teaching.

2. Concerning God's guidance, this chapter mentions the following factors: (a) the knowledge of the Scriptures, (b) the revelation from heaven, (c) the common sense of man, and (d) faith, waiting, and obedience.

3. Joseph had great faith because: (a) it is against natural law that a virgin should conceive, yet he could believe it (1.24); (b) Jesus the Son of God must flee for His life (2.14), but Joseph still believed; and (c) he returned to the land of Israel in obedience to God's command (2.21).

4. Herod was troubled (2.3), inquired exactly the time out of his pretension to go later to worship (2.7), and murdered all the little children in Bethlehem (2.16). He was like Satan, who disguises himself as an angel of light.

5. The wise men had (a) the knowledge of the Scriptures, (b) a seeking and waiting attitude, (c) the revelation of the Holy Spirit, (d) an expression of extreme respect, and (e) an obedience toward God as evidenced by their not returning to Herod.

6. The ways of God are higher than the ways of men.

7. The wise men worshiped only the young child (2.11), not the child's mother. This is something worth noticing.

THE GOSPEL ACCORDING TO MATTHEW

Chapter 3

As we turn now to chapter 3, a problem may arise immediately, for there are so many different views about the kingdom of heaven. In studying God's word it is necessary for us to rid ourselves of any preconceived idea or prejudice. Paul says that a Christian has the danger of being "tossed to and fro and carried about with every wind of doctrine" (Eph. 4.14), and his expression "foolish" in Galatians 3.1 actually means "senseless". We ought not approach God's word with our own presupposition, nor should we simply follow the opinions of men. Our Lord has promised that the kingdom would be revealed to babes (Matt. 11.25).

John Preaches Repentance, 3.1–12

v.1 John the Baptist commences his work. Does the beginning of his work shown here in this verse mark the beginning of the gospel age? When does the dispensation of the gospel begin? In order to know its commencement, we need first to determine when the dispensation of law comes to an end. If in fact the gospel age begins with the work of John, then what he preaches has much to do with us; otherwise there will be no direct relationship.

Now some people maintain that the dispensation of law ends at the cross. If so, the gospel age commences after the cross.

"Christ is the end of the law unto righteousness to every one that believeth" (Rom. 10.4). This cannot be quoted as evidence for the conclusion of the dispensation of law at the cross. For what is said here concerns the *demand* of the law, not its dispensation.

The basis for accepting the work of John as the beginning of the gospel age is as follows:

(1) Matthew 11.13 states that "all the prophets and the law prophesied until John" and Luke 16.16 declares that "the law and the prophets were until John: from that time the gospel of the kingdom of God is preached, and every man entereth violently into it"—and so the law and the prophets come to an end at the appearing of John; that is to say, at the beginning of his work, not at his death. Even though John himself belongs to the dispensation of law, what he preaches is grace and not law.

(2) "The word which he sent unto the children of Israel, preaching good tidings of peace by Jesus Christ (he is Lord of all)—that saying ye yourselves know, which was published throughout all Judaea, beginning from Galilee, after the baptism which John preached" (Acts 10.36–37). What John preached prepared the way for the preaching of the glad tidings of peace by our Lord Jesus.

(3) "When John had first preached before his coming the baptism of repentance to all the people of Israel. . . . To us is the word of this salvation sent forth" (Acts 13.23–26). The preaching by John of repentance is the word of this salvation.

(4) "The beginning of the gospel of Jesus Christ, the Son of God" (Mark 1.1). And the gospel begins with the preaching of John the Baptist.

(5) The "today" in Luke 4.21 shows that the gospel age is here (since verses 18 and 19 of Luke 4 give the essence of the gospel). Thus, by the time our Lord spoke these words the gospel age had already been ushered in.

(6) "But the hour cometh, and now is . . ." (John 4.23) in-

dicates that when the Lord uttered these words, the gospel age is already present.

(7) "The hour cometh, and now is, when the dead shall hear the voice of the Son of God . . ." (John 5.25). The time when the dead hear the things of the gospel age is now here.

G. H. Pember once commented on John 4.23 and 5.25 by saying that the word "hour" there is used in the Greek to stand for "age" or "dispensation", and hence another age arrives after the dispensation of law.

A few different views concerning the commencement of the gospel age are that it:

(1) begins with the time when John started his work;

(2) begins at the hour of the crucifixion of the Lord;

(3) begins with the descending of the Holy Spirit at Pentecost;

(4) begins with Stephen (Acts 7), for Acts 3.21 tells us that the Lord was waiting for the children of Israel to repent while Acts 7.56 reveals that in Stephen's vision the Son of man was now standing at the right hand of God because the Jews had rejected Him, and henceforth, the gospel was to be preached to the Gentiles;

(5) begins after the time of Acts 28, for then the gospel is to be preached wholly to the Gentiles; and,

(6) begins with the development of the church at Ephesus, because at that time the mystery of God was revealed to the apostles: Proponents of this view reject baptism and the breaking of bread, for they consider them as belonging to the Jews—They believe everything is predestinated and heavenly—They need only the three books of Ephesians, Philippians and Colossians.

What sort of work is the work of John? According to Matthew 3.3, John is doing preparatory work. Even though the gospel age has already begun, John's work is still preparatory in nature.

To what does "the kingdom of heaven" in 3.2 refer? Does it

mean the Messiah's kingdom which the Jews are expecting, such as was prophesied by Daniel, Ezekiel, and others?

According to C. I. Scofield, the kingdom of heaven is defined as the time during which Messiah will rule on earth, being the restoration of the throne of David. Is this scriptural? Do both John and the Lord specify at the outset that Christ comes to establish the kingdom? Scofield goes on to say that if the Lord had not been rejected by the children of Israel while He was on earth, He would have established His kingdom on earth.

"The kingdom of heaven is at hand"—John, the Lord Jesus, and Jesus' disciples all preach the same message. We find that this theme is developed in the following manner:

Matthew 1–4	The preparation of the coming of the King
Matthew 5–7	The law of the kingdom of heaven
Matthew 8–9	The Lord heals
Matthew 11–12	The Lord is rejected
Matthew 13	The mysteries of the kingdom of heaven

Some interpreters adhere to "the postponement theory" of the kingdom, which holds that due to Christ's rejection by Israel the Messianic kingdom is postponed to the millennium, and thus it today becomes a kingdom shrouded in mystery. However, if Christ really came to establish His Messianic kingdom, would the Jews have had any reason to reject Him? Does not John 6.15 tell us how they tried to compel Him to be king? Should the Lord have indeed come the first time with the purpose of setting up the Messianic kingdom, He would no doubt have come to *reign* and not to die.

If the kingdom of heaven is in fact the Messianic kingdom, then the cross would have been a matter of expediency. In other words, salvation through the cross is improvised after the kingdom is postponed because of its rejection by the Jews. Yet the death of Christ is something predetermined by God even before the foundation of the world. Through the prophets the Holy Spirit "testified beforehand the sufferings of Christ, and the glories that should follow them" (1 Peter 1.11). The Lord himself declared: "Behooved it not the Christ to suffer these things, and to enter into his glory?" (Luke 24.26)

Both the first and the second chapters of Matthew show us that our Lord has a relationship not only with the Jews but also with the Gentiles. (Let it be pointed out here that during the millennium there will be two aspects: one is the kingdom of heaven and the other is the Messianic kingdom. The kingdom of heaven sets forth the relationship of the Lord with believers; it is spiritual in nature. The messianic kingdom describes the relationship of the Lord with the Jews; it is physical in character.)

Does Matthew 3.2 really speak of the kingdom of heaven as the Messianic kingdom? John set out in his preaching with the call to "Repent" (v.2). This is the very first work in connection with the kingdom of heaven, revealing thereby that the kingdom of heaven is not something physical, but spiritual and heavenly in character. So far as the Messianic kingdom is concerned it is to rule the nations with an iron rod, so that this matter of repentance is out of the question. It too will come in power and great glory.

3.3 mentions making ready the way of the Lord and straightening His path. This means preparing the heart of the people to turn to the Lord.

3.4–12 are words spoken by John. Naturally, these words are related to the theme of "the kingdom of heaven is at hand"; and from this passage we may learn the nature of the kingdom of heaven:

(1) that it has nothing to do with the Jews: "Think not to say within yourselves, We have Abraham to our father . . ." (v.9);

(2) that it must serve as a way to flee from the wrath to come (v.7);

(3) that it requires holy and righteous works (v.8);

(4) that whoever is not rightly related to the kingdom of heaven shall be cast into the fire (v.10);

(5) that John baptizes in order to cause the people to believe in the One who is to come (v.11); and

(6) that there is a relationship between Christ and the kingdom of heaven, which is: (a) that the beginning of the kingdom of heaven comes in by His baptizing with the Holy Spirit, and (b) that the end of the kingdom of heaven comes in by His baptizing with the fire (3.11–12).

There is a basic argument that can be given as to why the kingdom of heaven and the Messianic kingdom are greatly different: In Matthew 13.11 it is said that the kingdom of heaven is a mystery which was unknown by men but is now being revealed; moreover, 13.35 goes on to say about this kingdom that there are "utter things hidden from the foundation of the world" —all this showing that before its revelation no one knew anything about it. The Messianic kingdom, on the other hand, was known to Balaam, Isaiah, David, and the other prophets.

When does the kingdom of heaven begin? It begins with the sowing of wheat seed (Matt. 13.3), and thus the kingdom of heaven is parallel to this dispensation.

The passage found in Matthew 16.13–19 tells us that the Lord Jesus will build His church "upon this rock"—that is to say, upon the confession of Peter with respect to Him. In this same passage, "keys" in the phrase "the keys of the kingdom of heaven" is plural in number, and they are obviously used to open doors. Peter used these keys to open doors both on the day of Pentecost and in the house of Cornelius so as to bring in both the Jews and the Gentiles. And hence it can rightly be said that the church begins simultaneously with the kingdom of heaven.

The church is the believers' position, whereas the kingdom of heaven is their responsibility. The contrast between the two can be simply outlined as follows:

The Church	The kingdom of heaven
Related to the Lord	Related to men
Pertains to the giving of life	Pertains to the receiving of disciples
Speaks of position and grace	Speaks of responsibility

In conclusion, we ascertain that the nature of the work of John the Baptist belongs to grace. The messages he preaches concerning Christ are:

(1) "The Lamb of God" (John 1.29), and

(2) "He shall baptize you in the Holy Spirit and in fire" (Matt. 3.11).

According to the prophecy of John's father Zacharias (Luke 1.67–79), what John will do will be "to give knowledge of salvation unto his people in the remission of their sins" (v.77). John is to (1) call people to repent and (2) cause them to be baptized; while the Lord Jesus is to (1) bear our sins and (2) baptize with the Holy Spirit and with fire.

A call for people to "repent" automatically places them in the category of sinners. Repentance is linked to confession, because as soon as a person realizes his place as a sinner he will naturally confess his sins.

And to be "baptized" is to signify death and resurrection. In baptizing people John in effect is telling them how they ought to die and to be raised from the dead. He exhorts them to believe in the One who is to come. So then, the work of John is for the preaching of the gospel and not for the Messianic kingdom. He only mentions "kingdom" once as recorded in Matthew 3.2, and even in that instance he has not said that the Lord shall be King. He only asserts that the Lord shall be as the Dayspring from on high, as the Bridegroom, as the Lanb of God, and as the One who shall baptize with the Holy Spirit. For the Lord to be the Lamb and for Him to baptize with the Holy Spirit, He must die and be resurrected.

In the story of Acts 11 Peter recognizes that the gospel begins with John the Baptist (v.16), and in the record of Acts 13 Paul acknowledges the same thing (v.24). Apollos began to speak and teach correctly the things concerning Jesus, knowing though only the baptism of John. Accordingly, Priscilla and Aquila came to his aid, expounding to him the way of the Lord more accurately (see Acts 18.24–28).

John aimed for people to believe in the One who should come after Him (Acts 19.4). He preached the gospel before Christ died on the cross. And hence, after Christ had accomplished the work of redemption, John's mission was viewed as having been fulfilled.

Neither Peter nor Paul, who come after John, ever subvert his work.

The people mentioned in Luke 3.7–10 who came to John were repentant, desiring to flee from the wrath to come; therefore, John told them what they should do (see Luke 3.11–14).

In the four Gospel accounts John is the only one mentioned who in effect preached that Christ died as our substitute (see John 1.29).

The emphasis of John's work is different from that of our Lord's work. John stresses repentance, because he is sent to prepare the way of the Lord. For this reason he stands in a different position from that of the Lord with respect to the world.

John makes the wilderness his home, whereas the Lord accepts the city as His inn.

John comes to make people weep, but the Lord comes to make them dance.

John causes people to weep, as though he were wearing sackcloth; the Lord, however, causes people to dance, as though He were supplying the music. A complete salvation is first to weep and then to dance. In other words, repentance plus belief.

Unlike Jesus, John stands on a ground which condemns the world.

John begins his preaching in the wilderness of Judea because salvation comes from the Jews.

v.2 "The kingdom of heaven is at hand"—Since this is a fact, repentance is imperative. It does not say if you repent the kingdom of heaven will then draw nigh.

The word "heaven" is plural in the original. It is really "the kingdom of the heavens" in the verse. Why is it the kingdom of the heavens (plural), and not the kingdom of heaven (singular)? Let us see that when the word "heaven" is mentioned, people most often think of it in terms of location—that is to say, in heaven as a place; but "the kingdom of the heavens" is a phrase that conjures up the thought of authority and dominion, as for example when Daniel once declared that "the heavens do rule" (4.26). For we must note that before Christ died, and Satan being in the air, there never was any kingdom on earth that was under the rule of the heavens. The kingdom that is now being brought in by God is alone distinct from all the kingdoms on earth, in that it is a spiritual kingdom capable of communing with God.

v.3 Although John the Baptist is a prophet, he did not prophesy much. Although he is the greatest of all the prophets, he does not parade his greatness, he is merely a "voice" instead.

Why does Luke (in 3.4–6) quote more from Isaiah than does Matthew (in 3.3)? Because Matthew writes to the Jews he cites only that which is directly related to the Jews, whereas Luke in presenting the same Jesus repeats more of the prophetic utterances which have bearing on the Gentiles.

v.4 As his message is centered on repentance, so he stands on a ground opposite from the world. Both his eating and his clothing are different from that of the world.

Today's Christians are not required to imitate John in this respect, for the Lord himself is not different from the people in this relationship (see Matt. 11.19). This does not suggest, however, that Christians should be conformed to the world.

vv.5–6 Such baptism is unknown to the Old Testament. What Hebrews 6.2 says "of the teaching of baptisms" relates to the Old Testament teaching on washings.

The baptism of John is aimed at leading people to believe on the One who is coming after him.

Since baptism is a personal act, so confession too is a personal act. Matthew 3.6 cannot be used as argument for public confession.

v.7 The Pharisees are self-styled fundamentalists and the Sadducees are agnostics and modernists.

"Offspring of vipers"—Both the self-styled fundamentalists and the modernists end up in the same hell.

Such self-styled fundamentalists believe only in the creed and do not know the power of God. They hurt the church as much as do the modernists, for they are not only old but also dead. How undependable it is to trust in this kind of fundamentalism.

v.8 speaks of the fruit worthy of repentance.

v.9 The approaching of the kingdom of heaven is not something mechanically related to the children of Abraham. What is necessary is repentance, because repentance is associated with the kingdom of heaven.

v.10 This is a test. What is required is not simply a certain kind of behavior, but such a behavior as is worthy of repentance.

v.11 Three different kinds of baptisms are mentioned in this one verse: (1) water baptism, (2) Spirit baptism, and (3) fire baptism. The fire here points to hell-fire.

"Baptize you in the Holy Spirit and in fire"—The word "and" is a coordinate conjunction which shows a comparison in the things connected. Since the Holy Spirit is literal, the fire must also be literal. At that time those who stood before John the Baptist were of two classes; one had a real desire for the Lord and one had no desire for the Lord. The baptism of John will not differentiate them but the Holy Spirit and the fire will.

Some may take the word "fire" here as referring to the tongues of fire on the day of Pentecost. But this is unlikely, for it would constitute a vain repetition of thought if 3.11 in this case were now to read: "baptize you in the Holy Spirit and in the Holy Spirit"! "Fire" is mentioned three times in 3.10, 11 and 12. Since both the first and the third instances of fire refer to hell-fire, how can the middle reference to it mean something else? Such being the case, it seems that the kingdom of heaven commences with the Lord baptising people in the Holy Spirit and concludes with the Lord baptising people in fire (cf. 2 Thess. 1.7–8).

v.12 Here, people are divided into wheat and chaff.

"Threshing-floor"—This is usually a raised or elevated ground. After the ox has trodden the corn (1 Cor. 9.9) the farmer uses a winnowing fork to clean the floor.

A "garner" is not built in the field; it usually is located near the house. The field represents the world. Harvest in the Scriptures almost always points to rapture or sometimes resurrection.

Jesus Is Baptized, 3.13–17

v.13 John the Evangelist does not record the baptism of our Lord, for in his Gospel Jesus is presented as God; but the other three Evangelists do report His baptism.

v.14 Only Matthew records these words—"but John would have hindered him"—because Matthew presents Jesus as King.

v.15 To what does "all righteousness" refer? When a

person enters the water he acknowledges that he is a sinner who needs to be baptized. The river Jordan represents the water of judgment. In stepping into the water the sinner admits the justness of such judgment. The Lord does it in order to save us. He fulfills God's righteousness by His death and resurrection so that sinners might be saved.

In the word "us" the Lord includes all the believers in Him.

Why should the Lord commence His work by being baptized? This causes us to see that at the very outset of His work the Lord stands on the ground of death and resurrection. Even though He does not die and is not raised from the dead until He has labored three and a half years, He wants us to know that all His works on earth are done on the basis of death and resurrection. He therefore receives baptism as a sign. So far as redemption is concerned, it is a work of death and resurrection. And such work also is done on the ground of death and resurrection. This is the principle of all spiritual works. All three aspects of self, namely (1) opinion, (2) power, and (3) glory must be delivered to death.

v.16 "Went up straightway from the water" proves that baptism is by immersion.

"Lo, the heavens were opened"—This is in line with the kindgom of heaven. As soon as the heavens are opened, the Spirit of God descends. All this indicates the meaning of the kingdom of heaven. It is none other than the communion of God and men. The Lord's death and resurrection opens the heavens. The heavens can only be opened on such basis. This death and resurrection is factual, therefore it only needs to be believed. But it also is a principle, hence it demands obedience as well.

"The Spirit of God descending as a dove"—When the Bible mentions the dove it is laying stress not only on the harmless character of Christ but also the fact that He is single-eyed, for a dove can only see one thing at a time. The Holy Spirit comes upon the Lord to give Him power to do one thing in His whole life before God—which is, to do God's will.

v.17 This is a testimony from God. God so testifies in order to show (1) that the Lord has indeed taken this way of death and resurrection, and (2) that what the Lord does is truly for the sake of righteousness. (It should be noted that during this time all people were being baptized for their own sins and therefore heaven was silent. The Lord alone was baptized for righteousness' sake, and hence heaven testified.)

THE GOSPEL ACCORDING TO MATTHEW

Chapter 4

Having received the testimony of God (3.17), there is no need for the Lord to prove himself (4.3).

The failure of Adam was in his not doing what God had ordered; the victory of Christ Jesus is in not doing that which God had not ordered.

This chapter deals with two important events: (1) the Lord suffers temptation (4.1–11), and (2) the Lord calls four disciples (4.12–25).

The temptation in this chapter follows immediately upon baptism. Why should baptism incite temptation? Because baptism means not only death but also resurrection. And by resurrection He is "declared to be the Son of God with power" (Rom. 1.4).

The resurrection of Lazarus is only a return to physical life. The Lord's resurrection is reckoned as firstfruits. In resurrection He is declared to be the Son of God. This is why Satan cannot but challenge Him.

This temptation is parallel to the temptation in the garden of Eden. After Adam was awakened out of his sleep he was tempted. Likewise, too, was the Lord tempted.

From Adam to Christ is approximately 4,000 years. Within these 40 centuries no one was able to claim himself to be the Son of God. But today a voice comes out of heaven, saying, "This is my beloved Son." Satan is therefore stirred to wage war against Him. As a matter of fact, Satan never lets any child of God go easily; he always attacks him. Sin, the world, and environment seem to be all at odds with God's children. Yet Christ is our forerunner.

Since Jesus proves himself to be the Son of God by going through great temptations, can we who belong to Him be exceptions? The first and foremost matter in the work of Christ is to prove himself to be the Son of God. Consequently, the beginning of the church is a confessing of Christ as the Son of God.

(Once someone was teaching the Gospel according to Mark. When it came to the place where the Lord asked His disciples, "But who say ye that I am?", a sinner who had never before exhibited any interest in the Lord suddenly repented and wept and confessed Jesus Christ as his Savior; for the purpose of the Gospel narratives is to lead people to such confession.)

As a point of principle, victory in work is not by fighting to victory but by standing firm on the right ground.

Henceforth, the Lord needs only to declare His victory over the enemy. For this reason the disciples whom He sends out can cast out demons in His Name.

Evan Roberts once said: Everything will be all right if Christians know how to stand firmly on the right ground.

The Lord Suffers Temptation, 4.1–11

v.1 After the Lord has received the witness from God that He is the Son of God, the first thing He encounters is not victory but temptation—which is battle.

v.2 The number "forty" always speaks of a period of temptation. This is the proper verse for fasting. Our Lord does not hunger for 40 days and 40 nights, rather He fasts for that period of time. What is a fast? Due to an excessively heavy burden in the spirit, one is unable to eat. The spiritual conflict is so intense that the body does not feel the need for food even though he naturally *should* be hungry. The Lord does not feel hungry while fasting, but instead He feels hungry only after He has fasted for the 40 days and 40 nights.

In the garden of Eden it was a case of lusting for more even after being filled with the fruits of the other trees. Here, however, it is a case of fasting by the denial of a legitimate need. If we cannot gain the victory in the matter of eating and drinking, how can we possibly overcome in other things? (see Phil. 3.19, Heb. 13.9) Food is for nourishment, not for pleasure. He who serves his own belly does not buffet his body. And in that event God can do very little with him.

v.3 This verse mentions the tempter, who is pointed out later as being the devil. In Genesis 3 he is called the serpent.

When the Lord was baptized the voice out of heaven said, "This is my beloved Son": but Satan stubbornly refused to accept the fact: instead he continuously probed to see if this One were indeed the Son of God. How significantly related is this event to Hades! For please note that the first part of Matthew 16.18 records Jesus as saying, "Upon this rock I will build . . .", whereas in the latter part he says, "And the gates of Hades . . ." What Satan with all his power cannot shake is the Son of God. If we stand on this testimony, we too shall overcome.

The Lord always is the Son of God. After baptism He is declared to be just such a One. And thereafter He refuses to be provoked to prove again who He is. For Him, the testimony of God is sufficient. And we too need God's testimony, not man's explanation.

The Lord declines to do anything without God's command. What God has not ordered, that He cannot do. Even though He is hungry and it is legitimate for Him to turn stone to bread, He will not do it.

In the garden of Eden man did what God had said "no" to. Here the Lord does not do what God has not ordered. We too, therefore, must obey God and do what He has commanded; but we must never act presumptuously without God's command. We should never walk ahead of Him.

Presumptuousness is just as sinful as rebellion. Moses was barred from Canaan, not because of doing less but because of doing a little more than what was commanded of him by God. Both the doing and the not doing of our Lord are miracles.

Using up all one's power is according to human nature, expecting thereby to derive glory from it. Reserving strength, on the other hand, is the nature of God.

Satan speculates that even though Jesus is the Son of God, if He acts outside of the Father's will by turning stone into bread, He will be finished.

v.4 "But"—The Lord's answer is exactly opposite to Satan's query. Satan takes one line, but the Lord adopts another line of thought to oppose him. "It is written" is one of His battle weapons. When temptation comes, resisting will not only help to hold ground but will also usually cause the devil to flee. But there are occasions when the situation appears to be a standoff; declaring the word of God at such times will surely make him flee. The word of God is the sword of the Holy Spirit. The battle will be won by wielding it. Yet it is essential to wield it with faith. God's word is like the verdict of the Supreme Court.

vv.5–7 But Satan still will not let "the Son of God" go. He too begins to cite scripture. In the first instance it is the Lord quoting scripture against Satan. The second time around, however, Satan cites scripture. But then the Lord invokes the scripture again to refute Satan. Scripture ought not be quoted carelessly. What the Lord means to teach us here is that at the first instance He refuses to turn stone into bread because God has spoken, and that at the second instance, if He leaps without God's word, He will be tempting God.

Faith is doing what God has said. Following temptation is

acting presumptuously without God's word. Faith works along one principle only, which is, I believe, for God has said it.

"Again" (v.7)—Let us remember well this word. When we seek the will of God it is rather dangerous if we have only one scripture but fail to find another verse to confirm it.

vv.8–10 Satan is willing to forfeit all the things in the world and their glory, but he is loathe to give up the worship of man. Satan is now the prince of this world. His lifelong wish is to receive man's worship. He hides behind the idols of many religions to receive human worship. This explains why many idols have spirits, since Satan is behind them all. Satan aims at depriving God of man's worship. For this reason, the Bible states over and over that our God is a jealous God. It is written: "Yea, ye have borne the tabernacle of your king and the shrine of your images, the star of your god, which ye made to yourselves. Therefore will I cause you to go into captivity beyond Damascus, saith Jehovah, whose name is the God of hosts" (Amos 5.26–27). The word "seek" in John 4.23 is an emphatic verb in Greek. God seeks for worshipers because Satan schemes to rob God of worship. "Nor take their names [those of other gods] upon my lips," said David (Ps. 16.4). During the Old Testament period a sorcerer or a necromancer must be stoned to death. Even if the wife of a man's bosom should be the one to entice him to go and serve other gods, she too must be stoned to death. And her husband was required to cast the first stone.

This time the Lord reprimands him and calls him by the name of Satan because of his attempt to rob the Divine of worship. And the Lord ends by invoking this scripture: "Thou shalt worship the Lord thy God, and him only shalt thou serve" (v.10). The Lord is coming soon. We must reject all attempts at depriving God of His worship.

v.11 The ministration of the angel is the portion of every believer (see Heb. 1.13–14). During the time of Jesus' temptation the angels were standing by. Hence we should ask God to send His angels to camp around and protect us too.

The Lord Calls Four Disciples, 4.12–25

vv.12–17 Although John was now imprisoned, the Lord continued preaching John's message. Despite the imprisonment of the first herald of the message of the kingdom of heaven, the nature of the message underwent no change in the preaching by the Lord Jesus.

vv.18–22 Peter was called while he was casting a net; John was called when he was mending nets. It so happened that later on Peter did the work of casting a net and John the work of mending a net every time. Peter first cast a net upon the Jews and second upon the Gentiles. In the case of John, he wrote the last of the Gospels at a very late hour in early church history. Although the Lord was no longer seen on earth, John nevertheless brought people to the source of all things. When John wrote his epistles he led people back to know Him "who is from the beginning" (1 John 2.13), because there were agnostics at that time. He came to mend the net because the church had fallen away in apostasy. Had the church remained faithful during the time of the apostles we would not have known how to cope with the situation of a fallen church. God permitted the church to fall away in apostolic times and raised up John to mend the net, thus teaching us how we of a later era are to behave in such an hour. Hence it can be said that what one's status is at the time of his salvation usually governs the character of that one's later work and ministry.

vv.23–25 That which the Lord preaches is none other than the gospel of the kingdom of heaven. This is the same as the gospel of grace, except that here it carries with it a special emphasis.

All who follow the Lord will become fishers of men. If anyone is saved and subsequently fails to lead another to Christ, he has not followed the Lord: for note that the Lord says explicitly, "I will make you fishers of men" (Matt. 3.19).

Jesus healed many sick, and many followed Him. Now that people's spiritual diseases are healed, there should be many following the Lord.

THE GOSPEL ACCORDING TO MATTHEW

Chapter 5

Chapter 3 records John the Baptist as proclaiming the kingdom of heaven, chapter 4 tells of the Lord himself announcing
the kingdom of heaven, and chapter 5 enunciates the law or
principle of the kingdom of heaven as declared by the Lord.

Is the long discourse given in Matthew 5–7 addressed to
Christians? Matthew 5.1 mentions "disciples"; Matthew 5.22,
28, 34, 39 and 44 all repeat the refrain, "I say unto you"—
which implies a command; and Matthew 5.16, 22 and 48 use the
intimate terms of relationship like "Father" and "brother" and
"heavenly Father".

vv.1–2 A. Since "his disciples" are prominently mentioned, we may say that this discourse is spoken to Christians.
The following observations give support to such a view:

(1) According to 5.1–2, and though there are the multitudes,
only the disciples follow the Lord up the mountain. He does not
speak to the multitudes (although doubtless they overheard what
was said), but He spoke to the disciples. And disciples are
Christians.

(2) Some people suggest that the "disciples" cited in Matthew 5.1 are Jewish disciples. The Bible, however, does not endorse such an interpretation. Compare this verse: "Unto you it is
given to know the mysteries of the kingdom of heaven, but to
them it is not given" (Matt. 13.11). The "you" here are obvi-

ously disciples, and the "them" are the Jews; this thus shows that the disciples are different from the Jews. When the Lord charges His followers to "make disciples of all the nations" (Matt. 28.19), He means making disciples of the Gentiles, not having Gentile disciples. And it is clearly stated in Acts 11 that "the disciples were called Christians" (v.26). From Matthew to Acts, therefore, whenever a Gentile or a Jew believes in the Lord, he is called a disciple.

B. We may further say that this discourse is addressed to Christians in view of the Lord's repeated word of command. Please note the following:

(1) What is meant by "teaching them to observe all things whatsoever I commanded you" (Matt. 28.20)? Of all which the Lord has commanded as recorded in the Gospel according to Matthew none can surpass what is given to us in chapters 5–7. For what is said there is the heart of all that Jesus has commanded. It constitutes His foremost commandments. And hence, it is given to Christians to keep.

(2) One of the works of the Holy Spirit as described by the Lord Jesus himself is to "bring to your remembrance all that I said unto you" (John 14.26). The Holy Spirit will remind the disciples of what the Lord has said while on earth. This is a major part of the Holy Spirit's operation—to lead us to the word of Christ.

(3) Now what does Paul say regarding the Lord's word? In Colossians he calls it "the word of Christ" (3.16) rather than "the word of God"—because "the word of God" includes the whole Bible. And it should be noted that he wrote the Epistle to the Colossians while in prison, long after the mysteries of the church had been revealed.

C. And we may say that this discourse is directed to Christians, finally, because of its contents, as follows:

(1) Taking into consideration the oft-repeated statement—

"Ye have heard that it was said to them of old time . . . but I say unto you"—we can readily know that what is enjoined in Matthew 5–7 is *not* Old Testament law. Christians are not under the law of the Old Testament; yet they are not *without* law, either, because they are under the law of Christ (see 1 Cor. 9.21, Gal. 6.2).

(2) Since Matthew 5–7 frequently uses words such as "Father" and "brother", this discourse shows that the people in view here have the life of God in them and can therefore no longer be considered to be in the time of the Old Testament dispensation of law.

(3) We can find in the New Testament epistles many teachings which are identical to those found in Matthew 5–7. The injunctions of Romans 12 form a typical example.

(4) If Matthew 5–7 refers to the law of the millennial kingdom, where in that kingdom can we ever find "the evil", "the unjust", the oppressor, and the adulterer?

The Beatitudes, 5.3-12

v.3 "Poor in spirit"—This means having no wish to be rich. Here we find no definition of the kingdom of heaven; we can only see that what is in view is a reward, or something which is greater than a reward.

v.4 "Mourn—God wants us to be pessimistic concerning the world, for it will grow worse and not better.

v.5 "Meek"—This word means non-resistant, able to endure. Such people will surely lose ground today, but they shall inherit the earth in the future.

v.6 "Righteousness" here points to our personal, righteous conduct. It does not say "Blessed are the righteous"—for who can say they are righteous? It rather says "hunger and thirst after righteousness"—that is to say, a real seeking after righteousness. And those who do such shall eventually be satisfied. It is unrighteous to take advantage of other people.

v.7 To do righteousness is to give what is right to people; to show "mercy" is to give to people that to which they have no right.

Christians today should not seek to gain the upper hand on earth. We ought to look for mercy at the judgment-seat of Christ, for the Lord will recompense what we dispense to others. Our prayer will certainly reach the judgment-seat (see 2 Tim. 1.16,18).

v.8 The so-called nine beatitudes do naturally govern the present, but they shall even more so govern the future. "Pure in heart" means a having as one's single objective the glory and the will of God. Such a man seeks nothing but what God may gain. God is the finality as well as the pursuit. Since he looks for only one thing, he therefore only sees one thing: he seeks God, and hence he sees God. "They shall be priests of God and of Christ" (Rev. 20.6). Priests are those who see God. May no one lose this blessing of seeing God.

v.9 This verse relates to present days. "Peace" is what God undertakes to work out on earth; today we are only proclaiming it.

"Children of God" (John 1.12) refers to all believers. All who are in Christ are God's children, including both the male and the female. To call someone a brother in the Lord is due to his being in Christ, not because he is a male.

"And ye shall be to me sons and daughters" (2 Cor. 6.18)— This is something special. "Sons" (which is the correct translation of this beatitude) are grown-ups; it implies "sonship": it was a Greek custom to call by the term "children" all who were born to the family; but after they had grown up, the father would choose from among them one who was to be placed as "son"—that is, he was to receive sonship.

v.10 "For righteousness' sake"—For the sake of justice and equity. "Have been persecuted"—This phrase refers to the past, hence these people are probably the Old Testament saints. This phraseology differentiates them from those mentioned in verse 11, since the latter suffer directly for the sake of Christ.

Such terms as "enter into the kingdom", "theirs is the kingdom" and "in the kingdom" are synonymous; otherwise there would be confusion.

vv.11–12 Christians suffer persecution through three different forms of treatment; namely, by means of (1) reproach—to one's face, (2) persecution—all kinds of environments, and (3) saying all manner of evil—behind one's back by creating rumors. Since the ninth beatitude speaks of "reward" all the other preceding eight beatitudes likewise refer to a reward. The Bible adopts the method of consequential relationship: in this case the first part of each beatitude mentions a form of conduct while its second part cites a reward.

"Rejoice, and be exceeding glad"—The Greek original implies a leaping for joy. Since the Lord says "great is your reward in heaven", the reward cannot be small. An added comfort lies in the realization that the prophets who had gone before had all been so persecuted.

The Nature of a Christian on Earth Today, 5.13–16

In this section two things are stated: (1) that believers are the salt of the earth, and (2) that believers are the light of the world. Salt speaks of the character within, whereas light speaks of the conduct without. The first is directed towards one's self, the second is related to other people.

v.13 The Lord does not say "Ye are the salt" but "Ye are the salt of the earth"—The earth is full of refuse. Fortunately, though, there is salt in the rocks, in the rain, and in the ocean water. Salt is able to purify the uncleanness; otherwise, the whole earth will smell rotten. Christians, as spiritual salt, should be able to influence others on earth.

"If the salt have lost its savor"—This does not mean that believers have fallen away from truth. It simply points to the fact that they have lost that peculiar taste they once possessed (see 2 Cor. 6.14–16): They dress as the worldly people dress, and eat as the worldly people eat: In these and so many other ways they are no different from the people of the world. And thus have they become as savorless salt. Let us see that believers do not need to commit any serious sin to become savorless.

"Good for nothing" is a conclusion as seen in the eyes of God. "Cast out" means an entering into tribulation. "Out" and "trodden" are words which describe tribulation, both present and future.

vv.14–16 What about "the light of the world"?

(1) It can be likened to "a city set on a hill [that] cannot be hidden"—Believers ought not to seek distinction among their fellow-believers, and yet they should let the world know that they are Christians.

(2) It can be likened to "light [ing] a lamp, and put [ting] it . . . on the stand"—To what was said before ("cannot be hid") is now added the words "should not be hidden" (the thought of v.15). "City" speaks of a relationship to those outside, whereas the word "stand" speaks of a relationship among those within a household—the household of faith. God has special use for our light. If the light is hidden He will not be able to be glorified through us. Light can shut out darkness: the very nature of this world is darkness, but light is able to drive the darkness out.

"Glorify your Father who is in heaven"—Glory is not attributed to you and me, it is ascribed to the Father. This proves that the people in view here must be regenerated persons.

The Significance of the Law, 5.17-20

vv.17–18 The law cannot be destroyed.

v.19 This verse is in regard to people in the Old Testament times.

v.20 Here it is in respect of people in New Testament times. "To fulfill" (v.17) is to fill full what is incomplete in the law. It does not refer to the "It is finished" statement of Jesus on the cross. Verse 19 treats the question of "destroy" or "not destroy" in a general way. On the other hand, verse 20 so deals with the phrase "to fulfill" that it is specifically directed towards a certain class of people. The second part of verse 19 represents the height of righteousness the scribes and Pharisees may achieve. Yet unless the righteousness of the disciples exceeds that of the scribes and Pharisees, they cannot enter the kingdom of heaven. What is it that the Lord prescribes to be "fulfill [ed] "? None other than all which is given by Him as recorded in Matthew chapters 5–7. "To fulfill" is to fill full what is incomplete in the law, not to add more articles to the law.

The law demands three things:
(1) A keeping of the law from the first article to the last. Christ is the only person who has kept the law so perfectly.
(2) Punishment. If a man is punished, he is viewed as having fulfilled the law: he who sheds blood shall have his own blood shed.
(3) Instruction. Since the law is not perfect, it needs to be fulfilled. This is the meaning of the phrase "to fulfill" found in Matthew 5.17.

Christ, having fulfilled the first demand of the law, is qualified to fulfill its second demand by taking punishment for us as our substitute. With these two demands completed, the Old Covenant passes away. Now there remains the third demand for us to keep.

"Fulfill" in 5.17 has a different meaning from "accomplished" in 5.18. The first means to replenish; the second means to consummate.

With respect to fulfilling, verse 17 mentions the law and the prophets. With respect to accomplishing, though, verse 18 refers only to the law, not to the prophets as well; for what the law teaches reaches only to the kingdom, but the prophets (such as Isaiah) prophesy concerning what extends to the new heaven and the new earth. The law never speaks of eternity. "Till all things be accomplished" alludes to the time of the kingdom.

"Be reconciled"—5.21–26

vv.21–22 The judgment in verse 22 is of the same kind as the judgment in verse 21. Though it is not the judgment of the Jewish court, it nonetheless proceeds from the preliminary judgment given at the city gate to the judgment of the council until it finally reaches the very judgment of God. These words are spoken to Christians. Due to the fact that those who stood before Him at that moment were Jews, the Lord naturally used expressions with a Jewish background.

"Angry" is a boiling up within. Mark records that our Lord got angry. The Bible has not taught that *all* angers will be judged. It only states that some angers offend brethren as well as God. The verse "Be ye angry, and sin not; let not the sun go down upon your wrath" in Ephesians 4.26 is suggesting for us not to be angry to the extent of sinning nor to be controlled by anger. Also, there is a time limit to any anger: one ought to control his temper.

Why equate anger with killing? Because frequently it is only our position or physical environment or ethical teaching that keeps us from actually killing; but the thought of killing is already conceived in our heart.

Since judgment is mentioned here, how can we say that Christians will not be judged at all? We cannot agree with some people who advocate the theory of no judgment for Christians. The word "brother" is used here and the demands are high here —all indications that these words are not addressed to non-believers.

The Presbyterians, the Episcopalians, and the Brethren follow the thought of John Calvin, who promoted the teaching that salvation is predestinated and that therefore all who are saved will never perish. On the other hand, the Methodists and some of the Pentecostals follow the teaching of Arminius, who stressed the position that man has a free will. Seeing from the Bible that many Christians do fall or have fallen, the Arminians today uphold the view that Christians may yet perish.

Though Calvin seems to have gained the upper hand in his exalting of God, it must also be said that Arminius has his ground too. I do not believe we should overturn a concept which seems to have less scriptural support (the Arminian) with a concept that apparently has more scriptural support (the Calvinistic). On the contrary, we should put all the Scriptures together and let the Scriptures themselves decide all issues.

"They shall never perish," says the Lord (John 10.28). Eternity exists before the creation of the heavens and the earth, and it extends beyond the events of the book of Revelation. In between these two is the temporary period which can also be called time. Between creation and the events of the book of Revelation Christians may receive punishment during this period. In 2 Corinthians 5 we read: "we must all be made manifest before the judgment-seat of Christ; that each one may receive the things done in the body, according to what he hath done, whether it be good or bad" (v.10). Some will receive bad recompense. If this is not punishment, what is it? Likewise, Luke 12 states: "And that servant, who knew his lord's will, and made not ready, nor did according to his will, shall be beaten with many stripes; but he that knew not, and did things worthy of stripes, shall be beaten with few stripes. And to whomsoever much is given, of him shall much be required: and to whom they commit much, of him will they ask the more" (vv.47–48). The beating is before the judgment seat. It incurs not only the loss of reward but also the possibility of being beaten. With regard to the words "suffer loss" in 1 Corinthians 3.15 someone has said that any loss without the inflicting of suffering cannot be reckoned as the suffering of loss. The consequence of "abide not" is to "cast them into the fire" (John 15.6). This without a doubt speaks of punishment. Revelation 2.11 declares: "He that overcometh shall not be hurt of the second death"; in other words, he who does not overcome will be hurt of the second death. Who shall reign with Christ for a thousand years? The answer: "Blessed and holy is he that hath part in the first resurrection: over these the second death hath no power; but they shall be priests of God and of Christ, and shall reign with him a thousand years" (Rev. 20.6).

According to the original rendering of John 10.28, "they shall never perish" should be translated "in no wise shall they perish for ever"*—in other words, if believers should sin and fail to repent, they will suffer temporarily what the unbelievers will suffer eternally.

Purgatory as promoted by the Roman Catholic Church commences, in its view, at the time of death; and indulgence is promised by the Church through the Mass and other means. To this thought we vigorously object. Nevertheless, we cannot use heresy, either, to oppose the fact that Christians may receive punishment. We can only rely on the Scriptures to prove that the Matthew passage before us has reference to the judgment-seat of Christ.

---

*See *The Englishman's Greek New Testament with Interlinear Translation* (London, Samuel Bagster and Sons, Ltd., 3rd ed., n.d.).—*Translator*

One sister in the Lord has said it well: Sin in an unbeliever is sin, but so too is sin in a believer sin.

Robert Govett translates "raca" in verse 22 as "useless"; others, as "stupid" or "worthless". "Moreh" (v.22 mg.) is probably Syrian, and it is more appropriate to translate it as "rebel". Judging by the context, calling a brother "raca" is a deeper reaction than getting angry with a brother, and the judgment of scolding a brother by using the term moreh is stronger than all, even to the extent of placing oneself "in danger of the hell of fire". Hence the meaning of moreh must be weightier than that of raca. If raca means stupid, moreh, according to G. H. Pember, should mean rebel.

The very mentioning of the hell of fire here indicates that Christians may not escape judgment. This situation cannot be applied to unbelievers, for they do not go to hell just because they denounce people.

v.23 This is not offering sacrifice, but offering gifts. Offering sacrifice is for the sake of sin; offering gifts is to please God, an action completely dissociated from sin. "Hath aught against thee" shows that the person has done something wrong.

v.24 The demand here is several times stronger than what is required in the Old Testament. Not only the person and the gift must be right, even the spiritual condition must equally be right. It should also be pointed out that when the Lord spoke these words, ceremonial law had not yet been abrogated; so that in using the words "offering thy gifts at the altar" He gave His hearers some local background.

v.25 The "adversary" is the plaintiff. The word itself implies that there is something against you. "In the way" means that there is still opportunity for you to be reconciled before you appear before the judge.

Three reasons why you should be reconciled with your adversary quickly are:

(1) Perhaps he may die and you will never have the chance to be reconciled with him.

(2) Perhaps you may die and so you cannot be reconciled to him.

(3) Perhaps the Lord may come back, and likewise you will have no opportunity to be reconciled with your adversary.

If you have done anything wrong against someone and have not made it right, his sigh or cry will prevent your prayer from reaching God. The voice of Abel made Cain restless.

"The judge" points to the Lord; "the officer" points to the angel; "prison" is where freedom is deprived you and where darkness prevails.

Those who are "cast into prison" shall not live gloriously as does that group of people who follow the Lamb wherever He goes. However, this is not a being permanently cast into prison. It merely indicates the possibility of Christians being judged.

v.26 Since sooner or later the debt must be repaid, why not pay it today? "Come out"—This will happen in the age to come, which is the millennial age. This is called forgiveness in the age to come.

Concerning Adultery, 5.27–32

v.28 "Looketh" here is an intentional act. "A woman" in the context means someone's wife. What Christ condemns is not the sudden thought which Satan may thrust in upon a person's mind, nor is it some improper thought that arises impetuously in the mind, rather is it an intentional look. An action without the approval of the will may not be reckoned as sin. Action which is taken after the will agrees to the temptation is sin. The Lord is here teaching us how we need to keep our heart. Otherwise, we will certainly commit adultery if there is not the involvement of ethics, environment, or position. For "he whose spirit is without restraint is like a city that is broken down and without walls" (Prov. 25.28)

v.29 An unbeliever will still go to hell even if he plucks out his eye. Thus what is spoken here is not for unbelievers but for Christians.

v.30 The cutting off of the hand and the plucking out of the eye are not to be interpreted literally. They simply signify eliminating the opportunity of sinning. (Did not Peter cut off the ear of the servant of the high priest? And yet his hand was not cut off.) We must be ready to pay any cost in order to get rid of the opportunity of sinning.

v.32 When the Lord speaks on the matter of divorce He is standing on an entirely new ground. He recognizes that the husband and the wife are one body. Before this oneness is broken, nothing is allowed to terminate this oneness. A writing of divorcement is but a recognition that the oneness has already been broken. Unless divorce is based on adultery, such oneness remains intact in the sight of God; and therefore, if either married partner is remarried to another person, then he or she breaks the oneness and commits adultery.

Concerning Not Swearing, 5.33–37

The apostle James declares: "But above all things, my brethren, swear not, neither by the heaven, nor by the earth, nor by any other oath . . . " (5.12) Why is the apostle emphatic on this matter? Because the whole book of James lays much stress on speech. People always like to use other means to prove the honesty of their words.

v.34 "Swear not at all"—Swearing includes "whatsoever

is more" (v.37) than yea and nay. The word of a Christian should be most simple. He does not need to employ other outside means to prove the accuracy of his speech.

"Resist Not Him That Is Evil"—5.38–42

Today is the period of our patience. The following observations elaborate upon three different forms of coercion:

(1) Regarding the physical body—To endure the first strike is not the characteristic of a Christian; to be ready even for the second strike is peculiar to a Christian. A Christian does something deeper than non-resistance; he joyfully offers himself to be smitten again.

Strength is not measured by what a person can do but is measured by what he can endure. For this reason Colossians chapter 1 concludes its list of all the virtues required of a Christian with these words: "unto all patience and longsuffering with joy" (v.11).

v.39 "Turn to him the other [cheek] also"—This signifies being patient to the utmost degree. To be ready to be struck again is the spontaneous expression of an inward life, not the unnatural act put on by oneself.

The implication of turning the left as well as the right cheek is the showing of one's willingness to be smitten again. Such is the life of the Lamb.

(2) Regarding property—Such a lawsuit is most unnatural. What the Lord here suggests is that even if the accuser spares nothing, not even the coat, let us be so gracious as to give him also the cloak. Apart from the protection given us by the love of God, we will not even lift up our hands to defend ourselves.

(3) Regarding work—The word "compel" is a special military term. The blessing of a Christian lies in the other cheek, the cloak as well as the coat, and the second mile. This is the principle of the second. How often we are not able to go even one

mile. Only those who follow the principle of the second will receive glory with the Lord. All who would reign with Christ in
the future are unable to reign now.

v.42 This verse sums up all that has been said before.
Here Christ has not taught us to choose whom we will give to;
He merely charges us to do our part. We can only be responsible
for what God has required of us; we cannot interfere with what
He requires of other people.

The Motivation of Love, 5.43–48

The aforesaid actions are taken because there is love. If we
are fretful, we will not be able to pray for our persecutors. The
love in view here is neither due to liking nor to familiarity,
rather it is because of mercy. (There are four kinds of love: intimate love, preferred love, respectful love, and merciful love.) We
should never shut up a heart of mercy.

By acting according to verse 44 we may be sons of the heavenly Father, since we have exhibited His nature. Verse 45 shows
us how liberal is the way God treats mankind. Were He like us,
none would ever be saved. Only God can forget man's evil. Man
does not possess the ability to forget evil; he does not have absolute forgetfulness. "May be sons of your Father who is in
heaven"—The words "may be" imply the thought of our being
manifested to be such.

vv.46–47 These verses tell us that without the various
modes of conduct mentioned before, we will not receive any reward. A certain heart condition always needs to be present.

v.48 The word "perfect" here refers to being perfected in
love. We will never be perfect as God is perfect in nature,
power, wisdom, glory, and holiness. But we *are* required to be
perfect in works of love.

The "perfect" mentioned here is not the eradicaton of the root of sin, for this secton does not dwell on punishment but on works of love.

"Be ye merciful, even as your Father is merciful" (Luke 6.36). Luke's account of these words by Jesus serves as a comment on this idea of "perfect": it is in the area of mercy. This agrees with what is said in Matthew 5.48.

We are not told in this passage to be perfect in righteousness as God is perfect. No, the Bible exhorts us to be righteous towards ourselves and to be perfect in love towards other people.

Some Principles of Interpretation to Be Garnered from Chapters 1–5

Principle 1 Words joined by coordinate conjunctions must be interpreted either spiritually or literally together.

Principle 2 A scriptural truth with less verse support should not be sacrificed for a scriptural truth with more verse support.

Principle 3 All the words of the Bible should be interpreted literally unless such interpretation would approach absurdity. Naturally, parables, visions, and signs cannot be interpreted literally.

Principle 4 A single scripture verse is insufficient to decide on a truth. There must be an "Again it is written" to support it.

Principle 5 Two similar terms within different contexts should not be similarly interpreted.

Principle 6 Parallels are identical.

Principle 7 Interpretation should not be controlled by background, nor can it overlook background either.

Principle 8 Never take one verse as inclusive of all the truth. For example, in the matter of the law, search must be made throughout the Bible in order to discover all the truth about it. No one verse will be sufficient.

THE GOSPEL ACCORDING TO MATTHEW

Chapter 6

"Righteousness" is the general theme of verses 1-18. It is treated in three divisions: (1) alms, (2) prayer, and (3) fasting.

v.1 This verse points out the theme. There must not only be righteousness, but such righteousness must be done in secret. In other words, one needs to control his heart in every undertaking.

In the previous section we are told to love our enemies. Now in this section we are taught not to do righteousness before men.

During one of the wars in Germany a company of enemy soldiers arrived at a certain place where a group of true believers lived. They asked a believer to lead them to the best field for cutting wheat. He led them through many fields till they came to one particular field. There he told them to cut. When the believer was asked why he did not allow the enemy soldiers to cut the wheat standing in the fields on the other side, he replied that those were not his but that this particular field was his own. This is what is meant by going the second mile.

One central teaching in Matthew 5–7 is reward; and this thought recurs often in this passage, as will be seen below.

Alms, 6.2–4

v.2 "Sound not a trumpet"—This is probably a proverbial expression.

v.3 "Let not thy left hand know what thy right hand doeth"—Obviously this is not to be interpreted literally. It simply suggests how one ought to avoid as much as possible doing alms before men.

v.4 "Recompense" is reward.
Therefore all righteous acts should be done before God as though in secret.

Prayer, 6.5–15

v.5 "And when ye pray"—The Lord has not charged us to give alms, to pray, and to fast, for these are the basics to believers. What He says here is *how* we can do alms, pray and fast so as to receive God's pleasure.

"Hypocrite" has in its root meaning the idea of an actor performing in a play. Hence a hypocrite is an actor. When there is no zeal to pray and yet one acts as though there is much zeal in his praying, such performance is condemned by the Lord.

"Synagogues" are where the zealous people assemble; "corners of the streets" are where the people gather. Both synagogues and street corners serve as theatrical platforms for the hypocrites. Actors must perform before men. Thus will they receive glory of men both within (the synagogue) and without (the corners of the streets).

"That they may be seen of men"—This reveals the motive behind such performance. It is natural to a man of flesh and blood to hide his shortcomings, but grace enables one to hide his strength.

A new Christian always likes to hide his weakness. As he grows deeper in the Lord, though, he is willing to let his weakness be exposed before others. When he grows still more, he will have his weakness eliminated by the grace of God.

There are two different times for reward: (1) now, and (2)

in the future. There are two different kinds of reward: (1) that which comes from man, and (2) that which comes from God.

No one can have both rewards. If we wish to receive man's reward now we will not be able to obtain God's reward in the future. We cannot seek to enjoy great fame on earth and then have high position in the kingdom to come. If today's zeal and alms are for the purpose of getting fame and praise, there will be nothing to gain in the future before God. For this reason we should refuse today's reward.

As worldly people are zealous and suffer long for today's gain, we need to be careful in our giving alms and offering prayers lest we fall into the same disposition.

What, after all, can the praise of man add to us? If we have our eyes opened we will seek only the glory before God and the angels; the rest will not count at all.

v.6 "Enter into thy inner chamber"—Some people would suggest that prayer is restricted to a certain location and that there is therefore the need to build a prayer room. Yet Paul's word to Timothy is to "pray in every place" (1 Tim. 2.8). "Inner chamber" is the bedroom, which is occupied by very few people. In the daytime people go out to work; hence the bedroom is quiet. In the night after people have gone to bed, it is again quiet. We are here enjoined to seek out some place where few people are and to pray there.

When our Lord was on earth He had no resting place. Accordingly, He took the wilderness and the mountains as His inner chamber. Did not David say, "I watch, and am become like a sparrow that is alone upon the housetop" (Ps.102.7)?

"And thy Father who seeth in secret"—How natural for man to draw attention to his strength. But God sees in secret, and He will not forget even a cup of cold water. The assets we remember today may not be regarded by God in the future, and what we often forget now may be recalled by God then.

"Recompense" is reward. This does not refer to what is commonly deemed to be answer to prayer; instead, it points to future reward. God accounts prayers made in secret to be righteous acts, and He will thus reward them in the future.

v.7 "Repetitions" means using many meaningless words to prolong prayer. This in no sense forbids the use of the same words in prayer. Even the Lord Jesus prayed three times in the same words; hence it shows that when there is burden in the spirit, the same words are frequently uttered in His many prayers. Those who know best how to pray are rather creative in their prayers.

There is a poor habit among us believers today. We tend to pray long prayers, stretching out our prayers with many words and so thinking that we shall be heard for much speaking. However, prayers recorded in the Bible are most straightforward and concise. For example, "Save, Lord" (Matt. 8.25). A very short prayer is often quite acceptable. In a time of distress, in witnessing to a sinner, in an hour of need, short prayers are most effective.

"For they think that they shall be heard for their much speaking"—Probably believers think the same way as do the Gentiles. Of course, if we have time we should pray much. But do not imagine we will be heard for our much speaking.

v.8 Some people say that since God knows what things we need of before we ask Him, we do not need to pray at all. Not praying is therefore even better than short praying. Yet this verse does not tell us not to pray, it simply teaches us not to make a report before God. Although God knows our needs, He nonetheless waits for our prayer but not for our report. "Lord, we perish" (Matt. 8.25) is an example of a report, but "Lord, save me" (same verse) is a prayer. We should not notify God, but we can ask Him. Hence prayer in the form of a report is best to be avoided.

v.9 "After this manner therefore pray ye"—What follows upon these words was never meant to serve as a prayer form or liturgy for us to say but as an example for us to follow. The disciples are to learn to pray after this manner.

vv.9–13 Only this once does the Lord on His own initiative teach us to pray. On another occasion, given in Luke, the Lord's teaching is the result of the disciples' request, "Lord, teach us to pray" (11.1). Even though the words generally are the same, these are two different occasions.

Here we are given a hint. Though the prayer the Lord teaches us is few in words, it still includes all the will of God, all He desires to fulfill speedily, and all He expects His church to pray about during these thousands of years. This prayer expresses God's eternal will as well as His heart desire for man. It contains "thy" three times and "us" four times.

"Hallowed be thy name. Thy kingdom come. Thy will be done, as in heaven, so on earth" (v.10). On earth, men do not hallow God's name. Neither do they respect authority nor carry out His will on earth. The purpose of God is to have His will done on earth as it is done in heaven. In heaven God's name is hallowed and His will is done. Yet on earth another name is honored, and there is the kingdom of darkness with its hostile will. Satan is the prince of this world and the god of this age. The whole world lies under his hand.

We must preach the gospel in order to deliver people out of the hand of the evil one so that they may hallow God's name and submit themselves to His authority. This will cause God's kingdom to come to that particular ground on which we stand.

Christians today should take up a monumental responsibility: the bringing in of the kingdom upon the earth through prayer.

Why is it that Satan still remains on earth today? Because those who belong to Christ have yet to experience the victory of Christ.

At least one of the reasons why God creates man is that He in His capacity as the Creator does not himself want to drive out a created being—Satan. Man is to do this. At the beginning God charged man to keep the garden of Eden, thus indicating there was an enemy around. The dominion which He gave to man was the dominion which He formerly assigned to the archangel Lucifer who later turned himself into Satan.

The serpent was cursed to eat dust all the days of its life. As man was made of dust, so he came under the power of Satan.

The first man Adam failed to cooperate with God. So God raised up the second man Christ to overcome Satan. The Lord Jesus redeems us, His people, by means of His death. As He has done God's will, so He unites all who are saved to himself in order that together they may exalt God, do God's will, and defeat Satan's kingdom. In Christ these form the second man who causes the will of God to be done on earth as it is done in heaven.

Evan Roberts speaks of the wheel or cycle of prayer as (1) God initiates, (2) man prays, and (3) God accomplishes.

Ezekiel 36.26,37 gives us a great principle. God says first that He will give the house of Israel a new heart, and next He says that He will be inquired of by them (prayer) to do it for them.

v.9 "Our Father who art in heaven"—The "our" includes all Christians. "Father who art in heaven" is the exclusive claim of believers. The world cannot address God by this appellation.

"Hallowed be thy name"—This is what God enjoins His people to do throughout the centuries, to hallow His name.

v.10 "Thy kingdom come"—On the one hand, we may say it is already in our midst; on the other, its appearing still awaits the prayers of the believers.

vv.11–13 This is "asking"; "us" is mentioned four times: verse 11, verse 12, and verse 13 (twice).

v.11 "Give us this day our daily bread"—Because the Christians do not hoard on earth, therefore they must ask for their daily bread.

v.12 "Forgive"—Some people maintain that this word is directed at the Jews, thus making it different from the "forgiving each other" phrase in Ephesians 4.32. However, we consider such teaching to be incorrect, for the following reasons:

(1) If this is directed to the Jews, how can God be addressed as the Father in heaven? (Adam is called the son of God because he is created by God.)

(2) Words such as "debts" and "our Father who art in heaven" indicate that there already exists the relationship of Father and children at the time of sinning. Hence this speaks of those sins committed after being saved.

(3) The sin of the Jews is not forgiven through forgiving others. One day their sin will be washed away in a fountain opened to them (see Zech. 13.1). The forgiveness in view here is not the forgiving of sins in the first instance; it instead has to do with the covering of the daily weaknesses and faults of the saved. These require our forgiving others in order to obtain the Father's forgiveness. If a believer fails to forgive his debtors, he will forget how he himself has been forgiven by God. Will God allow two believers who are at odds with each other to enter His kingdom together? Either neither of them enters or else one of them fails to enter.

v.13 Since we stand for the kingdom of God and really desire to keep the teachings on the mount, we must ask God to "deliver us from the evil one" and keep us from temptation.

Many authorities, some ancient, but with variations, add: "For thine is the kingdom, and the power, and the glory, for ever. Amen" (v.13 mg.): "kingdom" is the realm in which God rules, "power" is the operation of God, and "glory" is the effulgence of God's personal glory.

On Fasting, 6.16–18

Fasting is:

(1) an expression of humbling oneself before God.

(2) an expression of buffeting one's body and bringing it into subjection.

(3) an expression of seeking the grace of God.

Fasting should therefore not be abolished; yet it should be kept secret as much as possible. It is a matter of motivation.

On Treasures, 6.19–24

Treasures include not only money but also clothing, food and all which one cherishes.

v.19 The word "rust" is the same Greek word *(brosis)* translated "eating" in Romans 14.17. Literally, then, it simply means completely eaten up or consumed:

Where "moth consumes"—points to clothing.

Where "rust" or "eating" consumes—points to food.

Where "thieves steal"—points to money.

"Lay not up for yourselves treasures upon the earth"—This is a commandment of the Lord. However, it does not suggest we must use up our money and eat up our food every day so that nothing is left. Lay up means that which you plan to depend on.

v.20 Whatever may be consumed by moth and rust or stolen by thieves displeases God, for He condemns all idle treasures. It is not right to waste things, yet neither is it right to lay up things on earth.

Laying up in heaven may be done by helping the poor

among the saints. If there is a laying up in heaven, you may draw on God—not ask of Him—when you have need. Such laying up is like changing banks from an earthly location to a heavenly one.

v.21 As treasures are shifted in position to heaven, so the heart changes direction. If we wish to translate our heart to heaven we should first distribute our treasures to people. The treasures go before the heart.

v.22 The function of each member is for the whole body's benefit; therefore each member also represents the body. If a man is blind in the eyes, he is blind in the body, he is a blind man.

"Single"—Though there are two eyes, both focus on the same object at one time; otherwise the vision will not be exact.

Some believers think of laying up treasures entirely on earth, but they feel uneasy in their heart; yet they find it impossible to wholly lay up treasures in heaven. Consequently, they try to do a little of both, causing them to lose spiritual sight. What the Lord shows us here is that we cannot gain both worlds.

Apprehensive lest people might not understand His speech in verse 21, our Lord uses the word in verse 22 to explain the word just spoken: if the eye is not single the heart is divided, and thus there will be no light. "Light" is to make manifest everything (Eph. 5.13) so that we may see clearly. "Full of light" means to be filled with the knowledge of the thing manifested— in other words, *spiritual* sight, vision or discernment. This enables people to see accurately as to what is the way of the cross, which is a strait or narrow way.

v.23 "How great is the darkness!"—A person whose eye notices two different things and whose heart has two divergent desires lacks spiritual insight. He is like a blind man walking on a narrow path between two chasms. How perilous will that be!

v.24 "No man can serve two masters," says the Lord. Yet the heart of a believer always seems to consider it a possibility. Love's strength is as limited as the strength of the other members of the body. If one's strength is spent on non-essentials, it will leave no strength for the absolutely essential. If love is all spent on "mammon" (v.24), where is there strength when it is to be used on God? The human heart has place only for one.

The principle of mammon is diametrically opposite to the principle of God. A Chinese proverb runs as follows: To be rich is to lack compassion. This does not imply that the rich are cruel, it merely implies that the rich are selfish.

Not Being Anxious, 6.25–34

v.25 Here the Lord changes His tone. Since in the preceding passage He has commanded people not to lay up for themselves treasures on earth, the problems of clothing and eating cannot help but arise in the hearts of men.

The previous passage dealt with idle money which ought to be given away; here from verse 25 onward it tells of the proper use of, and right attitude towards, clothing and eating. The Lord mentions eating and drinking first, and then clothing, because the demand for the first is stronger than the second—it being more urgent and more difficult to solve.

"Therefore" implies a deep meaning. As the preceding verse warns us not to serve mammon, so here we are cautioned not to be anxious about our needs such as eating, drinking, and clothing. For in being anxious we may fall into serving mammon, since it is quite possible that the serving of mammon commences with these very things.

"Life" is "soul" in the Greek original. Out of the soul comes the demand for eating, drinking, and clothing. In a number of places the Bible connects the soul with eating and drinking. Experiencing a lack of these supplies, the soul faints.

"Is not the life more than the food, and the body raiment?"

—This intimates that believers should possess noble ideals. "Can God . . . ?" and "Will God . . . ?" (Ps. 78.19,20) express the unbelief of men.

v.26 Anyone who asks "Can God?" or "Will God?" reveals his unbelief. How burdensome it is for men to live without faith in God. Our anxiety can only be alleviated through trusting Him.

In order to stimulate people to think, the Lord frequently uses questions.

For five days God restores the earth, and then on the sixth day He creates man. He prepares everything man needs before He makes him. Too often we imagine we were created on the first day!

v.27 This is the third question asked. In other words, if we know how helpless it is to be anxious, then why be anxious at all? If there is help, there is no need to be anxious. If there is no help, it is equally useless to be anxious.

Verses 26–27 dwell on the problem of eating and drinking. The birds can be seen by lifting up one's eyes. So the Lord says, "Behold the birds of the heaven" (v.26).

vv.28–30 These verses treat of the problem of clothing. The lilies of the field are rare; therefore, "Consider," says the Lord. Oh how careful is our Lord. The lilies spoken of here are probably very colorful.

"O ye of little faith"—This shows that these words are spoken to the saved ones.

George Muller based his whole life of trusting God on these two great promises concerning the birds and the lilies.

To exercise faith is to be the characteristic in this age.

v.31 "Therefore" is used one more time, for here comes the conclusion. The reason the Lord uses birds and lilies as examples is to teach us not to be anxious. He certainly has no intention for us to follow the birds and lilies in not laboring. Has He not warned us through the apostle Paul that "if any will not work, neither let him eat" (2 Thess. 3.10)?

"Sow . . . reap" (v.26)—This is man's work. "Toil . . . spin" (v.28)—This is mainly the woman's work.

v.32 "For your heavenly Father knoweth"—These words show again that this passage is addressed to believers.

"Ye have need of these things"—God will supply our needs, but He is not bound to satisfy our demands, that is, whatever we would like to have.

v.33 What is the "kingdom"? It points on the one hand to a spiritual state, such as is indicated in this statement: "The kingdom of God is not eating and drinking, but righteousness and peace and joy in the Holy Spirit" (Rom. 14.17); it points on the other hand to the future reign during the millennium. In the parable of the ten pounds (Luke 19.11–27), the idea of the kingdom includes both the spiritual living today and the future reward. Today's spiritual condition decides the reigning in the future. The "kingdom" to be sought here in Matthew 6 stresses a present spiritual condition, but even more so in the future.

The "righteousness" spoken of here is to be attained through seeking; thus it cannot have reference to justification or to the righteousness of God as is presented in the book of Romans. The righteousness in Matthew 5–7 exceeds the righteousness of the scribes and Pharisees. It is the righteousness specified in Matthew 6.1. Hence it denotes especially the Christian conduct presented in Matthew 5–7.

"Added" here means something given in addition to what you have already. Because you seek God's kingdom and His righteousness, you gain His kingdom and righteousness with a bonus of food and clothing. "To give" means there is nothing beforehand; "to add" means that something is already there.

v.34 The word "evil" is the same word found in 6.13, indicating that the Lord has not promised believers easy days.

Chapter 7

The Matter of Judging, 7.1-5

v.1 "Be ... judged" (v.1) is the very opposite of "ye judge" (v.2). It does not mean to be judged of men; rather, we know that it conveys the thought of being judged by God.

The word "judge" does not refer to that act of discerning which is both proper and legitimate. For please note the following observations:

(1) We should exercise a certain degree of discernment. The Lord himself, although He declared most emphatically that He did not come to judge but to save the world (John 12.47), did not hesitate to call the Pharisees hypocrites. Paul reprimanded the Corinthian believers as being carnal and unspiritual, yet he could at the same time exhort them not to judge anything (see 1 Cor. 4.5).

(2) We should tell the person concerned. To discern is not only an inward attitude; sometimes we have to tell what we have seen. Whenever a person comes to ask about a third person, the first thing to learn from him is whether he has any connection with the person he inquires after. If his inquiry merely represents an itching ear, there is no need on your part to confide in him. But if the inquiry relates to a given spiritual situation, there may be ground for fellowship. Our Lord enjoined His disciples to practice and observe whatever the scribes and the Pharisees taught but not what they did (see Matt. 23.3). Paul in

his last letter mentioned Alexander (2 Tim.4.14), Demas (4.10), Phygelus and Hermogenes (1.15) in order to help the receiver of his letter to guard against these people.

The word "judge" here does include, however, the following two thoughts:

(1) To act as a judge. The earliest mentioning of "judge" in the Scriptures is found in Exodus 18.13–27, at which time able men among the children of Israel were appointed rulers to judge. Hence the word carries a sense of judging as ruler. "Judge not" —Do not be judges, nor be political appointees; for if a Christian becomes a judge or political appointee, he is unable to be merciful or to be meek, and thus he will lose two of the promised blessings.

"That ye be not judged"—This does not suggest that all who are not political appointees shall escape the judgment-seat of Christ. To be judged is to be condemned.

(2) To be critical and hairsplitting. Many actions one might take may be characterized as border actions. For example, to "be angry" is permissible, yet it borders on "sin" very closely. The least carelessness will result in stepping over the boundary and falling into the realm of sin.

Such critical, hairsplitting judgment is usually due to (a) some bad intent such as having jealousy towards others, (b) harboring sin in one's self, or (c) not knowing one's self. The more people know themselves the more liberal they will be towards others.

The Lord and Paul, however, were perfect models in being able to speak the truth in love whenever it was profitable to others.

v.2 This verse shows the reason not to judge. In the Bible there are two cardinal principles: one is righteousness, the other is mercy. If you choose to treat others according to righteousness, none of your fame, position and property will suffer loss because you are able to protect yourself with righteousness. But what about the ultimate consequence? The answer given here is that "with what measure ye mete, it shall be measured unto you"— Does not James 2.13 concur by saying that "judgment is without mercy to him that hath showed no mercy"? But if you choose the principle of mercy—that is to say, the mercy which overflows as seen in Matthew 5—then in the future God will also measure out to you according to the measure of mercy. Consequently, we find that James concludes with these words: "mercy glorieth against judgment" (v.13b).

v.3 In the preceding verses the Lord warns us not to judge but instead exhorts us to be merciful. Here He tells us how improper it is to judge. As He dealt previously with future consequences, now He touches on the present situation. There is no question about the beam in one's own eye, for if he sees the mote in the other's eye it is certain that he has a beam in his own eye. And why? Because:

(1) To be able to see the mote, which is so tiny, in your brother's eye proves that you must be an expert in this respect. Because you have had experience in such sin, you can most easily recognize it. As an old Chinese adage goes: To catch a robber, use an ex-convict.

(2) It reveals one's own improper attitude towards God. Due to the multitude of one's own sins, a person tends to be more critical of his brother's fault.

Since the word "brother" is employed here, we have a further proof that the so-called Sermon on the Mount is doubtless addressed to Christians.

v.4 The preceding verse speaks of beholding the other's sin, but here it speaks of *telling* the other of his sin.

v.5 It is all right to cast out the mote in another's eye, but one needs "to cast out first the beam" in one's own eye before he can get rid of the mote in his brother's eye.

Dogs and Swine, 7.6

Verse 6 is a fragment by itself. The dogs and swine mentioned here refer especially to those people cited in 2 Peter 2.21–22. Such people are fairly near the door of the church. They have received some spiritual education, yet they are never saved. The "had washed" in 2 Peter symbolizes a kind of noble ideal; it is not a cleansing through the forgiveness of sins.

The Old Testament mentions swine a great deal, and the New Testament has much to say about dogs. Both swine and dogs are unclean. Swine are cloven-footed, but they do not chew the cud; and the dog neither parts the hoof nor chews the cud. Hence both are unclean. The spiritual symbol for a Christian is the sheep.

Outwardly the swine may look better than the dog, for it is at least cloven-hoofed. This observation may be applied to churchgoers who seem to know, yet do not know, the truth. The dog has neither the appearance nor the reality of cleanness. The Letter to the Philippians warns us of dogs (3.2); and the book of Revelation (22.15; cf. 21.8) tells of the dogs which are in the lake of fire without the Holy City.

"That which is holy" (v.6) belongs to God. How do people come into possession of holy things? These holy things—possibly they are truths as revealed in the book of Revelation or are such truths as baptism, breaking of bread, and so forth—are spiritual things which come from God.

"Pearls" are "*your* pearls"—which denote things you personally have received from God. Thus holy things represent truths in general which come out of God, whereas pearls represent those experiences which you specifically receive from God.

God's Promises

vv.7–12 This section enters upon a new situation. Although this so-called Sermon on the Mount consists mostly of commandments, it also contains God's promises. Though it mainly declares the laws of God, it equally proclaims the grace of God. In giving charge as to what one ought to do, it tells in addition how God grants the power to fulfill such a charge.

"Ask" concerning the conduct expected of you and such conduct will be given to you. "Seek" after the kingdom of God and His righteousness, and you shall find them. "Knock" at the narrow gate and it will be opened to you.

"To "ask" is an asking generally, but to "seek" is a seeking specifically, and to "knock" is a knocking closely. Hence each action is a step further on than the previous one.

vv.7–8 The first of these verses is the promise, the second is the principle.

The promise in verse 7 has a two-fold application:

(1) In order to practice the teaching of Matthew 5–7 the power must be obtained through prayer.

(2) All prayers of faith shall be answered.

v.11 "If ye then, being evil, know how to give good gifts unto your children"—"Evil" because you are born in sin. The phrase "being evil" includes in its thought all people, for no one is good.

Matthew 5–7 may be divided into three parts: (1) 5.1–20, the characteristics of the kingdom of heaven and their relationship to the law of old; (2) 5.21–7.12, the Ten Commandments or Decalogue with its new counterpart; and (3) 7.13–27, exhortations.

v.12 Here is the concluding word to the second of these three parts. "Therefore" sums up the *new* "decalogue" as pronounced in 5.21–7.12. The teaching on the mount is most practical. "All things therefore . . . " shows that 7.12 states a principle. What is given here is all positive, therefore it is different from the Ten Commandments of old. And yet it does not contradict the law and the prophets but stands on the same line with the law and the prophets. It tells us what we ought to do.

Two Gates and Two Ways

vv.13–14 What is the difference between the "gate" here and the "door" in John 10.9? In the latter passage it is the door of grace, whereas here in Matthew 7.13 it is the gate of the principles of the kingdom of heaven.

"Enter in" speaks of a choice. "By the narrow gate" indicates a transaction. "The way" represents the daily life. "Narrow" refers to the strictness of the Lord's commandments. "Narrow" is a comparative term. If the above-mentioned new law is the narrow gate, there must be a more lenient law. And thus we see that the demand of the teaching on the mount surpasses even that of the Mosaic law of old.

Here we are confronted with two gates and two ways. One is described according to its inward condition, while the other is expressed by its outward appearance. A Christian may select whichever gate to enter and whatever way to travel. His current choice is none other than to choose the life principle of today. No one can walk along the strait way without first entering by the narrow gate. Whoever does not enter in via the gate of Matthew 5–7 is definitely not walking in this way.

Why is it so important to "enter in by the narrow gate"? The word "destruction" may mean either perdition or ruin. In the case at hand, it is better to translate the word as "ruin" or "waste"; in other words, what is meant here is that everything will be demolished or ruined if the wide gate and the broad way are chosen. And even should the word "destruction" be translated as "perdition" it can only refer to temporary, not eternal, perdition.

Those who seek only to be presentable morally to the eyes of men will no doubt prefer the wide gate and the broad way.

v.14 "Straitened the way"—Because it is the way of the will of God. It is so straitened that only the will of God can get through. There is absolutely no place by which to squeeze into it the flesh, the world, or today's glory.

"Few are they that find it"—Truth often is found among the minority. The narrow gate and the strait way need to be found, indicating that many do not even know about it.

The word "way" in Acts 9.2 ("any that were of the Way"), in Acts 19.9 ("speaking evil of the Way"), and in Acts 19.23 ("there arose no small stir concerning the Way") is the same word used here in Matthew 7.14. The book of Acts thus enjoins us to believe and walk in this way.

False Prophets

vv.15–20 What kind of people are the "false prophets"? Let us see that those who were used of God to write the Bible were called prophets. According to 2 Peter 1 they were men who "spake from God, being moved by the Holy Spirit" (v.21). They were moved to speak the words of another Person. Similarly, these false prophets speak the words of another person (only they do not speak the words of God) as they are moved by the spirit (yet not by the Holy Spirit).

Being false prophets, they are directly involved in teaching. Sheep are rather innocent, but these sheepskins ("sheep's clothing") are stolen. Ravening wolves probably point to evil spirits. Neither the outside nor the inside really belong to these false prophets.

v.16 "Fruits" here refer to teachings, for the fruits of false prophets are teachings and not modes of conduct. By our hearing their teachings they shall be recognized as false prophets.

"Grapes" and "figs" are considered excellent fruits among

the Jews. How can the true preaching of God be heard from the mouths of these false prophets?

v.19 These must definitely be people of eternal perdition.

Conditions for Entering the Kingdom of Heaven, 7.21–23

v.21 This verse tells us positively that in calling Jesus Christ as Lord we shall enter the kingdom of heaven, though not everyone who so calls will enter in. The emphasis is laid on the words, "not every one"—"If thou shalt confess with thy mouth Jesus as Lord," says Paul in Romans 10.9, "thou shalt be saved"; thus indicating that the first condition for entering the kingdom of heaven is being saved. However, not everyone who is saved enters the kingdom automatically; for not all Christians have part in the kingdom. There is a second condition; namely, that "he that doeth the will of my Father who is in heaven" shall enter in.

Consequently, the general conditions for entering the kingdom of heaven are (1) a being saved, and (2) doing the will of God.

7.21 lays down the general conditions for entering the kingdom of heaven. 7.22 illustrates the special exclusion from the kingdom. And 7.23 tells of the special consequence thereof for such people.

The word "knew" in verse 23 is the past tense for the same Greek word translated "know" in Romans 7.15. In the original it means to recognize or to understand. "I never knew you" may therefore be translated as "I never recognized you"—which means "I never recognized what you did as right."

Now the people in question here are definitely Christians, for the following reasons:

(1) The context in which these words of Jesus are found is the so-called Sermon on the Mount, which, as we have continually seen, is primarily spoken to believers.

(2) The teaching of the mount from beginning to end never instructs us as to how we can be saved since it is obviously addressed to those who are already saved.

(3) This small section from verse 21 to verse 23 does not deal with the question of faith; rather, it treats of the matter of conduct. We know we are saved through faith and not by work. Hence what is said here has nothing do with eternal perdition of the unsaved.

(4) "In that day" (v.22)—What day is "that day"? These words refer to the day of judgment at the judgment-seat of Christ before which the saved alone will appear. This is *not* the judgment before the Great White Throne.

(5) The people in question here have called on the name of the Lord; therefore they are the Lord's.

(6) Notice the works they perform: they prophesy by the name of the Lord, and by the same Name they cast out demons and do many mighty works.

"That day" is a specific term in the Bible. As today is the day of man (see 1 Cor. 4.3: "or of man's judgment" which in the original is "of man's day") when man judges, so "that day" is the day of the judgment-seat of Christ when all the saved—and no one but the saved—shall be judged (see 2 Tim. 1.12,18; 4.8).

v.22 "Many" shall not enter the kingdom of heaven. "Lord, Lord . . . "—They call on His name once again.

"Prophesy by thy name, and by thy name cast out demons, and by thy name do many mighty works"—All these are considered to be great gifts in the church: to prophesy is to do the work of a prophet; to cast out demons is to bring in the kingdom of heaven; and to do mighty works is to exercise the power of the age to come. Those who perform such acts specifically cite these things because they think by these things they are most qualified to enter the kingdom.

v.23 The word "confess" in Matthew 10.32–33 points to

the saved ones. If we do not confess the Lord before men now we will be denied the glory of the kingdom of heaven. Similarly, the passage here rendered as "then will I profess unto them, I never knew you" is better to be translated as "I never recognized or approved of you"; and the reason for His disapproval is given in the words "ye that work iniquity"—wherein "iniquity" in Greek actually means "lawlessness" and means not working according to the rules of the kingdom of heaven.

"Depart from me" simply denotes that they have no part in the glory, a glory which is very different from what is mentioned in 2 Thessalonians 1.9.

Hence the general conditions for entering the kingdom of heaven are a being saved plus doing the will of God.

The Holy Spirit who *dwells in* man is the *Person* of the Holy Spirit, and therefore He is there to rule over man. But the Holy Spirit that *falls upon* man is without personality, and hence it obeys man: "The spirits of the prophets are subject to the prophets" (1 Cor. 14.32). The Holy Spirit dwells only in the saved ones, but His power may fall upon the unsaved such as Balaam.

It is possible to be lawless even in prophesying, in casting out demons, and in doing mighty works. There is the danger of not doing the will of God in all these things. We need to ask the Lord to deliver us from the iniquity of the sanctuary (see Num. 18.1). Let us realize that in the last days these same things shall be greatly increased.

The Wise and Foolish Man, 7.24–27

vv.24–27 The Lord adopts the use of parables here to reinforce what has been spoken before.

v.24 The problem cited in this verse is not a matter of hearing but doing. We have already heard; whether or not we do depends on each individual.

"These words"—Broadly speaking, they have reference to the entire teaching on the mount. In a more restricted sense, they refer to the emphasis previously laid down above of doing the will of God.

"Rock" signifies doing the will of God. Here it does not point to the Lord himself.

v.26 "Foolish" does not mean "wicked"; it instead agrees with the thought of the "foolish" virgins spoken of in Matthew 25.2. Neither does it refer to the unsaved, since the entire subject here is building.

vv.25, 27 "The rain descended, and the floods came, and the winds blew, and beat [smote, v.27] upon that house"—Not a beating upon the person but only a beating upon his work is in view here. Hence he must be a saved person.

"Who built his house upon the rock"—The man in question thus built, not because he was good but because he was wise. This is in parallel with the wise virgins cited in Matthew 25.2.

"Every one therefore that heareth these words of mine, and doeth them"—That is, a doing according to the Lord's words. The foolish person is not one who does nothing, since he too goes and builds; but he does things according to his own will instead of according to God's words. One pathetic trait among believers is their inclination to imitate the world.

What is the difference between the wise and the foolish? They both spend the same time and they are all engaged in building. Yet what a pity that the foolish builds upon the sand. The wise, though, has his eyes on the judgment-seat of Christ.

"Rain" and "floods" and "winds" speak of great tribulation. The rain comes from above, and so it beats upon the head. The winds blow in all directions, and the floods strike against the foundation. Thus, "rain" refers to the works of the evil spirits, "winds" allude to the leadings of the evil spirits (see Eph. 4.14), and "floods" signify the power of the evil spirits.

THE GOSPEL ACCORDING TO MATTHEW

Chapter 8

v.1 This follows immediately after the end of chapter 7.

The Cleansing of the Leper, 8.2–4

v.2 "And behold, there came to him a leper"—It should be noted that the cleansing of this leper actually happened before the teaching was given on the mount. This we may gather from other Gospels.

It should be remembered that the Gospel according to Matthew is not written in strict chronological order; but Mark's Gospel is. Each Evangelist has his own way of arranging the order of recorded events. Matthew records both the actions and the words of our Lord, whereas Mark narrates mainly the Lord's actions and rarely touches on Jesus' words, since Mark presents the Lord as servant; and it is not for servants to say much.

Mark uses especially the word "straightway", while Matthew repeats the special term "the kingdom of heaven" some 32 times. Now since Mark uses "straightway" so frequently it is quite natural for him to narrate the events according to historical order. So that if the exactness of historical order is desired, Mark is the best source for this among the Gospels. In this connection, it should be remarked that John in his Gospel often uses the words "on the morrow"; and this is a clue to the fact that his record is chronologically more exact than that of Matthew. So far as chronological order is concerned, we may conclude that Mark is more exact than Luke, and John is more exact than Matthew.

The criterion of Luke's order is moral or ethical in nature; that of Matthew is doctrinal or didactical; and that of Mark is historical or chronological.

According to the order of events in Matthew 8 (as rearranged by the Evangelist), they are listed as follows:

(1) the cleansing of the leper,

(2) the healing of the centurion's servant, and

(3) the healing of Peter's mother-in-law.

But according to historical order, they should be:

(1) the healing of Peter's mother-in-law,

(2) the cleansing of the leper, and

(3) the healing of the centurion's servant.

Why does Matthew record these events in such a way? Because from beginning to end his Gospel unveils to his readers the kingdom of heaven. Matthew uses this theme as the backbone to his entire narration; that is to say, he relates everything to the kingdom of heaven. Hence he groups events together meaningfully instead of simply following an historical order.

Since Luke makes the moral aspect—that is, how God shows grace to man—the controlling feature of his narrative, then naturally, in every section of his Gospel we are shown God's salvation.

John, on the other hand, tells his readers much of what the Lord Jesus does in Galilee. Now Galilee is sometimes called "Galilee of the nations"—and therefore John selects the world as that which governs his choice of material, and eliminates all unnecessary background to his Gospel account.

Why does 8.2 begin with a "behold"? For the sake of attracting people's attention, because what follows is a matter of special interest. In the case of Naaman, Elisha did not dare to touch him, but commanded the Syrian general to go and wash in the river Jordan (see 2 Kings 5.10–11), thus adhering to the Old

Testament law concerning the cleansing of leprosy (see Lev. 14). Here, though, the Lord both touches and heals the leper.

Matthew narrates events in this order because of their typological significance, as we shall see below.

Many there are who have leprosy, but only one among them is healed. The Jews are like men with leprosy—they have all sinned; yet those who receive grace are but a remnant—the one man healed.

The servant of the centurion is a Gentile. As the children of Israel refuse to accept grace, salvation comes to the Gentiles. In Luke's narrative we find that the centurion sends the elders to the Jews to ask the Lord, thus indicating that salvation is from the Jews. On the other hand, Matthew, who writes to the Jews, omits the sending of the Jewish elders in order to show how the Gentiles can come directly to the Lord.

Note too that the leper is healed through the touch of the Lord, which act symbolizes the fleshly relationship of the Lord to the Jews. By contrast, the servant of the centurion is healed without the Lord touching him at all, in fact he is healed merely by a word being spoken by the Lord while a great distance away. And the centurion hears the word and believes, yet he has not seen the Lord perform this act of healing. This signifies how the Gentiles will be saved through faith. Thus, what God has decreed for us is to believe that which we have not seen (John 20.29).

Leprosy denotes the uncleanness of sin; it speaks particularly of the Jew. Palsy signifies the infirmity of sin; it refers especially to the Gentiles. And fever represents the feebleness of the flesh in obeying God.

Sin causes weakness as well as it defiles.

Uncleanness needs to be washed before God.

Weakness needs to be countered with strength.

Peter's mother-in-law is healed because of the intimate relationship between Peter and the Lord. This shows how after the Gentiles have received grace (as represented by the centurion's servant being healed), the Lord will again be gracious to the children of Israel (symbolized by Peter's mother-in-law being healed) for the sake of Abraham and for the sake of David.

Fever here may allude to the situation that will obtain during the Great Tribulation, for tribulation is like a fiery furnace.

Matthew narrates these incidents in such a way because of their significance in the truth.

Charles H. Spurgeon comments on Matthew 8.2 by saying that if a person has leprosy and does not come to worship the Lord his leprosy is indeed incurable.

"Lord, if thou wilt"—In Mark 9, the father whose son has a dumb spirit is recorded as saying to the Lord, "If thou canst" (vv. 22–23). This is a question of power. And the Lord reprimands him for doubting His power. Here in Matthew it is "Lord, if thou wilt"—a matter of the Lord's heart. The man with leprosy does not at all doubt the Lord's power; he simply does not know if the Lord is willing to heal.

v.3 "I will"—The Lord is definitely willing. This reveals the Lord's heart towards the sick.

v.4 At that time the law has not as yet been abrogated. Only through the death of our Lord are we delivered from the requirements of the law (see Rom. 7.4). Since the Lord at that period is yet to die, everything has to be in accordance with the law of Moses.

The Healing of the Centurion's Servant, 8.5–13

Fever speaks of abnormal power. Palsy speaks of abnormal weakness. And leprosy speaks of abnormal uncleanness.

"So great faith" (v.10) is an evidence of believing God's authority. God's authority is closely related to His word. When God said, "Let there be light"—light indeed came into being. He created the heaven and the earth by His authority.

Power is dynamite (from the Greek word *dunamis*).

Authority (Greek, *exousia*) is absolute, unrestricted freedom of action or right to act. It denotes that incomprehensible strength to which everything must bow. People today stress power but neglect authority. Man sinned because he tried to overturn the authority of God. Lucifer became Satan because he wished to overthrow God's authority. He not only does not himself submit to the authority of God but also instigates men to rise up against Him too. When Christ shall come, however, He will crush Satan with His authority. The sword which comes out of His mouth is the power of His authority.

God does not use power as His direct way of controlling the universe.

Christians today ought to learn to submit themselves under the authority of God.

vv.11–13 "In the kingdom of heaven"—The Lord has not specified whether this refers to the present or to the future. Some people think it alludes to the present, but if so it is hard to explain how the many will come from the East and the West to sit down with Abraham, Isaac and Jacob. Yet from the words of Matthew 11.11–12 it seems as though the kingdom of heaven does exist today. Matthew 5.3, however, points to the future, because the kingdom of heaven is related to reward in that passage.

The term kingdom of God is used five times in Matthew (6.33, 12.28, 19.24, 21.31 and 43). The kingdom of God is the sovereignty of God. There must be a distinction between the kingdom of God and the kingdom of heaven, otherwise the Lord would not employ another term. The kingdom of God has its future, as well as its present, aspect.

The Healing of Peter's Mother-in-Law, 8.14–15

v.14 This verse is related to the Jews, for this word has its special significance in the Bible.

We should pay particular attention to the word "house" in Matthew 13.1 and 36. In the Gospel of Matthew the wise men are shown as having seen the Lord in the house (2.11) whereas in Luke's Gospel we are told that the shepherds found Him in the manger (2.16).

The Lord heals the leper under the open heaven and not in a house, for a house conveys the thought of intimate communication. At the first coming of the Lord relatively few among the Jews are saved. Note, though, that the Lord healed Peter's mother-in-law in the disciple's house, which indicates intimacy and affection—thus signifying how in the future the whole nation will be saved.

In the cleansing of the leper and the healing of Peter's mother-in-law the Lord touches both of them, showing how He has a special relationship with the Jews.

The Many Sick Ones Healed, 8.16–17

vv.16–17 This foretells what the Lord will do in the coming kingdom. This completes the cycle of the order according to the teaching which Matthew adopts.

The touch of our Lord (8.15) is powerful. As He touches, His power counteracts our weakness. Where He touches, Satan has no more ground.

The "many" in 8.16 means a great many, a great multitude. Here the Lord casts out demons with a word, and thus we can see echoed here the word that was spoken to the leper for his cleansing.

"Brought unto him" (v.16)—that is to say, brought to the place of the blessing of the Lord.

v.17 "Himself took our infirmities and bare our diseases" —This quotation from Isaiah 53.4 is potentially fulfilled at the time when the Lord Jesus healed the sick and actually fulfilled at the time when Christ was crucified.

There are two extreme views regarding the relationship between sickness and the Lord:

(1) the scope of the Lord's bearing sickness is as broad as the scope of His bearing sin, and

(2) the Lord bears only sins, but not sickness.

Both of these views are faulty. The Lord indeed bears our sicknesses today, but his bearing such sicknesses and infirmities is quite different from that of His bearing our sins—both in scope, in degree, and in meaning. (The "infirmities" in 8.17 is the same word in Greek as is translated "weakness" and "weaknesses" in 2 Cor. 12.9). For example, people may have the same faith towards forgiveness of sins and the healing of sickness, but they may not receive or experience the same result today. Believing in the forgiveness of sins will result in having sins forgiven; yet believing in the healing of sickness may not result in the experience of healing. And why? Because the work of bearing our diseases will not be fully realized until the Lord's second coming.*

Spurgeon once commented that each time the Lord healed a sickness there flowed out power from Him to the sick, He himself thus becoming weak.

On earth, our Lord as Son bore the appellation of four persons; namely, (1) the Son of God, (2) the Son of man, (3) the Son of Abraham, and (4) the Son of David. In the four small sections of 8.1–17 just described, we find the Lord displayed as the Son of the following four personages:

(1) in the cleansing of the leper, Jesus is presented as the Son of God—this is a looking towards the Jews;

(2) in the healing of the palsied, Christ is shown to be the Son of Abraham, on the principle of faith—this is a looking towards the Gentiles;

(3) in the healing of Peter's mother-in-law, the Lord is ex-

---

*For more on this subject by the author the reader is advised to consult Watchman Nee, *The Spiritual Man* (New York: Christian Fellowship Publishers, 1968), vol. 3, pp. 183–185. Translated from the Chinese. —*Translator*

hibited as the Son of David—this is a looking towards future Jews; and

(4) in the casting out of demons and in the healing of many sick, Jesus is portrayed as the Son of Man—this is a looking towards all mankind.

Faith Put to the Test, 8.18–27

v.18 It was the habit of the Lord to depart whenever there were great multitudes. He did not seek for curious people to throng Him.

"The other side" is that situation where no people are. Our Lord does not seek the crowds. To look at men, to draw men's attention to self, and/or to seek out multitudes are too often the common ills of God's workers. As we labor for God, let us not consider how to gain people to ourselves, for this is the Lord's business. As soon as the work is done we, as the Lord did, should leave; for if we linger longer, it will soon be strange fire. Human attraction may become stronger than divine order.

vv.19–20 The "scribe" may represent the zealous. He volunteers without condition to follow the Lord. But when the Lord shows him how He fares worse than the birds and the foxes, the scribe realizes the hardship and draws back. Consequently, whoever does not count the cost can never follow the Lord. The scribe may therefore also stand for all who wish to establish themselves instead of sacrificing themselves.

v.21 A "disciple" is one who has already been called. "Bury my father" is the duty of a son, but how can one who has been called shrink back?

v.22 The first "dead" is the dead described in Ephesians 2.1 ("when ye were dead through your trespasses and sins"). Here is a demand of the Lord which is far more important than the burying of one's father. The burying can be done by other people. Thus we are given a principle, which is, that the call of the Lord outstrips all. He will not allow anything other than His own self to govern or manipulate our lives.

"Suffer me first"—This is undoubtedly a great mistake; the Lord's call transcends everything.

The difference between these two men is that whereas the one has not counted the cost, the other has overestimated the cost.

In following the Lord it is plain foolishness not to count the cost; but it is equally idiotic to count it all the time, for that will hinder us from going on. We should avoid both of these errors.

If the Lord calls us to go, we should count the cost and say to Him, "I am willing": let us leave all things behind. The path of obedience takes obedience as finality; it does not wait until all difficult problems are finally solved. "Follow me" is the solution to "bury their own dead" (v.22).

If the Lord has called you, then even if you consider drawing back because of difficulties, He still commands you to follow Him.

Actually, verses 19–22 are a parenthetic section. Luke records something similar, though it may belong to some other occasion.

vv.24–27 Their prayer is "Save, Lord" because "we perish"—when they see they are perishing, then they are to be saved.

Due to their little faith they cry "Save, Lord"! Due to their cowardice they presume that they "perish" indeed.

A little faith seems somewhat better than no faith at all. It is a small step forward.

Amid all the confusion the Lord is still teaching His disciples, for it is easier for Him to deal with environments such as winds and waves than for Him to deal with the disciples.

All fears and apprehensions are due to unbelief.

The Lord reprimands them because of their little faith. Has not the Lord already said, "Let us go over unto the other side" (Mark 4.35)? This is a command which also is a promise. Yet they still cry out, "We perish"—thus revealing their unbelief as though the Lord had said, "Let us go down to the bottom of the sea"!

The word of the Lord is closely linked with faith.

We may conclude that many prayers are simply expressions of little faith. Prayer is not acceptable on the basis of their number.

Twice is the word "arose" used in this section: "There arose a great tempest in the sea" (v.24) and "he [Jesus] arose and there was a great calm" (v.26).

The little faith is in contrast to the great calm.

Verses 2–17 gather up several miracles together. Verses 18–27 relate the effects of the Lord's presence.

To rebuke the winds and the sea implies that these elements have intelligence. Since neither of them *has* intelligence, the Lord must be rebuking the demons behind the winds and the sea.

The Gadarene Demoniacs, 8.28–34

v.28 This fulfills what the Lord had said previously; namely, "he commanded to depart unto the other side" (v.18).

Matthew then recounts that two were possessed with demons, whereas Luke reports only one (see Luke 8.27). Being himself a physician, Luke is often found giving more detail in his Gospel record, especially when his narrative turns to the cases of the sick. For instance, Matthew speaks of a leper (8.2) but Luke says a man full of leprosy (5.12). Again, Matthew tells here of the two possessed with demons; Luke, on the other hand, reports the man as being possessed with legions of demons (Luke 8.30). Being a professional man, Luke has his own observations of the sick.

The reasons why Luke records only one demon-possessed man are as follows:

(1) Since the two cases are alike, a report on one is sufficient.

(2) Since Luke has not personally followed the Lord on earth, his writing is done through careful investigation of eyewitnesses and ministers of the word: he therefore narrates only that which he has researched.

(3) Because Matthew presents the Lord as King, he frequently reports two instead of one inasmuch as a plurality adds a tinge of majesty to the event being described. Luke on the other hand presents the Lord as man; hence the presentation of one evidence is quite adequate.

(4) Because Matthew writes to the Jews, he has in mind the Jewish custom of requiring the presence of two witnesses to an event. But Luke writes to the Gentiles, among whom there is no such rule; therefore, it is not necessary for him to report more than one demon-possessed man as being present.

(5) Since Matthew writes from a doctrinal and didactic point of view, he does not concern himself so much with what happens "afterwards" in the life of a person who has been touched by the Lord. Luke, however, writes from a moral or ethical stance, and so he is very much interested in singling out one individual and giving the details of his life and the "afterwards" of his walk.

The men possessed with demons are neighbors to the dead.

v.29 Ignoble as they were, the demons still recognized the Lord as the Son of God. In this respect they are better than men.

"Before the time" is indicative of a definite time. The demons well know the time of their torment. All this shows that God has set aside a definite time for tormenting the demons.

v.30 The Lord made no reply to the demons. The less anyone talks to the demons the better.

v.32 The Lord said but one word: "Go"; and then , the whole herd of swine rushed into the sea by their own will. They cast themselves into the sea because they did not want to be possessed by the demons. In this particular respect, the swine are better than men.

v.34 The people of the city begged the Lord to depart from their borders. (Interestingly, their "prayer" was not much different from the request of the demons.) Since they begged Him to leave, He departed from their borders. The Lord never forces himself upon anybody.

In this third major division of Matthew's Gospel (chapters 8–9, with chapters 1–4 being the first and 5–7, the second), we learn how the Lord manifested himself and how He was rejected by men.

In the first small section (8.2–17), we see how the Lord acted in the capacity of His fourfold sonship. But in the second small section (8.18–9.8), we are shown how the Lord manifested His authority in four different realms: (1) the realm of nature, (2) the realm of the demons, (3) the realm of man, and (4) the realm of the believers. In all of these realms, two things are quite evident to the reader: His power, and the intents of the human heart.

THE GOSPEL ACCORDING TO MATTHEW

Chapter 9

The Healing of the Palsied Man, 9.1–8

v.1 The city is Capernaum.

v.2 Mark states that "it was noised that he was in the house" (2.1). Matthew's account is stated more simply, since his purpose is to present Christ as King. Accordingly, he chooses not to record the details but to give only the broadest outline of events. For Matthew, wherever the Lord is, He cannot be hidden.

"And Jesus seeing their faith"—Faith is something which can be seen.

The Lord has manifested His authority among His disciples. He has also demonstrated His authority over the demons as well as over natural elements. If He should now show forth His authority towards sinners the cycle of His manifestation would be complete. It is for this reason, therefore, that 9.1–8 was shown earlier to be inseparable from chapter 8.

"Be of good cheer"—How can one be of good cheer if his sins are not forgiven?

Although the scribes have learned the *doctrine* of forgiveness found in the Old Testament, they are totally ignorant of the *reality* of forgiveness. They have the teaching but not the experience.

v.3 This is the first indication of Christ's rejection. The Lord's action reveals the hidden thought in the heart of the scribes.

v.4 The Lord will not overlook the thought of the heart. Hence we should strive to have the meditation of our heart acceptable in the sight of God (cf. Ps. 19.14).

v.5 "For which is easier . . . ?"—On the Lord's side, both are equally easy. To the mind of the Jews, however, uttering empty words such as "thy sins are forgiven" is much easier, for who can prove the outcome? Yet by causing the palsied man to walk, the Lord intends by this action to prove to the Jews that the sin of this man has indeed been forgiven.

v.6 The walking of the palsied man confirms the trustworthiness of our Lord's words. If what is *seen* is true, then what is *un*seen must likewise be true.

v.7 "And departed to his house"—The great principle of the gospel is that forgiveness precedes walking.

The Old Testament principle is to walk and live; the New Testament principle is to live and then to walk. The one is work, whereas the other is grace.

v.8 Before the time of chapter 16 of Matthew's narrative the Lord never calls himself the Son of God. He instead continually styles himself the Son of man after the event of His temptation but prior to that of Matthew 16. The highest peak in the entire Gospel of Matthew is reached in this chapter 16. Although the Lord has not said in so many words who He is, yet from what He has done He can be known. Once Peter confesses Him as the Son of God and as Christ as recorded in chapter 16, the Lord begins to speak of His death and resurrection.

"Glorified God"—Such glorifying of God here is quite different from the glorifying of God done by believers, because the people in question here have not yet repented.

The Call of Matthew, 9.9–13

This small section reveals the grace of God. Now the Lord himself comes forth to seek man. Other Gospels give more details regarding the call of Matthew. As usual, Matthew omits the particulars. Besides, he does not wish to write too much concerning himself.

v.9 "A man, called Matthew"—By the way this phrase is worded, it would appear as though Matthew has never seen the Lord before. As the Lord calls, he immediately follows. There must have been something quite special in the voice and eye of the Lord to cause people willingly to follow Him.

The Lord does not say, Believe Me; He instead says, Follow Me. And why? Because believing the Lord is included in the following of the Lord. The life of a Christian lies in following the Lord. Christ requires not only believing but also following. And following means doing God's will in the way of the cross. God has little use for people who believe and yet do not follow the Lord.

To follow the Lord is to partake of the Lord's tribulation, patience, and kingdom. Patience denotes no straining of one's own strength.

v.10 This feast is prepared by Matthew.

v.11 Though men themselves are unrighteous, they nevertheless enjoy seeing God mete out His justice upon others who are unrighteous. But because they do not know the grace of God, they blame the Lord for being gracious towards the world. A gracious manner is often censured by men.

v.12 What the Lord purports to say is that if publicans and sinners are not permitted to come to Him, then the whole world cannot come to Him. The publicans and sinners know and acknowledge their own plight, and hence they draw near to the Lord. But because the Pharisees account themselves to be righteous, they criticize the Lord for being gracious toward the others.

v.13 The world has only self-righteous people such as the Pharisees. "Mercy" is part of grace. Grace comes only from above. Instead of welcoming grace, men like to offer up something as a sacrifice to God.

God wants man (just as he is) to come and receive grace. This is the only way of communication, for repentance uncovers one's true face. A person admits what he really is.

This verse shows us, though, how grace incites the gainsaying of men.

Though at that time our Lord continually maintained friendly intercourse with sinners, the Scriptures nevertheless tell us that He was "separated from sinners" (Heb. 7.26). Only those who are separated from sinners may draw near to sinners.

In the case of the calling of Matthew, the Lord answered the protests of the Pharisees. From 9.14 to 9.17 He is found replying to the predicament of the disciples of John the Baptist.

The Question about Fasting, 9.14–17

v.14 John was inclined to be ascetic.

v.15 The "bridegroom" is the Lord, the "sons of the bridechamber" are disciples. These disciples will later on become the bride. But during the transitional period the Lord looks upon them as the sons of the bridechamber. "Taken away" points to the Lord's rejection, not to His ascension; for the ascension of the Lord is for the purpose of obtaining glory, and there is therefore no need to fast.

v.16 "Undressed cloth" speaks of the outward conduct and "new wine" in verse 17 refers to the inward life; for whereas cloth is exposed outside, wine ferments within. The one relates to living, the other to life itself. One is objective, the other is subjective.

What the gospel of the New Testament gives to man is an inner life as represented by the new wine. What it gives to man outwardly by way of conduct is symbolized by the undressed cloth.

The statutes and ordinances of the law are likened to the old garment. One among them is the matter of fasting.

To mix up the new and the old is to call on the gospel to help the law. The best that can be expected from such action is but a patching up, not to say also that this will equally cause to occur a worse rent to the garment. For example, circumcision is a cardinal rite; yet the Galatian letter of Paul shows us how we have no need for it. As Paul's Letter to the Romans tells us that none can be justified by law, even so, Galatians informs us that neither can anyone be sanctified by law. The law can neither justify nor sanctify anyone. And this is just what the Lord Jesus is teaching us here in Matthew 9.

The law has its aspect of commandment as well as its aspect of principle. So far as its commandment goes, the Lord fills it to the full. But as to its principle, He sets it aside completely: whenever the New Testament epistles use the phrase "by faith" it means by the *principle* of faith, such as "the righteous shall live by [the principle of] faith" (Rom. 1.17; cf. Darby footnote).

v.17 The reason why "wine" points to the inner life is because "new wine" continues on with the power of fermentation. The life which the Lord puts in us is like the new wine.

The phrase "old wine-skins" points to the ordinances of the law. The words "put new wine into old wine-skins . . . the skins burst" shows what will happen to those ordinances. We may ask, for example, how one with new life can practice the Old Testament commandment of an eye for an eye? Putting the new life of the Lord into the old ordinances of the law will without fail burst them.

Matthew 5–7 discloses to us not just new wine-skins but new wine-skins that have new wine in them. The commandments given on the mount, which are to govern our outward conduct, are but the highest expressions of our inward life. Hence Matthew 5–7 reveals what we have received within, thus making it possible to live in this totally new manner (whereas old wine represents the carnal or fleshly manner of life).

"Both are preserved"—That is, both the new wine and the old wine-skins.

The Dead Raised and the Issue of Blood Stanched, 9.18–26

v.18 The name of the ruler (Jairus) is not given, neither is given the name of the demons (Legion) who possess the two men in Gadara. (These names are supplied to us by other Gospel writers.) Matthew seldom mentions other peoples' names since before the Lord the King these names are insignificant.

"Jairus" is a Hebrew name which means "whom Jehovah enlightens".

Matthew says the daughter is even now dead, whereas Luke reports that she "was dying" (8.42). This apparent discrepancy is due to the fact that the former records the scene after her death while the latter narrates the situation from the start of her desperation. Each Gospel has its unique characteristics. Each Evangelist presents only that material which is related to his special viewpoint. Since Luke writes to the Gentiles, therefore he brings in moral issues. But because Matthew writes to the Jews, what is thus typified by the raising up of the daughter of this Jewish ruler is the future restoration of the Jewish nation.

v.20 The ruler's daughter is twelve years old, but so has

the woman had an issue of blood for twelve years (see Luke 8.43). This shows that the woman began to experience bleeding at the time of the birth of the girl. The woman with an issue of blood represents the Gentiles. This flowing of blood means the extinguishing of life. The Gentiles are indeed like dead dogs. This is thus another indication that while the Jews are still under God's gracious care the Gentiles have no part with God.

The death of the ruler's daughter typifies the rejection of the Jewish nation even as the nation herself has rejected the Lord. The Lord is on His way to Jairus' house. At this moment, therefore, the Lord's intent is not to heal the woman with an issue of blood but to go to the ruler's house. He heals the woman on the way only incidentally. All this signifies how the Lord comes for the Jews, but when the Jews themselves reject Him the Gentiles are blessed instead.

The resurrection of the ruler's daughter points to the millennium. This is what Paul means by the grafting again of the natural olive branches into their own olive tree (see Rom. 11.23–24).

In raising Jairus' daughter from the dead the Lord took her hand, just as He laid His hand on the leper for his cleansing. The woman with an issue of blood, however, was healed by herself touching the Lord's garment. This is faith.

v.21 Faith requires the word of God. "She said within herself"—Is this merely psychological? "If I do but touch his garment, I shall be made whole"—The word "but" here is a word of comparison. Perhaps she believed in the Lord the moment she noticed how He was willing to go, as requested, and lay hands on the daughter of Jairus. She does not ask the Lord to lay a hand on her, she instead reckons that if she merely touches the Lord's garments she would be healed. This is no guesswork; it is her expression of faith.

v.22 "From that hour" are Matthew's own words. The

hour refers to the time of the entire incident. The reason why to this woman the Lord said "Thy faith hath made thee whole" was to give her a word by which she could resist any future attacks of temptation to disbelieve the fact that she has indeed been healed by the Lord.

Here again we notice how scanty in detail is the narrative of Matthew. This is his characteristic way of writing.

vv.23–25 The Lord says only the damsel is asleep. He does not say that all the dead are sleeping.

"And the crowd making a tumult"—The world offers little help to the living, but it seems to give much help to the dead.

"The crowd was put forth"—The Lord appears to put out all who believe that the damsel is dead. The spiritually dead are shut outside the door of life.

The Two Blind Men and the Dumb Man Possessed, 9.27–34

vv.27–28 Blessed are those who say "Yea, Lord"!

vv.29–30 Here, we have eyes opened. In the next verse (v.31), we have mouths opened.

v.31 In the realm of spiritual work the most essential thing is to obey the Lord's word; otherwise, we will hurt the Master's affairs.

vv.32–34 This event proves how the Jews reject our Lord.

The healing of the woman with an issue of blood and the resurrection of Jairus' daughter have their doctrinal and dispensational representations. The death of the damsel represents the death of the Jewish nation. The healing of the woman speaks of the salvation of the Gentiles. And the resurrection of the damsel signifies the restoration of the Jews. In the other Gospels the narration of these incidents lays more stress on the moral teachings involved.

When the Jews are willing to confess that the Lord is the Son of David—the Messiah—their blind eyes will open and their dumb mouths will speak.

The Mission of the Twelve, 9.35–10.42

This section records the sending forth of the twelve disciples after the Lord is rejected.

v.35 The reason for the sending out of the disciples is to cover the many cities and villages. After the Lord has begun His work, He notices the tremendous need of these cities and villages. So He sends His disciples forth.

"The gospel of the kingdom" includes the gospel of grace with the addition of the element of the powers of the age to come.

v.36 "Moved with compassion for them, because they were distressed and scattered"—The Lord shows no sympathy toward sins, for sins must be redeemed by His blood. He is only moved with compassion towards their distress and "scatteredness". So our Lord not only deals with sin but also shows mercy towards our distress. God sends Him to be Savior because of our sins; He additionally sends Him to be the friend of sinners because of their distress.

v.37 "The harvest indeed is plenteous"—So far as the nation of Israel is concerned, they reject Christ. But as regards individuals, the harvest to be gathered is still plenteous.

v.38 Here is one of the greatest spiritual principles: Whatever the Lord has in His heart to do, He first calls the disciples to pray. Only after they have prayed to the Lord of the harvest to send forth laborers are they sent out by Jesus.

The chain of prayer is (1) initiated by God, (2) prayed by men, and (3) the work accomplished in accordance with God's will.

God answers prayer so as to achieve His will. And this is why Gordon Watts once said that prayer is laying down tracks for the will of God to run on.

Jesus asked the disciples to pray that the Lord of the harvest would send forth laborers. After a while, those who were sent out were these very disciples. As we pray for a certain thing, God is preparing us to be willing to do the very same thing. If God cannot change the one who prays, how can He change the one who is prayed for? How can we ever expect God to send out others if we ourselves are unprepared for being sent out too?

THE GOSPEL ACCORDING TO MATTHEW

Chapter 10

The Mission of the Twelve (9.35–10.42), Concl'd

v.1 "Gave them authority"—This is the power of the age to come. At the same time that the Lord sends the disciples out to preach the gospel of the kingdom, He also promises to perform the works of the kingdom through them by means of divine power.

vv.2–4 The apostles are sent forth. The twelve apostles are paired as follows: Simon called Peter with Andrew, James the son of Zebedee with John, Philip with Bartholomew, Thomas with Matthew, James the son of Alphaeus with Thaddaeus, and Simon the Cananaean with Judas Iscariot.

The order in Luke 6 is slightly different since there the emphasis is on the calling whereas here in Matthew 10 it is on the sending.

Peter means stone, some suggest that Thomas and Matthew are twin brothers, and Bartholomew is almost certainly Nathanael.

"Matthew the publican"—Only in the Gospel of Matthew are the words "the publican" attached to the name Matthew. No doubt this is due to the fact that when Matthew was recording this event he recalled his own salvation. And it might very well be that he wrote this line with tears.

Kerioth (from which Judas gets his name?) is a place in

Judea. Of the twelve apostles, only Judas is a Judean. The rest
are all Galileans. "Iscariot" may mean "that which is exchanged
with a price"—and hence it can be translated as Judas the
trader: how he trades, with the Master as his commodity!

vv.5–6 This time they are sent exclusively to the house of
Israel. Although the nation rejects the Lord, He still sends disciples to preach the gospel of the kingdom to them. "Israel" here
includes all twelve tribes.
Why does the Lord use the words "the lost sheep of the
house of Israel"? Because in the sight of God, Israel *is* lost.

vv.7–8 "Heal the sick ... cast out demons"—These actions are to manifest the powers of the age to come.
"Freely give"—The spiritual power of the gospel cannot be
bought or sold.

vv.9–10 "Nor shoes"—The word for "shoes" is plural in
the Greek. The word "laborer" is the same as that found in
chapter 9.37,38; only here, it is cast in the singular number.

v.11 Stay in the house of the worthy one until you go
forth.

v.14 "Shake off the dust of your feet"—An action to indicate that they will have nothing to do with whatever place
wherein Christ is rejected.

v.15 This verse shows that there will be different degrees
of punishment.
Rejecting Christ is a greater sin than many other serious
sins.
Here the Lord ordered the disciples to go forth without
money or staff. This is the principle for working among the
house of Israel, not for working among the Gentiles. The prin-

ciple which applies to preaching among the gentile nations is set forth in the writing of the apostle John: "taking nothing of the Gentiles" (3 John 7). Accept only the supplies from the believers.

Carrying no wallet nor staff while preaching to the house of Israel also has its time limit (see Luke 22.35–38).

From the context we can readily perceive that this passage does not give us the principle of preaching to the Gentiles, if we consider the following:

(1) 10.5 explicitly states: "Go not into any way of the Gentiles . . ."

(2) "Search out who in it is worthy" (10.11)—Preaching to the nations is to preach to the unworthy.

(3) "And if the house be worthy" (10.13)—The Gentiles have yet to be reconciled to God. How, then, could any house of the Gentiles be worthy of peace?

However, there are a few basics in this passage which *may* be applied to today's preaching of the gospel among the Gentiles: (1) "freely ye received, freely give" (10.8); (2) trusting God for all needs; and (3) taking nothing from those who do not receive salvation.

v.16 The Lord mentions here not just the serpents but also the doves. He does not exhort us to be *like* serpents, only exhorts us to be *wise* as serpents, which means for us to not unnecessarily provoke people to our own harm.

"Harmless as doves"—Among the wicked, be wise lest you suffer needlessly. And do not ever hurt others.

vv.17–20 They will be persecuted.

v.21 For the sake of the gospel, the closest ties of human relationship will be broken. The greatness of the Lord will arouse the resistance of men.

v.22 Many are hated by people, but how many are hated for the sake of the name of the Lord?

No tribulation, no joy. Nothing on earth gives joy like tribulation (see Rom. 5.3). Yet without an obedient heart, none can suffer for the Lord.

"He that endureth to the end, the same shall be saved"— This statement is quite different from the one found in Acts 16.31, "Believe on the Lord Jesus, and thou shalt be saved, thou and thy house": for the first is spoken to the disciples whereas the second is addressed to the sinner. "Saved" here may refer to deliverance out of the hands of the wicked, or it may also allude to salvation at the coming of the kingdom age—that is to say, it may have reference to receiving reward in the millennium. Most probably this points to reward.

Salvation has relevance to three different realms and time periods: (1) today in the age of grace, (2) in the kingdom age, and (3) in the new heaven and the new earth.

v.23 To "flee" (not "resist") is a principle for Christians to follow when under persecution.

"Till the Son of man be come"—This cannot be applied to the coming of the Son of man before His disciples have at that time gone through all the cities of Israel, because when the twelve apostles were sent out to preach the gospel at that particular time, instead of being persecuted they were popularly followed by many people. And hence, this verse remains historically still unfulfilled.

The situation here appears to be quite similar to that found described in Matthew 24. This must therefore advert to the period of the Great Tribulation.

Here for the first time the Lord sends forth the disciples to preach the gospel of the kingdom to the Jews. But after His resurrection He sends them out to preach the gospel of grace. And when the fullness of the Gentiles shall come in, then all Israel shall be saved and will enter the millennial kingdom (Rom.

11.25). The order of God is accordingly from the Jews to the Gentiles and back to the Jews.

vv.24–25 The reproach which our Lord has borne reaches the utmost. No Christian, however much he may suffer, can surpass the Lord in sufferings. This gives us comfort. The Lord knows our tribulation on earth. He plainly tells us that the *most* we may suffer is still not above His.

"Beelzebub" may mean either "king of the fly" or "king of the house": demons often possess human bodies as their houses. People referred to the Lord as the king of the fly, and they will likewise call us mad.

This portion of the Scriptures shows us that on this earth we cannot expect to be kindly treated by the world. Whenever we are misunderstood, despised and persecuted, we should remember how the world treated our Lord. If we are to be like Him in this respect, our heart can be at rest.

v.26 The word in this verse is a principle—it does not have any special application. It is the same as Matthew 7.8. Because this is principle, it can be taken as a formula.

v.27 The word here is detail and therefore is to be applied, just as Matthew 7.7 provides the detail for the application of the principle found in Matthew 7.8; for it can be seen in Matthew 7 that the detail is placed before the principle because of the presence of the conjunctive word "for" at the beginning of verse 8.

Due to the principle laid down in 10.26, there is the practice found in 10.27.

On the one hand, 10.26 explains why there should be no fear, and this includes two senses:

(1) What you secretly keep for the Lord, even if it be misunderstood by men, will one day be openly revealed by God.

(2) The hidden hate, jealousy, harm, and sins of man will one day also be revealed.

On the other hand, 10.26 suggests that since such is the principle, the Lord adds the following word mentioned in 10.27. No one can be a Christian secretly. If one knows the principle stated in 10.26, it is most foolish trying to be a secret believer. No Christian who fails to confess the Lord may enter the kingdom.

Hence 10.26 in reality both concludes what goes before and introduces what is coming.

v.28 Those who are able to "kill the body" but "not ... the soul" are the people whom Satan uses. The utmost Satan can do is only kill the body.

To "kill the soul" deprives one of any enjoyment, that is, he suffers loss.

"Destroy" here refers to a being disciplined, not a being annihilated.

"Be not afraid of them" is the same as "fear them not" in 10.26.

v.29 "A penny" means highly cheap.

"Without your Father"—When man or demons intend to hurt, God stands near so as not to permit such a thing to happen.

Madame Guyon long ago said that everything which befalls us environmentally is permitted by God (although Jessie Penn-Lewis later commented that the French saint had the tendency of falling into the danger of passivity).

God notices the minutest detail, therefore He is the greatest. He who is most powerful is He who suffers long.

v.30 "But the very hairs of your head are all numbered" —There is nothing in our life too minute for God's care and concern. The number of your hairs registered in heaven is exactly the amount of hairs you have on your head. In this connection, the story is told of a widow who moved to a small upstairs apartment. She asked God for a carpet which would fit the room. Someone sent her a carpet having the exact dimension of the room, but also an iron pan and a fire fork. She commented afterwards that though she forgot to ask for these two other items, God had not forgotten. This is the meaning of God having our hairs numbered.

v.31 Even in the smallest matter God is never careless about His children. Once a couple encountered a storm while crossing the sea. The wife was much frightened, but the husband watched the roaring sea with perfect calmness. His attitude so agitated her that she scolded him. The husband therefore took a knife and gestured to kill her. The wife, however, showed no fear. So he asked her why she was not afraid. She answered that it was because the knife was in *his* hand—which thus gave him an opportunity to explain why he was not afraid of the storm, because it was in God the Father's hand.

vv.32–33 We have a great principle here. We must therefore witness for the Lord and go out to preach the gospel. The mistake believers make today is that the more people oppose, the less believers dare to testify.

God wants us to confess with our mouths. Without doubt conduct is important, but the thought of substituting conduct for the testifying with the mouth is a doctrine which originates in hell. If a Christian is ever kept out of the kingdom, it will be due to his own fault.

v.34 The word "sword" here bears the same meaning as that mentioned in Luke 2, "a sword shall pierce through thine own soul" (v.35). This points especially to the realm of the emotions.

"Peace" means reconciliation or harmony. Since men are at

variance with God, they will naturally be at odds with God's children. The Lord comes to give each believer a sword of suffering.

v.35ff. Here is set forth a love which demands more than loving father and mother. This reveals to us how impossible it is for us to live peacefully on earth with those who oppose Christ. Should it be otherwise, there must be something between us and the Lord.

v.36 The reason for such enmity lies in the fact of their making Christ their enemy. How jealousy produces animosity. None can love both. He who is loved as well will become jealous. Loving the Lord arouses the jealousy of the household.

v.37 The Lord demands us to give Him all. It will not do if we give Him a little less. It is not relative but absolute love He requires of us. Loving the Lord to the extent of wounding ourselves will bring us to the place of rejoicing in our loving Him.

If we love but do not rejoice in love, we have not loved to the extent of being wounded. But for those who do, their experience will be, that as they are bearing the cross, they shall commence to sing. There is a line of a hymn which reads: "I am entrapped by the goal."

Receiving too much satisfaction from men blinds our eyes from seeing the preciousness which the Lord gives. Being too close to men takes away the sense of the preciousness of the nearness of the Lord.

"Worthy" must first be considered from the Lord's side. Is the Lord worthy of your love? The whole problem revolves around whether the Lord is worthy: not how much we forsake for the Lord, but how much He is worthy of our service. If we regard as an extraordinary act a prince proclaiming the gospel, we remain ignorant of the glory and majesty of our Lord. Our Lord is worthy!—worthy to be served by all the elites of this world. He is qualified to receive absolute, complete, and unrestrained love from all men.

Work always follows after love. If there is not that perfect love towards the Lord, He will not commit the care of His sheep to us.

v.38 To love the Lord is His only demand. Without denying self, no one can love the Lord. Here He does not mention His own cross, although at His baptism He was already reckoned as having been crucified. The emphasis here is taking up the cross. To be *laid on* the cross occurs only once: there He carries us. To *take up* the cross is a daily affair: here we carry Him.

What is meant by taking up the cross? It is submitting to God from the heart. In the Garden of Gethsemane our Lord had his mind set on doing the Father's will. And so He went from there to take up the cross. Taking up the cross, therefore, is being determined to do God's will and nothing else.

v.39 "Findeth his life" refers to the present, "shall lose it" points to the future; "loseth his life for my sake" is now, "shall find it" is the future.

"Life" is "soul" in the Greek. "Findeth his life" means letting one's soul enjoy and rejoice without trouble. If this is the meaning of "findeth his life", then "shall lose it" must symbolize just the opposite; which is to say, that the soul shall neither have enjoyment nor joy. In other words, he shall suffer loss. This is the same loss as is mentioned in 1 Corinthians 3. A certain believer once remarked that if a person does not feel the loss, he in fact loses nothing. The loss referred to here in this passage must be something which is deeply felt.

Hence the meaning of "lose" is to be unsatisfied, while that of "gain" is to be satisfied. Salvation of the soul is quite different from salvation of the spirit.

v.40 As we stand on the ground of the cross, the Lord

will consider those who receive us as receiving Him, and consider those who receive Him as receiving the Father. Such therefore is the union which can exist between us and the Lord, just as is the union which exists between Him and the Father.

v.41 Here the Lord reveals the depth of the human heart.

The decision one makes concerning a truth will be expressed by him before God.

In receiving a prophet or a righteous man, your spirit unites with the prophecy of the prophet or the morals of the righteous man. Hence you will receive a prophet's or a righteous man's reward.

Whatever is done for the Lord shall be rewarded.

THE GOSPEL ACCORDING TO MATTHEW

Chapter 11

v.1 This verse should be put at the end of chapter 10. What the Lord commands the disciples to do is that which He himself does.

Jesus and John the Baptist, 11.1–19

vv.2–3 We are shown here the failure of John the Baptist. It appears that John ought not ask such a question. Had he not recognized most clearly at the beginning who the Lord was and is? How, then, does it happen that he asks this question today? From the answer the Lord gives, it is evident that John has stumbled. The cause of his stumbling is the lack of attention the Lord shows to him while he is imprisoned by Herod. In his suffering he becomes weakened.

Some people think his fall is due to his doubting the Lord. But whoever once knows something can never fall into a place of not knowing. So that John is not really doubting the Lord, for he has already known Him. His fall lies elsewhere—in his exasperation at being neglected by the Lord. The Lord never says that John doubts Him.

"Stumble" should be translated as "offend"—not receiving what he expects, John is offended at the Lord. Accordingly, he sends messengers to stimulate the Lord.

v.4 Perceiving how John is offended, the Lord asks the disciples to return and tell John two things: (1) the things which they hear, and (2) the things which they see.

What is heard is the teaching of the Lord. It is in words and pertains to doctrine. What is seen is the miracles of the Lord. It is in deeds and pertains to works.

What is heard is placed by the Lord above what is seen, thus indicating that doctrinal teaching is more important than works of miracles. Seeing ten miracles of God is less effective than hearing ten words of God, for His word operates much longer in the heart.

v.5 "The blind receive their sight"—The Lord lists this at the very first because this is something never seen in the Old Testament. He wants John to realize that none except the Messiah can do such a thing.

"The blind receive their sight"—this may point to the opening of spiritual eyes. "The lame walk"—the stress here is on walking. "The lepers are cleansed"—this refers to the repeal of crime before God. "The deaf hear" are words which speak of knowing God's will. "The dead are raised" indicates the receiving of life. And "the poor" includes all who have no personal relationship with God and to whom the gospel shall be preached.

v.6 John is offended at not finding the Lord doing things according to his own wish. Blessed is the man who is not offended at what the Lord has appointed for him, because not being content with the will of God is a major cause of falling. John does not doubt the Lord, he is only unhappy with the way God has arranged things for him: this is the reason for his fall.

In His reply, the Lord gives some hint to John so as to bring him to the knowledge of his own fault. At the same time, though, He still bears a witness for John before men.

What the Lord answers is nothing but what John has himself heard and seen before. But He adds one important word: "Blessed is he whosoever shall find no occasion of stumbling in me."

v.7 There are plenty of reeds in the wilderness—in other words, at that particular time John is being shaken as is a reed by the wind.

v.8 For the sake of the Lord, John once dwelt in the wilderness in disciplined strength. Today he is being weakened through long imprisonment. The people may therefore think that he now wishes to wear soft raiment and live in kings' palaces. The Lord, however, says that this is not the case.

v.9 "Much more than a prophet"—The Lord accounts John greater than all the prophets. Ordinarily, we classify the prophets as being either major or minor according to the length of the books written by them.

v.10 is parenthetical.

vv.11–13 "But little" is actually "lesser" in the Greek original; it is relative to the "greater" mentioned here.

John is termed greater than all the prophets, yet not in the sense that he surpasses all other prophets in faith, conduct, fame, work, and the Holy Spirit—he is greater only in a specific sense.

All the prophets prophesied until John. John himself does not prophesy, however; he merely points out Christ to man: "Behold, the Lamb of God"—it is just here that he is greater, for in time and opportunity he is different from the rest.

"Yet he that is but little in the kingdom of heaven is greater than he"—This does not mean that John's faith, conduct, spiritual life and work are small and that he is therefore unable to enter the kingdom of heaven. It merely signifies how those who are in the kingdom of heaven may testify to the fact that the work of Christ is already done. So that in this connection, John can be likened to a person who must wait in the city of refuge until the high priest has died (see Num. 35.25). Christ is our High Priest who has died on the cross. Hence John's being "lesser" is not a matter of a lack of personal spiritual attainment but is a matter of the difference in dispensation. For we must remember that John stands in the place of transition between the dispensation of the Law and Prophets and the dispensation of Grace. This thought can be simply outlined as follows:

(1) The prophets prophesied of the coming Savior (the dispensation of the Law and Prophets),

(2) John points out the Savior in person to the people (transition), and

(3) Christians have the Savior who has already accomplished the work of redemption (the dispensation of Grace).

The kingdom of heaven in the Bible refers to the reward part of the millennium—in other words, it is reigning with the Lord for a thousand years.

The kingdom of heaven is the manifestation on the earth of the authority of God from heaven. What is difficult to determine is the difference in time between the kingdom of heaven to come (its public manifestation) and the kingdom of heaven today (its spiritual reality).

Without engaging in any comparison we usually are unable to know accurately. Comparison gives us exact knowledge.

The scope of the church today is as big as the scope of the kingdom of God today. The scope of the kingdom of heaven is smaller than the scope of the kingdom of God and the scope of the church.

The province in which God dispenses grace is the church. It is a matter of position.

The kingdom of God is the sovereignty of God. All who believe in the Lord are under God's sovereign authority. This is true both now and in the future. Hence the church (all who believe in the Lord) and the kingdom of God are like the two sides of a coin. The kingdom of heaven refers to those who will reign during the millennium. Not all who are today in the church and in the kingdom of God can enter the kingdom of heaven. Only the faithful in the church may enter.

"Violent" means "desperate"; "take" is "seize"—that is to say, to take for one's possession. Since the Pharisees use force to prevent men from entering the kingdom of heaven, those who would enter need to seize it by force.

v.14 What God has prepared for men is laid out clearly before them, and He waits for them to decide.

The kingdom of God has its two aspects: (1) the spiritual realm, and (2) the future kingdom.

vv.15–19 John came with wailing but Christ came with piping. Yet neither of them received any sympathy and response.

The Lord indicates how both of these ways are rejected by men:

(1) God in righteousness calls men to repentance (John's way), but they will not believe.

(2) God in grace calls them to receive (Christ's way), but they will not accept.

John declares that God judges sinners, yet they do not mourn. Christ proclaims that God loves sinners, yet they do not dance.

"Wisdom" is Christ himself: yet not the Christ in heaven but the Christ among men, not the Eternal Word but the Word that became flesh.

"Her works" is translated "her children" in many ancient manuscripts. Who are these "children of wisdom"? Those who are saved, who have obtained wisdom; that is, those who justify the salvation of God. All who accept the Lord reckon God's salvation to be true, to be "yea and amen".

The Refusal and the Offer of the Gospel, 11.20–30

v.20 The time for performing mighty works and preaching the gospel will not last forever. It will be followed by reprimand.

vv.21–22 In the day of judgment many will suffer terribly. The extent of one's suffering and the degree of punishment will vary. The greater the opportunity today, the heavier the punishment to come.

vv.23–24 Whatever may be the correct interpretation, it is clear that up to our very day there has been no sign of God's work in Capernaum.

The design of chapter 11 is revealed in its last section (vv.25–30). The beginning of the Lord's rejection may be seen at the end of chapter 9. In chapter 10 the Lord is found openly declaring that He is rejected by men, for have they not called Him Beelzebub? In chapter 11 we see that He obtains for himself a remnant. And by the end of chapter 12 it is recorded how he is again rejected. The thread of teaching after chapter 13 is not as distinct as in the first twelve chapters. It may be helpful for us to review a little what has been covered thus far in Matthew, and to recapitulate briefly the contents of each chapter.

The Lord comes first as the Son of David, in which capacity he has a relationship with the Jews. But He also comes as the Son of Abraham, so He has a relationship with the Gentiles as well. Matthew is written to the Jews, but it is not exclusively for the Jews. It records the teachings of Christ. Mark is historical and more concentrated on events and geography of Galilee. Luke is morally oriented. And John, while also historical as is Mark, concentrates more on Judea and what happens there.

Chapter 1 speaks of Jesus as Emmanuel on the one hand and as Savior on the other ("for it is he that shall save his people from their sins").

Chapter 2 The word that He comes to be King of the Jews comes forth from the mouths of the Gentiles.

Chapter 3 John the Baptist speaks to the Jews, telling them to bring forth fruits worthy of repentance. This indicates God's relationship with the Jews. Later, he says that God is able to raise up children to Abraham of the stones. This signifies God's relationship with the Gentiles. Finally, this chapter mentions the Lord's baptism in the river Jordan—which typifies His death.

Chapter 4 The Lord commences His work.

Chapters 5–7 The demands of the spiritual kingdom are given. (At the end of chapter 7 the will of God is mentioned, but so is it mentioned at the end of chapter 12.)

Chapter 8 first narrates the healing of a Jew, then that of a Gentile, and finally the healing once again among the Jews.

Chapter 9 shows us how the Lord continues to heal the sick and cast out demons; yet He is being accused of casting out demons by the prince of the demons. Thus He has already begun to be rejected by the Jews.

Chapter 10 tells us how the Lord still sends forth His disciples to the house of Israel. This is His last call for them to go out and gather in a remnant.

Chapter 11 discloses the remnant, the first fruit garnered from the labor spoken of in the preceding chapter.

Chapter 12 At the end of this chapter the Lord is recorded as announcing the severance of His relationship with the Jews. This, however, is but a pronouncement in His teaching. It is not until the time of the end of chapter 23 that He officially announces such a severance in fact.

Chapter 13 The teachings which follow from chapter 13 onward are directed towards the church rather than to the Jews.

v.25 The Lord reveals to us that those who obtain the truth of the kingdom of heaven are the babes. The wise and the understanding are not really wise and understanding: they simply stand in contrast to the babes. Here is to be found an important principle: if people do not understand the Bible they read, it is not because of their lack of brains but because of too much brains. Our mind is spiritually ineffective in this task due to the hardness of our heart. We fail to study the word of God well due to the absence of a childlike attitude.

v.26 Who are these babes? They are the remnant whom the Lord has gathered. Though the whole of mankind has rejected the Lord, there is still a small remnant who follow Him in obedience. This is enough, for this is the good pleasure of the Father. Margaret E. Barber once said: Even though I desire to go to China to save souls, I am quite willing to be shut in for 20 years if the Lord so wills. To be a perfect servant depends not on the result of his work but on doing the will of God.

v.27 "All things" here refer to people, for the Lord said on another occasion that "no man can come unto me except it be given unto him of the Father" (John 6.65). Hence everyone who is saved is given to Christ by God. All who come to Christ are moved by God: "All that which the Father giveth me shall come unto me; and him that cometh to me I will in no wise cast out" (John 6.37). Although people do not know Him and even misunderstand Him instead, He nevertheless is satisfied because His Father knows.

The life of Christ may be divided into three periods: (1) from the manger to Jordan River, (2) from Jordan to the Mount of Transfiguration, and (3) from the Mount to Jerusalem.

By reading Hebrews 10.7 we can see that the aspiration of the Lord's life is to do God's will—namely, to die. The uniqueness of Christ with the Father lies in the fact that Christ has only One who knows Him, and that One is the Father. Love is undivided and most intimate, otherwise it cannot be reckoned as love. No one can come to the Father except those to whom the Son has revealed the Father. And no one can reveal the Father except He who knows the Father, even the Son.

v.28 The Lord does not say "ye who sin"; what, then, is the meaning of "ye who labor and are heavy laden"? Here, the lost sheep of the house of Israel are especially in view. They can find no satisfaction from the world. "I will give you rest"—Rest is one aspect of salvation. The laboring spoken of here comes from sin: for example, the Buddhists prostrate themselves every few steps while on a pilgrimage, the Jews fast twice a week, and the Hindus sleep on beds studded with nails. These are all labors as a result of sin. To "come" is our responsibility, the rest is done by Christ. We do not need to bear our own sins.

v.29 "Find rest unto your souls"—This means finding rest for our rebellious mind. The first "rest" is a receiving of rest from sin; this second "rest" is a finding of rest from a heart that is disobedient to God—it is a rest from self.

v.30 When there is obedience, the "yoke is easy"; what makes it hard is when there is no submission in the heart.

THE GOSPEL ACCORDING TO MATTHEW

Chapter 12

Chapter 12 is a transitional passage. What is said in it begins to decide the fate of the Jews. It occupies a most important place in the line of dispensation. We will be strangers to God's word if we fail to recognize the change in the Lord's relationship told of in this section. Before the time of this chapter the Lord is clearly for the Jews, and only in a hidden way is He shown to be for the Gentiles. But after the time of chapter 12 He is clearly for the Gentiles, thus intimating that the Jews have been rejected. In view of the fact that this chapter is transitional, the one thing which typifies the old relationship must be overturned. Since men have sinned, there can be no sabbath rest in actuality. Even God cannot rest. And if God has no rest, then men can have no rest either; for where there is sin, there can be no rest. This thought will become clearer as we take up the question of the sabbath below.

The Question of the Sabbath, 12.1–13

vv.1–2 Do the stories of the disciples eating grain in the field and the healing of a man with a withered hand follow chronologically after chapter 11? Time-wise, these two incidents occur before the time of chapter 11. Why, then, are they placed after? It is to show us how the Lord is rejected so as to lead us to what is in chapter 13. As we have pointed out before, Matthew emphasizes doctrine, therefore he tends to group together events or other matters which are similar in nature so as to substantiate more clearly this or that doctrinal point he is wishing to make.

Of the Ten Commandments nine are moral, but only one is ceremonial—the keeping of the sabbath. If the observance of the sabbath is set aside, it must indicate a change in dispensation: that somehow God's special relationship with the nation of Israel has been temporarily broken off.

In the Old Testament, the sabbath possessed special meanings: (1) that the keeping of the sabbath was to remember God's rest, (2) that according to Ezekiel 20.12 the sabbath was a sign of God's covenant with the children of Israel, and (3) that according to Deuteronomy 5.15 the observing of the sabbath by the Jewish people was to remember how they were redeemed.

For these reasons the Jews placed great emphasis on the sabbath. They regarded it as the sign of God's covenant with them as well as the remembrance of God's rest and redemption. If this were shaken, all would be lost.

To the Jewish tradition it was all right to pluck ears of grain out in the fields, but attention must be paid to the time of doing so; for no work was ever to be done on the sabbath. The plucking of ears was work to the Jewish mind, and therefore working on the sabbath was sin. And so, because the disciples of Jesus were found plucking ears of grain on the sabbath, they were guilty of violating the sabbath rule. Yet here we find the Lord declaring that the disciples were guiltless in working on the sabbath: He defends them by saying that even if they have violated the sabbath they are nonetheless guiltless (see 12.7).

In the section on the healing of a man having a withered hand, the Lord argues that healing does not violate the sabbath; and in the section on plucking ears of grain, He asserts that even one who does violate the sabbath is still guiltless.

vv.3–4 Christ has not said that eating while hungry is necessarily a pardonable act. The question He means to address himself to is whether or not the sabbath should be kept, not whether there is a special allowance for the sabbath. If the Lord should maintain that because David was hungry it was all right for him to eat the shewbread, where would this leave the law? Christ could never support such a conclusion. What, then, is He really saying in this section? He is simply intimating here that what was originally given to the priest to eat can now be eaten by the king also. But this is a change of dispensation. Let us understand that the communication of God with the children of Israel in the Old Testament time underwent three different periods: first through the priests, then through the kings, and finally through the prophets. David represented the nation of Israel. Though he was God's anointed, he at that time was rejected (he had to flee for his life). Yet God communicated with the children of Israel through David, thus putting aside the priests.

In former days, political persons such as Joshua were required to stand before the priest (see Num. 27.21–22), for that was the period of the priests. But later, according to 1 Samuel 2.35–36, the priest must walk before the anointed of the Lord. Hence the king becomes the first in order, while the priest now stands second.

The fact of David's eating the shewbread indicates how the priests and their functions had been downgraded. It was not at all an exception. David had not sinned. He could eat not only on that day but on every other day; for the time had changed. On the occasion when David had eaten the shewbread, it was at the time of his rejection. Likewise, the fact that here in Matthew 12.1 we see that the disciples of Jesus had plucked ears of grain to eat also suggests the rejection of the Lord. Moreover, the Lord mentions not only David but also his followers ("and they that were with him"), and thus the Lord is including His own disciples in His rejection as well.

Thus, verses 3 and 4 relate how the king profaned the sabbath, and so indicate a change in dispensation.

v.5 But this verse shows us how the "priests" have also

profaned the sabbath, for the word "Or" which introduces the verse brings in this other thought. How do the priests profane the sabbath? They offer sacrifices many more times on the sabbath than on ordinary weekdays. They do not violate the sabbath at home but in the "temple": Now the temple is for God—for His glory. It is the place which is filled with the glory of God. The priests are for the good of men. By offering up sacrifices the priests profane the sabbath, yet this is for the glory of God and for the good of men.

But the blame for this disregarding of the sabbath lies with the children of Israel themselves. The priests cannot rest in the temple; they must offer such sacrifices so that the children of Israel may not be judged and the glory of God may not suffer. And why a sacrifice? Obviously because of sin. For God tolerates no sin; and hence blood must be shed for their sins. Had the people not sinned, the priests could rest not only one day in a week, they could rest every other day in the week besides! Yet where sin is, there can be no sabbath rest, for where sin is present, the covenant is abrogated. Where sin is, there is no memory of redemption. To offer a sacrifice is for the sake of solving the problem of sin. The presence of sin—even that of the children of Israel themselves—is thus the cause for there being no rest to the priests on the sabbath. It is for this reason, then, that when the priests profane the sabbath in the temple they are guiltless.

v.6 "One greater than the temple is here"—The Lord himself is the place wherein the glory of God fills the most: for no matter what *He* does for the glory of God, He cannot be considered guilty. Thus the Lord is greater than the temple as well as the priests. Being as David, He reveals His person; being as the priest and the temple, He unveils the nature of His work. For the sabbath therefore, He substitutes His person and work. He sets the sabbath completely aside. If the problem of sin is not solved there can be no rest. As long as the Lord is rejected and people are still in sin, there is not going to be the sabbath. As long as He is as David and the temple, then what the Lord says here is that His disciples may profane the sabbath and yet be guiltless.

vv.7–8 These two verses give the conclusion. "Mercy" is what God gives to men, whereas a "sacrifice" is what men give to God. And thus verse 7 tells us that God is not interested in what men do for Him but that He takes great delight in doing things for men. And hence this provides the basic reason for Jesus Christ being called in verse 8 the Lord of the sabbath. If He desires to be gracious to people, why should anyone complain?

v.8 Yet up to the present, men still do not recognize the Lord of the sabbath.

In 12.1–8 we notice two turnings: from David to the king, from the king to the Lord.

vv.9–13 Here is another instance of profaning the sabbath, this time in the synagogue among the Pharisees.

v.10a A "withered hand" can do nothing. Please note that this is not a case of a man not having a hand but having a hand which is withered. In other words, the form is there but the power is absent. Spiritually speaking, this condition is true of all men: being dead yet still existing.

vv.10b–12 The Lord does not answer either yes or no. He instead asks a question himself. When we are confronted with difficult questions, the best response is not to answer but to ask. Truth can stand questioning, untruth cannot. Note that the Pharisees talk about man, but our Lord raises the question of sheep. The Pharisees bring up the question of the man with the withered hand, but the Lord brings up the matter of the sheep fallen into a pit.

How people highly esteem material, physical things, yet they despise sinners! They have more regard for sheep than for men.

By His words the Lord means to say that as long as there are pits in this world and (human) sheep that have fallen into them, the only reaction possible is to lift them out of their pitfalls.

"To do good on the sabbath day" are not words referring to any specific act: they touch, rather, upon a principle. Our Lord is always found speaking in this way.

v.13 The Lord acts by speaking the word. "And he stretched it forth"—The man with a withered hand acts according to the Lord's word. Life is behind the word of God. God's word is like a capsule, God's life is like the contents of the capsule. As a person swallows a capsule he at the same time swallows the powdered medicine within it. Even so, in receiving the word of God, one receives simultaneously the life of God.

"No word from God shall be void of power" (Luke 1.37). This means life is behind each word. "And it was restored whole"—How complete is the work of Christ! He restores sinners to life, even to a life far better than what Adam originally had.

The Pharisees Take Counsel for the First Time to Destroy Jesus, 12.14–21

v.14 The Pharisees take counsel to destroy Jesus. This is because the Lord has set aside the sabbath day. They recognize that the children of Israel will not be deemed God's chosen people if the sabbath is abrogated, for it is the sign of God's covenant with them. And if the covenant is annulled, it no longer is effective. They well understand the Lord's attitude towards Israel—in setting them aside. For this reason they want to kill Him.

vv.15–16 Those who are attracted by His fame and those

who seek Him out of curiosity are not always trustworthy.
Hence the Lord does not want them to speak His name.

vv.17–21 In this passage, which quotes Isaiah, the Gentiles are mentioned twice, strongly suggesting that God has set
aside Israel and has turned to the Gentiles. Isaiah 42.1ff. may
point to the millennial period, but the Holy Spirit adopts the
quotation especially for this age.

v.18 Whenever the Bible employs the word "behold" it is
calling people to pay special attention to something. The servant
referred to in Isaiah from chapter 40 onward points specifically
to the Lord Jesus. What is quoted in Acts 8.32–35 may serve as
proof of this statement.

"Chosen" is a matter of will. "Beloved" is a matter of position. "Well pleased" is a matter of affection.

v.19 How quiet is the Lord!

v.20 A "bruised reed" gives no sound when blown, yet
the Lord will not break it. The Gentiles are already bruised;
they are like dogs. Nevertheless, the Lord turns to them, expecting to hear music out of these bruised reeds.

The Jews often put flax in the ox horn and pour oil on it,
using it as a torch while traveling. If it gives forth too much
smoke, they will quench it. "Smoking" believers not only do not
help people but may even hinder others from seeing. They easily
become problems in a church meeting. Yet the Lord does not
quench them; He still expects them to give light again.

According to strict interpretation, this section points to the
unbelieving Gentiles. But according to teaching, it may refer to
all believers.

The Blasphemy against the Holy Spirit, 12.22–32

This section goes a step further. In the first section, the sign of the covenant is set aside. In the second section, the Pharisees take counsel to destroy Jesus. But in this, the third section, they not only plot to make Jesus suffer physically, they even blaspheme the Holy Spirit.

v.22 The Bible speaks of a spirit of infirmity, of a foul spirit, or of a blind and dumb spirit. Even though man may look at blindness as stemming from natural causes, here we are told that it is due to demon-possession. When the demon is cast out, the phenomenon which came with the demon disappears.

v.23 "Can this be the son of David?"—As if to say that if this is not the Son of David, who is He? This shows that the multitudes generally have already come into a degree of faith. For the title, the Son of David, is a noble name. Such a designation well fits the meaning of the book of Matthew.

vv.24–26 What the Lord does here is a real casting out. His authority comes from God. A kingdom must be united; otherwise, even the kingdom of Satan cannot stand.

v.27 The Lord gives the reason for His defense.

v.28 What is the outward manifestation of the kingdom of God? The kingdom of God is the sovereignty of God. Where His sovereignty is, demons have no power.

The Bible speaks of two things: the kingdom of God and the power of God. The kingdom of God represents God's sovereignty. The Spirit of God represents God's power. God has authority because there is power behind it. The Holy Spirit is the power of the kingdom of God.

How does the kingdom of God come? Through its power.

The Lord manifests power here, so there comes the kingdom of God.

Casting out demons is one of the most significant manifestations of the reality of the kingdom of God.

v.29 All spiritual works are public spoiling, not secret stealing. This holds true toward Satan.

"Goods" is a term that, strictly speaking, refers to all who are demon-possessed. Broadly speaking, it applies to all unbelievers. The "strong man" is Satan (cf. 1 John 5.19).

Every demon-possessed person or unbeliever is in the hand of Satan, who guards him as his goods.

Seeing the influence of Satan, the Lord comes to snatch publicly from Satan's hand the unbelievers, the demon-possessed, and the sick so that they may be liberated and healed.

"And then he will spoil his house"—Whatever is in his house will be taken as spoil by the Lord. In order to cast out demons, the first thing which must be done is to bind the strong man. "Spoil" is a verb which implies a taking by force against the will of the strong man. If it is a casting out by Beelzebub, it would be by peace talks and not by spoiling.

Binding the strong man is done through the Spirit of God. The power of the Holy Spirit is needed in casting out demons. They are cast out in the name of the Lord because the Holy Spirit is the power of that Name.

How is the strong man bound? Indirectly through the cross of our Lord Jesus. On the cross the Lord has crushed the head of Satan (see Gen. 3.15). (It is in the millennial kingdom that the *whole* body of Satan will be dealt with. The cross has dealt only with Satan's head, that is, it has destroyed his power and influence.) Satan will bruise the Lord's heel. He could not do anything to the Lord when the latter was on earth. Consequently, after the Lord's ascension to heaven, Satan now exerts his utmost energy to bruise the Lord's heel—that is to say, to shake the believers. But after our Lord arose from the dead and ascended back to heaven, the Holy Spirit came to earth to execute what the Lord had accomplished on the cross. Hence binding Satan is done through the power of the Holy Spirit on the basis of the cross. On our side, we can bind Satan through the prayer of faith. We should use prayer to bind the strong man.

One great principle in the Lord's work, then, is first to bind and next to spoil.

v.30 What has happened today is a positive issue which divides the two sides with absolutely no neutral ground. "With" means standing on the same side, a matter of ground. "Gathereth" means a gathering of others together—a matter of work. No Christian on earth is free not to stand on the Lord's side. (People such as Nicodemus and Joseph of Arimathaea are not total disciples of the Lord.) And neither is a Christian free never to gather anyone to Christ.

v.31 Every sin shall be forgiven. The sin here refers especially to sinful conduct. Even a word of blasphemy may be forgiven.

v.32 What is the blasphemy against the Holy Spirit? It is speaking against the Holy Spirit. This does not mean lying to the Holy Spirit nor quenching Him. It is speaking against the Holy Spirit.

Yet what is speaking against the Holy Spirit? This is a deliberate sin—not just saying something wrong, but speaking clearly that the Holy Spirit is Beelzebub. Speaking against the Holy Spirit is not sinning against the Holy Spirit in action, but rather it is sinning against the Holy Spirit in speech.

"It shall not be forgiven him, neither in this world, nor in that which is to come"—In our dialogues on the gospel* we men-

---

*A work of Mr. Nee's published in Chinese, and later translated into English and published as *Gospel Dialogue* (New York, Christian Fellowship Publishers, 1975).—*Translator*

tioned five different kinds of forgiveness: (1) eternal forgiveness, (2) forgiveness through God's people, (3) forgiveness for the restoring of fellowship, (4) forgiveness with discipline, and (5) forgiveness in the kingdom.

This present age is the age of grace. The age to come is the kingdom age. The sin of speaking against the Holy Spirit shall not be forgiven, neither in this age nor in the age to come.

Forgiveness in this age pertains to eternal forgiveness; forgiveness in the age to come pertains to one's position in the kingdom.

Every Idle Word to Be Judged, 12.33–37

v.33 By your fruit is your heart known.

v.34 Error in lips is preceded by error in heart. When the condition of the heart is questionable, the mouth speaks out.

v. 35 "Treasure"—This carries with it the idea of things kept in a bank safety box.

v.36 If even only their words are judged, men would still be looking for a place to hide.

When the Holy Spirit is evilly spoken of, He will not work anymore, therefore removing the hope of salvation. For this reason, the rebellious are the most difficult to repent.

Speaking against the Holy Spirit through ignorance is not considered blasphemy against the Holy Spirit. Speaking evilly against the Holy Spirit, knowingly and deliberately, is viewed as blasphemy.

v.37 Matthew 12.37 is different from Romans 10.10 The first is concerned with being justified before God, whereas the second is related to being justified before men—that is to say, to being placed in a new position—and hence is unto salvation.

*The Sign to an Evil and Adulterous
Generation, 12.38–42*

v.38 The moment covered by the "then" here in Matthew is at least several months apart in time from the time sequence as given in Mark 8.11–13. As we have said several times, because Matthew lays stress on teaching in his gospel, he does not allow chronological order to dictate the manner of his narration very much.

The New Testament Scriptures have three different Greek words associated with our English word "miracles":

(1) miracles *(dunamis)*—a power of supernatural source, a thing which God has done.

(2) wonders *(teras)*—something strange.

(3) signs *(semeion)*—miracles and wonders with objectives. "Sign" is the word used here.

v.39 The word is "generation" here, which means that as long as there are evil and adultery so long will the generation be.

At this point three different words from the Greek should be contrasted in their usage:

(1) world *(kosmos)*—which points to the organized world in the place called earth;

(2) age *(aion)*—which signifies a period in time of indefinite duration; and

(3) generation *(genea)*—which strictly refers to a period of a lifetime: say, 30 or 40 years; broadly, though, it refers to a period marked by special characteristics. And it is this Greek word in its broadest sense that is used here in verse 39.

"Evil" reveals the nature, while "adulterous" discloses the particular phenomenon which marks this generation.

v.40 Why does the Lord mention specifically the prophet Jonah? We need to remember that this chapter in Matthew continues to follow the main line of teaching that is evident at this point in the Gospel narration. Just as Jonah was not sent to the children of Israel but to the gentile Ninevites, so at this juncture our Lord has set aside Israel as a nation and is turning to the Gentiles.

Since they have blasphemed against the Holy Spirit, there will be no further prophet given to Israel. Yet individually, people may stand on the ground of sinners and be saved. Thus, during Pentecost three thousand—and shortly afterwards five thousand—were saved.

v.41 Previously, the men of Nineveh had heard what Jonah preached and they repented. The Jonah of today comes to the Gentiles through the Jews. Formerly, Jonah had been thrown into the sea because of his rebellion; now, the Jews cast "Jonah" into the sea as it were, because they reject the Lord of Life.

v. 42 The Queen of the South was also a Gentile. Ethiopia today is the nation of Sheba in ancient time. And this nation has continued on to the present day.

Jonah went to Nineveh as a prophet, but the Queen of the South came to Solomon. A greater than Jonah has gone to the Gentiles, and many a Gentile has been attracted to come to the One who is greater than Solomon.

The cross is a sign. The Jews ask for signs, the Greeks seek for wisdom, but the cross is wisdom as well as a sign. It is sufficient for us.

The incident of Jonah is a sign, the episode of Solomon is wisdom.

The Condition of the Unrepentant, 12.43–45

The demon-possessed man here signifies the Jews, for from the words "even so shall it be also unto this evil generation" (12.45), we may infer that this is spoken of the Jews.

This episode of the unclean spirit may be viewed in two different ways:

(1) According to the First Epistle to the Corinthians, demons are closely related to idols. For their sin of idol worship the children of Israel were taken into Babylonian captivity. It was there that they were cured of such idolatry. After they returned from captivity, the sect of the Pharisees seemed to prevail. Paul at first also belonged to this sect. Religiously they are viewed as the strictest group, yet they are empty spiritually. Hence the Jews are not much different from their previous state. The Jews reject the Lord when He comes, and thus their latter state becomes worse than before.

(2) Looking from the perspective of the possessed one, whenever the Lord sees a demon He casts it out. So during the days the Lord was on earth, the unclean spirit may be deemed as having gone out of the man. Yet the house is empty, for the people still have not received Christ. In the future, during the three and a half years of the Great Tribulation, the phenomenon of demon possession will be much more serious.

The previous section spoke of the repentance of the Gentiles; this section relates the condition of the unrepentant people.

v.43 "Dry" (the literal rendering of "waterless") means nothing that gratifies. Only human bodies make demons comfortable. The unclean spirit therefore wanders everywhere seeking a place of rest, which is to say that it is seeking out a person to possess.

v.44 The evil spirit takes a man's body as his house. "Swept" is negative, the action of removing inside things out. "Garnished" is positive, the action of adding things in. The Jews fit exactly these descriptions. Yet, says the Lord, they are empty.

Historically the Jews are absolutely cured of idol worship, but morally they have reformed themselves only a little bit outwardly.

v.45 Demons like to dwell in the bodies of moral persons. The most corrupted people are not only a problem to God and men but also a nuisance to the demons. A person with only some moral improvement yet who does not have Christ in him will find himself in even a worse situation than that of a completely corrupted person.

Some people have attempted, without clear justification, to translate the Greek word *genea* in this passage as "race" instead of "generation"; and hence they have assumed that this refers to the race of Israel. If so, however, will not all Israel be annihilated? Obviously, this is an incorrect interpretation. The generation in question here does not refer to race nor to a limited period of time of say 30 or 40 years; rather, it points to a period characteristically marked by evil and adultery. As long as evil and adultery persist, even that long will this generation last.

Severance of Relationship with the Children of Israel, 12.46–50

v.46 "Behold" is a call for attention. The Lord's mother and brethren represent the relationship with Israel in the flesh.

vv.47–48 Such relationship is completely cut off.

v.50 Brothers are for helps; sisters, for sympathy; and mothers, for tender care.

THE GOSPEL ACCORDING TO MATTHEW

Chapter 13

The first thirteen chapters of Matthew can be simply outlined as follows:

Chapters 1–4: Preparation for the Lord's coming as King
Chapters 5–7: The moral nature of the kingdom of heaven
Chapters 8–12: The Lord's allusion to the Gentile as well
    as Jewish side
Chapter 13: The mysteries or outward appearance of the king-
    dom of heaven

The primary objective of the Scriptures is not moral but doctrinal in nature. Only one verse in the entire New Testament
tells us of the usefulness of the Scriptures, and that is in 2 Timothy: "Every scripture inspired of God is also profitable for teaching, for reproof, for correction, for instruction [or discipline]
which is in righteousness" (3.16 mg.). The first item mentioned
is teaching, which should be translated "doctrine"; only afterwards is attention paid to the moral side: they are profitable for
correction and for discipline which is in righteousness.

Although Matthew 13 is so rich to the point of being inex-
haustible, the emphasis is not on morals but on doctrine.
Though the moral side is not overlooked, the position doctrine
occupies in its narrative is of paramount significance. The subject of Matthew's Gospel is the mysteries of the kingdom of
heaven. The word "mystery" is used a number of times in the

New Testament (some suggest there are seven mysteries, though this cannot be determined very exactly). All the mysteries are of the same nature except one, which is viewed from a different stance. They are called mysteries because unless the Spirit of God reveals them no man can understand. Of God's manifold mysteries those concerning the kingdom of heaven are all one. (The chief mysteries in the New Testament are found in the following passages: Eph. 1.9–10, 3.4–6, 5.32; Col. 1.27; 1 Cor. 15.51; 1 Cor 2.7; Rev. 17.5; Rom. 16.25; and 1 Tim. 3.16.)

Whatever mysteries there be that remain must be revealed in their appointed times (from the first coming of Christ to His second coming). They cannot happen either before or after that period. Hence the mysteries of the kingdom of heaven must transpire in this age and bear no relationship to the age to come.

From 13.35 we may learn that the mysteries which occur today were hidden during the Old Testament time.

v.1 "On that day"—the day in which the Lord severs His relationship with the children of Israel. "House" signifies belonging, boundary, calmness. Sea denotes openness, no limit, agitation. That the Lord comes out of the house proves that God has come out of a restricted boundary into an unlimited field.

The wicked are like the tumultuous sea, whereas the Pharisees are like a house that is calm and well-regulated. Nevertheless the Lord leaves the moral people and goes to the sinful. Or speaking more frankly, He leaves the Jews and goes to the Gentiles (see Rev. 13.1,2,11 and Dan 7.3—sea in the Scriptures always points directly to the Gentiles, while land points to the Jews.)

v.2 He comes out of the house; yet He does not go into the sea either, since we find that He sits in a boat (see Mark 4.1). The boat is in the sea, but it does not belong to the sea. Hence the boat denotes the church—which is in the world yet not of the world.

The Lord leaves the Jews and goes to the Gentiles. He reveals His thoughts in the church. He does not go to all the Gentiles, only those Gentiles who are in the boat.

Why does He speak in parables (see v.3)? Verse 11 points out plainly that it is given to the disciples to know the mysteries of the kingdom of heaven but to the multitudes it is not given. The disciples have believed and understood, so more is given in order that they shall have abundance. From the others, however, even what they have shall be taken away from them. They have seen the miracles and wonders which the Lord performed in their midst, but due to their unbelief no more miracles or wonders will be performed. The reason for speaking in parables is because seeing they perceive not and hearing they hear not. Since their hearts are waxed gross, their ears are dull of hearing and their eyes are closed. They reject the grace of God, therefore there is no way for them to be saved (see 2 Thess. 2.10–12). From this we know that all the parables in the New Testament are spoken to the believing disciples, not to the Jews. This is a principle to be remembered.

"The kingdom of heaven is like" [or "likened unto . . ."] — This introductory statement is used six times in this chapter. There are seven parables, and if the parable of things old and new is included, there would be eight. Please note that the first parable does not open with these introductory words. Three parables are spoken in the house, they being exclusively for the disciples; but three are spoken by the seaside where both the Jews and the disciples gather. Whenever the Bible uses the numbers three, seven, ten, twelve, and so forth, they all convey the thought of completeness. Three is the complete number of God; seven, the completeness in time (that which is temporary); ten, the completeness of man; and twelve (that number which signifies the intimate relationship between God and man), the completeness in eternity. Though the parables in Matthew 13 do not appear to be altogether positive, they nevertheless follow a progressive line (moving towards God). By contrast, the conditions of the seven churches spoken of in Revelation 2 and 3 follow a regressive line.

A very important principle to gain in studying the Bible is to recognize that the release of truth occurring in the time frame of the Scriptures has its dispensational restrictions. For this reason we must submit ourselves under the mighty hand of God, waiting for light to be given at the time of specific need.

Let us review the things we have already seen previously concerning the kingdom of heaven. After the birth of Christ, there comes one who prepares the way for Him. His name is John, and he proclaims that the kingdom of heaven is at hand. The Lord, together with the apostles whom He sends forth, announce the same news. What does it mean? Later on, as noted in chapters 8 and 9, we see that the Lord heals the sick and casts out demons, and that all these are closely related to the nearness of the kingdom of heaven. Matthew 5–7 speaks of the nature of the kingdom of heaven: which is, that those who belong to this kingdom are absolutely righteous towards themselves, absolutely gracious towards others, and absolutely pure towards God. In Matthew 10 we learn that the Lord sends out His apostles. And in Matthew 11–12 we see that a great transition begins occurring, as though the kingdom of heaven is now being taken away from the Jews.

Now with regard to the kingdom of heaven found spoken of in Matthew 13, some interpreters have asserted that the mysteries of the kingdom of heaven are the kingdom of heaven in mystery. Such an assertation is logically unsound when it is held up against all the things which we have just seen: how that both John and the Lord as well as His disciples proclaim that the kingdom of heaven is at hand, how that the Lord then announces the nature or character of this kingdom, and how after He is rejected by the children of Israel He in the thirteenth chapter is found declaring only the outward boundary of this kingdom (what we see in this age being but the outward appearance). So that chapter 13 does not deal with the character or nature of the kingdom of heaven, for this has already been described in Matthew 5–7.

Some, on the other hand, contend that all who desire to enter the kingdom of heaven mentioned in chapter 13 must possess the character of the kingdom of heaven as laid down in chapters 5–7. This interpretation again is impossible to accept, since in chapter 13 we have presented the tares, the leaven, and so forth as being in the kingdom of heaven. So that this chapter presents to us nothing but the outward appearance of the kingdom of heaven.

The kingdom of heaven is not the millennial kingdom; it is the *reigning in* the millennial kingdom. Let us see that the kingdom of heaven has three different aspects.

(1) an outward appearance, boundary, or scope as is shown to us in Matthew 13;

(2) a spiritual reality, that is to say, a kind of spiritual conduct which is formed as a result of learning righteousness and grace progressively under the authority of God and which is elucidated for us in Matthew 5–7; and

(3) a reigning with Christ in the future millennial kingdom as revealed in the fact of our future reward as told to us in Matthew 5–7.

Accordingly, we must first of all enter into the sphere or boundary of this kingdom of heaven by being sons of the kingdom; then secondly, we need to have the kind of conduct described for us in Matthew 5–7—which is to have real spiritual conduct; and lastly, as a consequence we may reign with the Lord.

Today there are three different kinds of people:

(1) those who have entered within the sphere of the kingdom of heaven and yet are unsaved; these are represented by the tares.

(2) those who have been saved and are in the domain of the kingdom of heaven, yet they fail to keep the teaching of Matthew 5–7.

(3) those who are saved and also keep the teaching of Matthew 5–7; they truly overcome, and therefore in the future they shall reign with the Lord in the third stage or aspect of the kingdom of heaven.

A Comparison between the Kingdom of Heaven and the Kingdom of God

The kingdom of heaven and the kingdom of God are distinguishable but are not separable. Let us consider in some detail these two descriptive phrases found in the Scriptures.

(1) With certain parables Matthew employs the statement "The kingdom of heaven is likened unto . . . "; but Luke uses the words "The kingdom of God is like . . . " for the *same* parables — thus indicating that the kingdom of heaven and the kingdom of God are one and the same. Both the kingdom of God and the kingdom of heaven in these parallel instances refer to the outward domain of the kingdom. On this level, it can be said that the outward appearances of both the kingdom of heaven and the kingdom of God are alike. Parables such as that of the leaven belong to this category.

(2) Yet the kingdom of heaven and the kingdom of God are not synonymous with respect to the second aspect of the kingdom of heaven, inasmuch as what is described in Matthew 5–7 speaks of actual overt behavior whereas "the kingdom of God is righteousness and peace and joy in the Holy Spirit" (Rom. 14.17). The one stresses spiritual conduct; the other, inner spiritual condition.

(3) Even so, in the third aspect the kingdom of heaven is again similar to the kingdom of God since both refer to the matter of reigning during the millennial period.

Though the kingdom of God and the kingdom of heaven are similar as regards the first aspect, the kingdom of God covers also the time of which the prophets in the Old Testament speak —for whenever the sovereignty of God is present, His domain is there at the same time. But this characteristic is not applicable to the kingdom of heaven.

With regard to the third aspect, it is true that the kingdom of God is the same as the kingdom of heaven in that both refer to ruling with Christ in the millennium; yet the kingdom of God extends further on into eternity since in eternity God also reigns —but by that time the kingdom of heaven will have passed away. With respect to the third aspect, therefore, the kingdom of God exists longer than the kingdom of heaven.

In a certain sense it can be said that the kingdom of God includes the kingdom of heaven, but not vice versa.

So far as the outward official history of the church on earth goes today, there can be said to be the Roman Catholic Church, the national churches, and the private churches. The Roman Catholic Church claims that the entire world is under her domain and that no national church is therefore allowed. The national church such as the Anglican Church asserts that every citizen of the nation belongs to the Church. But due to dissatisfaction with the national churches, there came into being the so-called private churches.

As regards the outward sphere, as long as people say they are Christians, no one can drive them out of the kingdom of heaven; for the Lord has not promised to weed out the tares today. At communion or the Lord's Table or the breaking of bread, however, the church may indeed weed out or separate the unsaved and the wicked from the saved ones. So that in the outward appearance of the kingdom of heaven, such as in a national church, unbelieving people may be included therein, but in the sphere of the believing assembly an unsaved person may be excluded from fellowship. This clarifies the two totally different spheres: that of the outward appearance of the kingdom of heaven and that of the church. Within the boundary of the outward appearance of the kingdom of heaven there may be tares; but within the church as the body of Christ there is only wheat but no tares.

The Parable of Sowing

Before proceeding to discuss this particular parable, it might be well to indicate that the parables to be found in this chapter may be divided into several parts:

(1) The parable of sowing heads up all the parables.

(2) The parable of the wheat and the tares is in contrast to the parable of the net. As in seeds with their good wheat and bad tares, so in fishes there are both good and bad.

(3) The parable of the mustard seed is parallel with the parable of the leaven, except that the mustard seed speaks of the external while the leaven speaks of the internal.

(4) The parable of the treasure runs parallel with the parable of the pearl. The treasure signifies the outside whereas the pearl signifies the inside.

Contrast is not for repetition but for emphasis.

(5) If the passage on things old and new is also considered a parable, it compares with the first one, the parable of sowing.

v.3 This parable does not begin with "The kingdom of heaven is like" because the work of sowing is done by the Lord himself. The outward sphere (or domain) of the kingdom of heaven does not appear until the Lord is rejected and the disciples begin to labor; so that this parable applies exclusively to the result of the work of our Lord Jesus on earth. The sowing occurs before "the kingdom of heaven is likened unto . . ." According to strict interpretation, this is the only possible explanation.

In 13.24–25 there are two classes of men mentioned: the first man is singular, which points to the Son of man; the second in the original is plural, and these men are the servants who sleep. The first man—the Son of man—does His work alone. Nobody shares in His labor.

How many kinds of seeds are there? Only one kind. But how about the soil? There are four different types. What is the seed?

The word of the kingdom. What is the soil? The human heart. And the sower is Jesus Christ.

"Went forth to sow"—If this is not the *beginning* of a new dispensation, then it must be the *preparation* for the new dispensation. In the Old Testament, God was seen as the One who planted. The Old Testament used the vine to represent the children of Israel. A vine is planted in a vineyard. Out of all the nations, God chose Israel and planted her in the vineyard. The root of a vine constantly draws water from the earth. Hence the vine typifies God's earthly people. The first evidence concerning Canaan brought back to the children of Israel was a branch with one cluster of grapes from the valley of Eshcol. The blessing Israel enjoyed was earthly in nature. Now although the Old Testament does mention the fig tree, it is not employed to represent the children of Israel. Instead it uses the vine to typify them. In the New Testament, however, the fig tree *is* used to represent the children of Israel. In Luke 13.6, for example, a fig tree is planted in a vineyard. Due to their unfaithfulness, God is going to set them aside temporarily from the place of election. The fig tree is to be watched for three years to see if it will bear fruit. The fig tree is therefore a type of temporary Israel, whereas the vine is a type of permanent Israel.

Yet here in this parable there is not found the type either of permanent or temporary Israel. What is found instead is the sowing of the seed of wheat. And when it ripens it dries up and so is harvested. This is none other than a type or picture of Christians.

vv.4,19 "By the way side"—The field is the world. The way side is that which borders the field, hence this description speaks of the air (that which borders the entire earth)—the habitation of evil spirits. "By the way side" typifies those who are near to evil spirits such as the necromancers, the idol worshipers, the demon-possessed, and the morally corrupt. These people will not accept the word of the kingdom of heaven. "Birds" stand for the evil one, even Satan. The word is preached to the heart, so Satan tries to blind the minds of the unbelieving so that the light of the gospel of the glory of Christ should not dawn upon them (see 2 Cor. 4.4). These people do not understand because their "heart is waxed gross" and "their eyes they have closed" (these words in 13.15 point to the Jews who reject Christ). This class of people are not saved.

vv.5,6,20,21 "Upon the rocky places"—Underneath is rock and above is a thin layer of soil. The seeds spring up quickly. This class of people shows the best appearance. After hearing the word, they respond most emotionally (cf. John 2.23–25). Revivalists should beware the rocky places and immediate sproutings. They should be afraid of people who cry too readily and are emotionally stirred too easily. They should not be satisfied simply with large numbers of people. (Many *throng* the Lord Jesus, but He feels nothing. But when one *touches* Him, immediately He senses power flowing out.) Those who are easily stirred emotionally exhibit instant enthusiasm; yet alas, there is no root and no life. They are alienated from the life of God because they have no way to draw nourishment. After revival meetings, many who seem to be stirred up fade quickly away. Why? because their stony hearts are not removed (see Ezek. 36.26). Soon they shall be withered. The sun represents tribulation or persecution. Sunlight is originally designed to help plant life to grow. Likewise, tribulation and persecution help the life of true believers to grow too.

vv.7,22 "Upon the thorns"—This class of people receives the word that they hear and thus have life. Unfortunately, they cannot later bear any fruit because they are choked. God's word needs sowing, but the thorns require no sowing. Believers do not bear fruit nor do they understand the Bible because their hearts are choked with the cares of the world and the deceitfulness of riches. Care seems to be so natural, yet the Lord says it ought not occupy our heart. Blessed are the poor in spirit. The poor in spirit are the poor in heart, that is to say, it is a heart that is not entangled by the care of this world and the deceitfulness of riches. The Lord requires us to bear fruit as well as to have life.

vv.8,23 "Upon the good ground"—That is, upon a good heart, one that obeys God's will. "Understandeth" means to understand in the spirit. For fruit bearing, more than faith is required. A hundredfold is perfect; sixty passes the half way mark; thirty is below half; but any below thirty is insignificant. Though the heart is good, there may yet be hindrance.

The Parable of the Tares

vv.24,36–38 The parable of the tares is the first parable of the kingdom of heaven that is qualified by the words "is likened unto . . . ": it is most comprehensive and it gives the outline of the kingdom of heaven. The parables are spoken by the seaside, yet the interpretations are given in the house. In the parable of sowing there are seed and earth, but the emphasis is on the seed which is the word of the kingdom. The parable of the tares lays stress on the good seed, and the field is one, which is the world. The parable of sowing speaks of the work of our Lord; it also serves as a prelude to our understanding of the kingdom of heaven. The parable of the tares refers to things which happen after the work of the Lord; it marks the commencement of the kingdom of heaven (all six parables relate to things following upon the Lord's work).

"A man"—The Son of man, who is Christ. The "field" is the world. The dimension of the world is exceedingly broad (cf. Matt. 28.19). It is quite different from the sending of the Twelve cited in chapter 10. The gospel is now to be preached to *all* the world. What amazing grace of God this is! Earlier, the sending forth was limited to the children of Israel. Now, it is not just to the vineyard but to the whole world. Thus do we see that the sphere of the kingdom of heaven is equal to the dimension of the world. Not so, however, with the true church. For the church is the gathering of people out from the world to God, while the kingdom of heaven is the coming from God to the world.

"Good seed"—These are the sons of the kingdom. This is different from the seed being the word of the kingdom. The sons of the kingdom are those who belong to the kingdom of heaven. After the word of the kingdom is received, it begins to grow in the people who receive it and transforms them to be sons of the kingdom of heaven. Not that these men change themselves into the sons of the kingdom of heaven. Not at all. What happens is that as soon as people receive the word of the kingdom of heaven, they are born again and become good seed—even sons of the kingdom (cf. 1 Peter 1.23). Regeneration is but the expression of the growth of God's word. In spite of the broadness of the sphere of the kingdom of heaven, only the good seed are sons of the kingdom of heaven, which means that they alone may inherit the kingdom.

"Then he left the multitudes" (v.36) should be rendered, "Then [Jesus], having dismissed the crowds" (Darby).

vv.25,38,39 "While men slept"—The word "men" is in plural. They are His servants and therefore refer to believers, especially to those during the apostolic age in the first century. Sleep is natural, it being the consequence of weariness. Sleep here, though, speaks of not being watchful, of a lack of knowledge. The enemy is Satan and the tares are the sons of the evil one—people who are begotten by evil doctrines, though not necessarily all the unsaved in the world.

The tares are sown among the wheat and they look like wheat (not unlike the mixed multitude who came out of Egypt with the children of Israel). A Mr. Thompson, who was most familiar with Jewish background, once remarked that the tare and the wheat are totally indistinguishable when they grow to one or two feet tall. It is not until the time of fruit bearing that they become distinguishable. At that time the tare is black while the wheat is golden in color. Before this occurs they look so much alike that even experts cannot distinguish them. There are therefore many tares today whom we have no way of distinguishing.

"And went away"—Satan leaves because he has accomplished his purpose. He feels safe and sure, for the tares do not need any watering but will grow by themselves. During the first century after Christ there were already tares (see 2 Peter 2, 2 John, 2 Thess. 2, and 1 Tim. 4). The apostle John was a mender of nets. And His ministry was always to lead people back to the beginning. Beholding the extensive spreading of heresy in his day, especially as it pertained to the person of the Lord Jesus, John paid special attention to Jesus as the Son of God. 2 Peter 2 foretells the destiny of the tares: the so-called modernists of our day are actually the progeny of the apostates of the early days. They embrace Satan's teaching yet call themselves Christians.

v.26 "When the blade sprang up and brought forth fruit" —The springing up of the blade has two meanings: (1) it points to the time of harvesting, and (2) it refers to a certain manifestation in conduct. Even though the servants did not know when Satan did his work, no modernist may be hidden forever. How subtle is Satan's work. If he cannot oppose, he imitates, "for even Satan fashioneth himself into an angel of light" (see 2 Cor. 11.13–15). When he finds out he cannot swallow up, he counterfeits and adds something more. He gives people that which is false. He may even give people false fellowship, false regeneration. Satan lays stress on "the knowledge which is falsely so called" (1 Tim. 6.20) and thus causes people to ignore the blood, the cross, and so forth. Experience *without* truth is false; it is merely psychological. Experience *with* truth is real; it is true salvation.

v.27 Due to the carelessness of the servants, tares are sown in the field. When they ask the master, the householder, it is already too late. How watchful must the workers be today, otherwise they will experience the same consequence.

vv.28–29 "An enemy hath done this"—Since the Lord calls Satan an enemy, Satan must be the true enemy. There is absolutely no comparison between Christians and modernists who are the messengers of Satan.

"Gather up" is a pulling up or a rooting out violently (cf. Prov. 2.22, Deut. 29.28). The Roman Catholic Church through the centuries has killed and burned many people, the majority of whom are wheat. The Lord definitely forbids such action. When James and John asked that fire be brought down from heaven to consume the Samaritans, the Lord rebuked them (see Luke 9.51–56).

vv.30,39 "Let both grow together"—This is absolutely impossible in the true church, for the church of the redeemed must maintain its pureness (see 1 Cor. 5). Hence this clearly applies to the outward domain of the kingdom of heaven.

"And the harvest is the end of the world"—The end of the world is the end of this evil age (Gal 1.4), and is also the end of the time of the Gentiles. Prior to the Babylonian Captivity God was called "the God of heaven and earth" whereas in Daniel 2.18,19,37 and 44 God was called "the God of heaven"; and Ezekiel 8–11 tells us how God gradually retreated from earth to be God in heaven because of the idol worship of His people. Thus Satan has become the god of this age. In the book of Nehemiah God was still only called "the God of heaven" even at the time of His restoration of Jerusalem and the temple. Since God is only God of heaven, we desire nothing on earth.

The post-millennialists and the advocates only of a social gospel expect the tares to turn into wheat. This is nothing but a sweet dream.

The "reapers" are "angels" as the verse itself tells us. "Bind them in bundles"—That is, gather the tares together. Today the tares are beginning to be gathered together.

*Helpful Collateral References for This Parable
of the Tares: Revelation 14 and Leviticus 23*

Revelation 14 may be divided into four parts:
vv. 1–4, the firstfruits—the first rapture;
vv.6–13, the situation during the Great Tribulation;
vv.14–16, the reaping of the wheat—the rapture after the Great Tribulation;
vv.17–20, the vintage of the earth—also the battle of Har-Mageddon or the great slaughter by the One mentioned in Revelation 19 who rides a white horse.
Leviticus 23 has eight set feasts:
Sabbath (which is also considered to be a set feast)—Redemption gives God and men rest.
Passover—The month of the Passover is reckoned as the first month, for redemption commences all spiritual experiences.
Unleavened Bread—It follows Passover and typifies repentance and abhorrence of sin accompanied by a desire to get rid of it.
Firstfruits—Three days after Passover. Christ is the firstfruits (see 1 Cor. 15.20,23). The sheaf of firstfruits points to the saints in Jerusalem who were raised from the dead with Christ as His companion firstfruits. This set feast speaks of the resurrection of the Lord three days after He was crucified.
Pentecost—It signifies the coming of the Holy Spirit after the Lord has ascended to heaven.
Blowing of Trumpets—This denotes a gathering together. In the future there will be a great ingathering to the Lord of both the Jews and the Gentiles.
The Day of Atonement—This refers also to the future. Even so, today we enjoy it beforehand (see Heb. 6.5).

Tabernacles—This leaving of houses and dwelling in booths with great rejoicing points to the millennium; it nonetheless is still temporary, not eternal.

Leviticus shows four stages with regard to wheat:

(1) Firstfruits—which typifies the resurrection of the Lord. (Although in the Bible many are raised from the dead, the Lord is reckoned as the Firstborn from among the dead.) Firstfruits ripen before the rest and are therefore reaped the first.

(2) Pentecost—the two wave loaves signify the first rapture, occurring before the Great Tribulation.

(3) The harvest—that rapture occurring after the Great Tribulation.

(4) The gleaning—whatever is left behind after the harvest has been reaped is to be gleaned individually. This refers to fragmentary raptures.

Matthew 13 compares wheat with tares and shows their diverse destinies. Both Revelation 14 and Leviticus 23 compare wheat with wheat and record their different consequences. Though they are all wheat, they are not all reaped at the same time; for if all will be raptured before the Great Tribulation, the Lord would surely have said something like: Blessed are you, for you are wheat. Also, there would be no need for watchfulness nor for patience. Let us see that the condition for rapture is more than simply having life, or else all the warnings of Scripture are meaningless.

Wheat needs to be dried (it is different from grapes, which need water). It therefore needs sunlight. The yardstick for being reaped is the percentage of moisture remaining. The stalk and root must be completely dried before reaping. Now we are all wheat, yet we all need to be dried, that is to say, to cease seeking the pleasure of the world. "Wheat dries towards earth but ripens towards heaven," D. M. Panton keenly observed. Now sunlight, which in its severity helps wheat to grow and to ripen, represents in a spiritual way the tribulation needed to dry us out from loving the world. (Let us understand that through tribulation sunlight stands for grace, whereas rain and dew stand for grace in blessing.)

Wheat is an annual not a perennial grain, signifying that the earth is not an eternal home. We are here only temporarily. Wheat is also not self-protective: it is neither thorny like a rose nor sturdy like a fig tree nor widespread like a vine: it is most tender, shaken easily by the wind.

How wise is our God in using wheat to represent the saints, the sons of the kingdom. He waits to see if we are ripened before He reaps. The time for the rapture of a believer is in a sense determined by his ripeness.

Before the coming of the Lord in the air there will occur the first rapture of relatively few saints (represented by the 144,000 mentioned in Revelation 14). Those who are raptured will take their place in heaven before the throne.

Revelation 14.6–13 Here we find the gospel of judgment and the warning is to be proclaimed during the Great Tribulation.

Revelation 14.14–16 The reaper—the Son of man—is in the cloud, which coincides with the scene set forth in 1 Thessalonians 4. "For the harvest of the earth is ripe" or "is become dry" (14.15 mg.): if the sunlight of tribulation is ineffective, then the Lord will have to use much stronger persecution and tribulation than sunlight to dry up the remaining wheat. Believers *will* eventually forsake the world, they *will* finally be dried; if not by sunlight, then by the fire of persecution and tribulation: for one day the world which believers love will turn against them. The chief difference in the five foolish and the five wise virgins lies in this matter of time, namely, which believers ripen first? The "sickle" is symbolic of the harvesting angels (cf. Matt. 13.39).

Revelation 14.17–20 The word "grapes" denotes the wicked (and is not a type of Israel, for today Israel is typified by the fig tree). These "grapes" are the slain mentioned in chapter 19 who fall at the battle of Har-Mageddon (Armageddon). What follows afterwards is the Feast of the Tabernacles (see Deut. 16.13–15).

And the gleaning occurs after the reaping, and hence represents various fragmentary raptures.

The coming of the Lord is imminent. Believers in the last days must pay attention to three essentials: (1) eternal life, (2) rapture, and (3) reward. Thank God, He has already provided us with the first essential. He has chosen us before the foundation of the world that through the death of Christ we should receive eternal life. The other two essentials are something required of us. Rapture is related to our manner of life as to whether we are watchful, patient, holy, and so forth. Reward is linked to our work. And these two are interrelated, such as is seen in the case of Philip the evangelist who was raptured while at work (a type).

Two passages of Scripture mention the conditions for rapture directly:

(1) Revelation 3.10 "Because thou didst keep the word of my patience, I also will keep thee from the hour of trial, that hour which is to come upon the whole world, to try them that dwell upon the earth"—It says "the word of my [i.e., the Lord's] patience" and not "my word of patience": today in this age people curse the Lord, yet the Lord does not strike them to death with lightning (in the millennial kingdom, however, such conduct will not be tolerated). Christians stand with the Lord on the same ground and refuse glory from men because the Lord is now rejected and has not received glory yet.

(2) Luke 21.36 "But watch ye at every season, making supplication, that ye may prevail to escape all these things that shall come to pass, and to stand before the Son of man"—"that ye may prevail": We need to watch at all seasons, not just be watchful for five minutes. We should not go to sleep, but instead discern the light of the Lord and the darkness of the world. And always praying that we may be counted worthy to be in the first rapture. If we do not resist the blessing of the world we cannot escape the woe of the Great Tribulation.

vv.30,39–42 The reapers are the angels, and so is the sickle. Otherwise, people may use this passage to justify the religious inquisitions of the Roman Catholic Church. "To burn them" is to be cast into the lake of fire (see Rev. 20.10, Is. 66.23–24) typified in the Scriptures by the Valley of Hinnom (which lies south and west of Jerusalem; please note, too, that the original New Testament word *Gehenna*—hell—is a corruption of Ge-Hinnom). "All things that cause stumbling" point directly to Satan and modernists, or broadly speaking, to those things which can serve as tools in Satan's hands to cause stumbling, such as idol temples, gambling, dancing halls, theaters, and so forth. During the millennium, none of these and other things which cause stumbling will exist anywhere.

v.43 "The kingdom of their Father"—Three different terminologies are used; namely, (1) the kingdom of heaven, which delineates the sphere or domain; (2) the kingdom of the Son of man (v.41), which means His millennial kingship over the Jews as well as the Gentiles; and (3) the kingdom of the Father (v.43), which points to the heavenly portion of the millennial kingdom where the believers or the righteous ones shall shine as stars even as the Lord who shines as the Sun of righteousness. "He that hath ears, let him hear," says the Scripture.

The Parable of the Mustard Seed

vv.31–32 This mustard seed is not the seed in the first and second parables. The emphasis here is on the smallest of all seeds. The Jews usually used the mustard seed as a simile for smallest (see Matt. 17.20), just as we often use the dust particle to portray anything tiny.

Mustard seed represents the principle of the word of life, for God's word *is* life. The man here is Christ, and the field is the world. The Lord unobtrusively plants the word of God in the world. Before 1828, the majority of commentators took this parable of the mustard seed as signifying the outward development of the church, for within a short period of time the church had spread over Asia. Further, they considered the parable of the leaven as representing the inner growth of the church, inasmuch as the three measures of meal are regarded as a symbol for the whole world. But since 1828,* people such as J.N. Darby and others have raised their voices against such an interpretation, deeming them totally unscriptural and of purely human imagination. For if the entire world were to be improved, then what is the explanation for why there are the tares and for why three-fourths of the soil is unproductive in the preceding parables? Moreover, if such improvement were to occur, there would not be mentioned the parable of the net which follows. Where in the Bible does the number three ever represent the world? Only the numbers two (the Gentiles and Jews) and four (Rev. 7.9—nations, tribes, peoples, and tongues) are used to suggest the whole world. Judging from the collective facts of all the parables, no good fruits are expected from the world.

How, then, should the parable of the mustard seed be explained? According to Genesis 1.11–12, whatever God created bears fruit after its own kind. The vegetables will always be vegetables, the birds will always be birds, and the monkeys will never become human beings. Yet this mustard bush grows abnormally into a tree. This is against the will of God. The church is ordained to be the smallest, the meekest, and the most inconspicuous. But alas, she has become a tree—she has developed today into the complicated entity known as Christianity. During the second and third centuries gnosticism invaded Christianity. This is typified by the parable of the leaven. Thereafter, the

---

*It should be noted that this specific year, mentioned frequently by the author throughout his study on Matthew, marked the beginning of the so-called Brethren movement, which has asserted a tremendous influence on the course of church history ever since.— *Translator*

church, under the Roman Catholic system, has performed mockeries of all kinds. With a royal decree, for example, tens of thousands of soldiers were baptized in one day. Becoming a Christian in those days meant for a person to have special privileges: a gain of four pieces of silver, two changes of suit, and so forth. The church has indeed become like a tree! And in the parable of the mustard seed we can see that the birds of the heaven denote the evil one, even Satan (see vv.4,19) and his influences. Satan is most clever. He knows where he can roost, and he will not let go such an opportunity. How preposterous has the Roman Catholic Church become—a headquarters of Satan! Yet today's Protestant church follows suit. Christmas, for example, is a bird which flew from the Roman Catholic Church into the Protestant Church.

What does the tree signify? And what are typified by the birds? In Daniel 4.20, 22 we learn that the tree represented the power and dominion of Babylon, and in Ezekiel 31.3–6 it represented the power and dominion of the king of Assyria. So that generally speaking, the tree points to earthly power—especially as it pertains to the political realm. Birds denote sins which come from Satan. The sins in the church today actually include all the sins of the world. Is there any sin which is not found in the church? The church has become Babylon, full of confusion; she has also become a large department store. Satan is most clever. If he devours the seed (v.4), he only partially succeeds. He therefore changes his tactic by inflating the church so as to make it possible for all the birds to come and roost. The brand trademark is Christianity, but the medicine sold is Satan's.

What has the Lord ordained for the church? She is to be unknown to the world (1 John 3.1), the world is to be crucified to her (Gal. 6.14), and she is to be a sojourner and a pilgrim (1 Peter 2.11). How very insignificant is the church in the eyes of the world. She has no relationship with the world. D.M. Panton once said that in life the world is a pathway, in death it at most offers him a coffin. Let me say here that if it does not even give me a coffin, I will not mind at all.

How does the church become abnormally large? In the same way that a plant does; namely, by sending its roots deep down into the earth and drawing profusely the nutrition in the soil. So that in this sense the church grows with the help of the world. (For this reason, Christians should not seek glory from the world.)

The differences between a vegetable and a tree are as follows:

(1) A vegetable is an annual or bi-annual plant requiring re-seeding over and over again, whereas a tree takes many years to grow and is therefore perennial in character. How the church, like the mustard plant in the parable, has lost her sojourner- and stranger-like character.

(2) Vegetables have leaves, but trees have branches. Let us observe how the activities of the church are so heavily advertised and how divided is the church into many sects!

(3) A vegetable root is only two or three inches, but the root of a tree is several times the height of the tree's own trunk and grows down very deeply into the ground. Similarly, the church has become worldly and is deeply rooted in the world. Unlike the vegetable which generally dies in three months, the tree lives a long long life.

How the church has lost her original quality of depending on God. God wants His church to return to the vegetable state as presented in Genesis, but she would rather be a tree. She has become a tree having an enormous outward form, yet she is so lacking in reality. She has lost her chastity, and is thus unable to lead the world to repentance. And in all of this, Satan gains the most profit.

Let us therefore maintain the appropriate "smallness". Do not admire the greatness of men. In honor prefer one another; in suffering, outdo one another. Let us have the will to suffer. Let our pocket *be* poor if necessary, if only our spirit may be rich.

The secret of victory lies in standing on the ground which the Lord has given us. When Saul esteemed himself as small, God used him. But when he became self-important, God sought for another person—David. The person whom the Lord seeks is a small vessel, not a big one.

The Parable of the Leaven

v.33 In the entire record of the Scriptures leaven always points to something bad. This is an irrefutable principle of the Bible (see Ex. 12.15, 19–20; 13.6–8; Lev. 2.4–5, 11; 6.17; 10.12; Deut. 16. 3–4; and Amos 4.4–5).

In the New Testament, leaven is used to represent the teachings of (1) the Pharisees (Matt. 16.12)—who, stressing outward grandeur in manners and rituals, are invariably proud; (2) the Sadducees (same verse)—who, by not believing in the supernatural, serve as ancient models for today's modernists who rebel against God; and (3) the Herodians (Mark 8.15)— who are the worldly ones.

"Leaven" may mean teaching (Matt. 16.12) or conduct (1 Cor. 5.6–18). These two are closely related. First improper doctrine, then improper behavior.

"Woman" here represents religious organization, and refers specifically to the Roman Catholic Church, although the word may also be broadly applied to all who propagate heresies.

"Three measures of meal"—This is the customary quantity for making bread (see Gen. 18.6; 1 Sam. 1.24—where an "ephah" equals three measures).

Flour is used in the oblation of a meal-offering. It typifies Christ as being the food of His people. The three measures of meal suggests the manifestation of Christ (one in the Scriptures is God's number, and three is the number for God's manifestations).

By joining all these symbols together we end up with a picture of the Roman Catholic Church having mingled the leaven of her teaching and conduct with the pure food which Christ gave to His people, so that the whole lump of the church is leavened. In the future the Roman Catholic Church and the Protestant Church will join hands. In having these heresies, Christianity appears to be prosperous. Yet hear the voice of the Lord: "Come ye out from among them and be ye separate, saith the Lord, and touch no unclean thing; and I will receive you" (2 Cor. 6.17). And again: "Come forth, my people, out of her, that ye have no fellowship with her sins, and that ye receive not of her plagues" (Rev. 18.4). Today there is leaven everywhere; it is easily encountered. Therefore, we must reject (1) outward grandeur, and (2) inward heresies.

vv.34–35 Without a parable the Lord speaks nothing to them. This is because the Jews have already rejected Him. Instead of speaking plainly as before He uses parables, so that hearing they may not hear and seeing they may not see and understand. Thus is the word of Psalm 78.2 fulfilled.

v.36 "Left" should be translated "sent away" or "having dismissed" (Darby). "Went into the house"—Note that the contents of verses 1–35 happen by the seaside, that of verses 36–52 occur in the house. This house points not to Israel but to the church. The seven parables may be divided into two groups: (1) those of sowing, the tares, the mustard seed, and the leaven are one group, and (2) those of the treasure, the pearl, and the net form a second group. The Lord begins with explaining the parable of the tares because it is the first of the parables of the kingdom of heaven. It is of great importance and has a very wide scope. So that if this one is comprehended, the other parables may easily be understood too. The parables spoken in the house are more precious and more intimate, and they are spoken to the disciples who have already understood what has been said before. Consequently, these latter parables must be more advanced in nature.

The Parable of the Hid Treasure

v.44 "The kingdom of heaven is like unto a treasure hidden [past participle] in the field; which a man found [past tense], and hid [past]; and in his joy he goeth [present] and selleth [present] all that he hath [present], and buyeth [present] that field"—Most commentators interpret this parable in one of the following ways:

(1) The treasure is Christ, the field is the gospel. So Christ hides the gospel. The man is the sinner. He forsakes all to follow the Lord. But we would like to ask the following questions: (a) The gospel is to manifest Christ, how can it then be hidden instead? (b) Where in the Scriptures does "field" ever point to the gospel? (c) What can a sinner buy? (d) Is Christ an article of merchandise which costs something? (e) "Found" and "hid" here are totally at variance with the facts. (f) How do you hide the gospel? (g) If the gospel may be bought, it no longer is the gospel.

(2) The field is the Bible, the treasure is salvation, and the man is the sinner. Hence salvation is hidden in the Bible, and when man finds salvation he forsakes all to obtain it. Again, we would ask some questions and make some observations: (a) Does the Bible reveal or hide salvation? (b) Does man find salvation or is salvation preached to men? (c) Must one pay a price to know the Bible? (d) As a matter of fact, it does not require such a great price to purchase a Bible. (e) There is no guarantee that one would gain Christ after he has purchased a Bible anyway. (f) And why should anyone hide Christ after he has come to know Him? Why should he be afraid of being discovered by somebody else?

(3) The field is the world, the treasure is the church, and the man is Christ. Having seen the church, Christ forsakes all to buy her. Nevertheless, we would like to inquire into the following matters: (a) When and where did Christ discover the church while He was on earth? (b) Or if the treasure signifies the glory

of the church, then while the Lord was on earth when did the church ever manifest her glory? (c) Or if the treasure speaks of sinners, the Lord met sinners everywhere he went and there was therefore no need to find them. (d) Why should Christ hide the sinners once He has found them?

Now if the above interpretations are faulty at various points, how then *should* we explain the parable of the treasure? Since the Lord has not himself explained it, we must interpret it by the use of other Scriptures. In 1 Chronicles 27.25 the word "treasures" is an expression for the glory of the kingdom of David. In Ecclesiastes the term "treasure" is used to show forth the abundance of Solomon's kingdom. The glory of a kingdom lies in its treasures. Even in the time of the Hebraic theocracy—that is to say, from Moses to the last of the judges—treasures represented glory. When the nation was strong, she kept her treasures; while she was weak, her treasures were taken as spoil.

"Field" is the world (see v.38). Why is the treasure hidden in the field? The glory of the kingdom of God has never been manifested on earth. Especially after the Jews were taken captive to Babylon, God was called the God of heaven. Men could not see that God actually ruled the universe. Even before the Captivity, the glory of God's kingdom was hidden to all eyes except to a relatively few. It was not unveiled appreciably until the time of John the Baptist, who began to proclaim that the kingdom of heaven was near. How long was the glory of the kingdom of heaven hidden? From the time of creation until John the Baptist (see Matt. 13.35, 25.34). Who had hidden the glory of the kingdom of heaven? God himself had (see Prov. 25.2, Rom. 11.33). The field is the world as explained in verse 38, else the Lord would certainly have said otherwise here. All this goes to show that in the future the kingdom of heaven will be connected with the world, for the kingdom of heaven shall one day be manifested on earth (see Zech. 14.5,9; and also Ps. 8. 6–9—this latter Scripture being a psalm of the kingdom). The domain of the future kingdom of heaven shall be the earth (though its rule shall indeed be from heaven), for the world will not be destroyed until after the millennial kingdom is ended.

"Which a man found"—This refers to the work of Christ on earth. During the days of confusion in the world, there came one who cried in the wilderness, saying, "The kingdom of heaven is at hand"; and both the Lord and His disciples proclaimed the same message. The power (as manifested in healings and miracles) as well as the teaching of the kingdom of heaven were even then being made manifest (the word "found" in verse 44 actually means to have discovered without the necessity of earnest seeking). The Lord first discovered it; none before Him had even unearthed it. Therefore, the man here is Christ. Neither angels nor prophets could have disclosed it (see Heb. 2.5–8). And if the angels could not disclose it, who else but Christ could?

"And hid"—All actions which occurred before and including this one are cast in the past tense, indicating that the "hidden" and the "found" and the "hid" are all accomplished facts. The actions which follow in the verse are the things the Lord will do thereafter. But why is "hid" again mentioned? Because the Jews have rejected Christ and His kingdom (please recall that this rejection had already begun in the time of chapter 11 and is now fully manifested in the time of chapter 12). For this reason the glory of the kingdom of heaven is now hidden. Henceforth, the Lord does not perform many mighty works among the Jews (and if He does, He does so only for individuals). He also hides himself (see John 8.59, 12.36; Luke 4.30). And why does He hide? Because something is wrong (which points to the rejection of the Jews), and because there is now danger (which indicates the conspiracy of the Jews). He hides himself from the Jews as a nation, not from individuals or from His disciples. He may reject the nation of the Jews, but He never rejects any individual.

"In his joy"—For verses on the joy of the glory of the kingdom we must turn to Luke 10.17–20, 21: the latter verse being the only place in the Gospels where the joy of the Lord is recorded.

"He goeth"—Christ goes to the cross at Jerusalem.

"And selleth all that he hath"—A price must be paid. It costs Christ His life. When the Lord came to this world, He had already forsaken the greater part of His possessions (yet not all). Soon at the cross, He is to sacrifice all, even His life.

"And buyeth that field"—Buy (see Acts 20.28, 2 Peter 2.1, Rev. 5. 9). The purpose in buying is for the treasure in the field. The scope of the purchase is the world. According to 2 Peter 2.1, even the unsaved are also bought. Sin-offering is for believers, propitiation is for the whole world (1 John 2.2). God expects great things on earth, and so He purchases it. The future kingdom is connected with the earth, because the kingdom shall be on earth (see Rev. 11.15, Matt. 6.10). The Lord's heart is also upon the earth (see Matt. 6.21); therefore, He will come again to establish the kingdom of heaven on earth.

The Parable of the Pearl

vv.45–46 Most commentators chiefly interpret this parable in one of the following ways:

(1) The pearl is Christ (this interpretation has persisted from Luther to the present), the man is the believer. But how can Christ be bought? How can He be only a pearl of great price among many pearls?

(2) The pearl is the elite of the church, scattered throughout many churches. But men do not need to sell all in order to seek truth. Both the rich and poor may find the truth.

(3) The pearl is the righteousness of God (this was suggested a hundred years ago).

(4) The pearl is the church (this is partially correct).

How should this parable of the pearl be explained? The pearl stands for the beauty of the church. Such a beauty comes from life, not something manufactured by human effort. Pearls are found in the sea. As we have learned previously, the sea represents the Gentiles—the many peoples—while land represents the Jews. The mystery in Romans 11.25,26 is concerned with the Jews, but the mystery in Ephesians 3.5,6 is mainly concerned with the Gentiles. Treasure is either nationally- or family-owned, but a pearl is individually owned. Do take note of the following verses: Job 28.18 mg.; Matthew 7.6, 13.45–46; 1 Timothy 2.9; and Revelation 17.4, 18.12, 21.21. From such passages as these we may conclude that a pearl is for ornament, to give people beauty and satisfaction.

And the man in the parable is Christ. The Lord intends to obtain many pearls (finding pearls, in fact, is the work of Christ). He does not say He has not found any other pearls; He only states He has found a pearl of great price, for the beauty of the church surpasses all: "a glorious church, not having spot [no sin] or wrinkle [always fresh, never aging] or any such thing; but that it should be holy and without blemish" (Eph. 5.27). She is like the little child in Matthew 11.25. "One pearl of great price"—Note what the Bible says in 1 Corinthians: "Ye were bought with a price" (6.20). "Sold all" speaks of the Lord's death. The beauty of the church is the Lord's ornament. People will see this beauty and will praise the Lord.

The story of the making of a pearl is most interesting. Pearls are produced by certain mollusks in the sea which are rather ugly-looking. This signifies how the church comes from a most humble Christ. A smooth, lustrous, varicolored secretion, which is the very life of the mollusk, issues forth and surrounds a grain of sand or other foreign matter that finds its way into its shell. The mollusk must therefore be hurt if a pearl is ever to be formed. The roundness of the pearl depends on the tenderness of the mollusk. The more tender and sensitive the mollusk, the rounder the pearl. How soft and tender is our Christ. Now pearls are found in the sea. And the divers for them must search and kill the mollusks if they are to get any pearls. Unlike the preceding parable, the man in question (the merchant) must truly seek with effort for pearls.

The Parable of the Net, 13.47–50

This parable is most easily misunderstood. First of all, what are the common interpretations for it? They are as follows:

(1) The net is the gospel, the sea is the world, the fishermen are the preachers of the gospel, the good and bad fishes are the good and bad people who are mixed together in the church.

(2) The sea is the Gentile world, the fishermen are the preachers of the gospel who rescue the unsaved from the world and get them into the boat of the church. The good are to be gathered into vessels, but the bad are to be cast away. Hence just to be in the boat is not enough.

The above two interpretations were the most popular ones in the medieval centuries.

However, this parable has two special features: (1) that the men are angels (to say that the men are preachers of the gospel is to contradict the explanation given by the Lord, else He would have stated otherwise); and (2) that the time for drawing the net is the end of the world. Considering these two features, it becomes evident that the above two interpretations are faulty.

The errors in these interpretations are as follows: (a) the fishermen are not preachers of the gospel, since the drawers of the net are the very ones who cast the net; (b) "cast" in the original is in the past tense: "was cast"; (c) the drawing of the net is at the end of the world and thus occurs only once, but the drawing of the gospel net today happens every day at any time; (d) the drawing is once and for all; (e) if the sea stands for the Gentiles, would not the church be composed only of Gentiles and none of the Jews? (and yet Romans 9.24 plainly states that there will be Jews); (f) as to the way of judgment, tares are bound into bundles for burning, but the fishes are selected one

by one—bad fishes are therefore not limited only to false believers; (g) "when it [the net] was filled"—yet when is the gospel
filled? (h) what does "the beach" represent? (i) the preachers
of the gospel have no right to choose; (j) what is "gathered" is
the gathering "of every kind" and not just fishes; (k) because
obviously a gospel net would be drawn daily, can we at all say
that every day is the end of the world? (l) who can decide to
throw away the bad fishes?—certainly not men; (m) the Lord
simply declared that we shall be fishers of men, but never did He
describe a saved person as being caught in a net; and (n) the se-
lection is done in the net—yet the gospel of grace accepts, never
judges, people.

A comparison between the parable of the net and the parable
of the tares yields this interesting contrast: The parable of the
tares speaks of the beginning when men slept, whereas the parable of the net speaks of the end, that is, the fullness of time. Thus
the parable of the net is placed at the conclusion of the series of
parables.

v.47 "Again"—This shows that there is new light, hence
this parable is different from the parable of the tares.

"Sea"—On the earth three fourths of its surface is sea
(representing, as we have said, the Gentiles—see Daniel 7.2–3
and Is. 60.5) and one–fourth is land (again representing, as we
have said, the Jews). As the land is different from the sea, so the
children of Israel are a people who "dwelleth alone" and are not
"reckoned among the nations" (Num. 23. 9).

"Net, that was cast into the sea"—"Net" here is the gospel of
judgment (see Rev. 14.6–13). "The end of the world" is the
Great Tribulation. The angel shall proclaim the eternal gospel
at the time of the Great Tribulation. It is therefore a gospel of
judgment. The angel casts the net, that is to say, the angel proclaims the eternal gospel to the nations (which include both the
believing and the unbelieving): "Fear God, and give Him glory;
for the hour of His judgment is come" (Rev. 14.7).

"Gathered of every kind" means all the Gentiles (cf. Ez. 47.10).

vv.48–50 "When it was filled"—When the eternal gospel is adequately proclaimed and the time is up.

"Drew up on the beach"—This speaks of judgment. The word of God gathers them, and everyone is compelled to leave his original habitation.

"Sat down" has two meanings: (1) having authority (1 Kings 1.13,20; Matt. 5.1 with 7.29; Matt. 20.21); and (2) judgment (Ex. 18.13, John 19.13).

"Sever the wicked from among the righteous"—This is a severing according to the rule laid down in Leviticus 11.9–13ff.

"The furnace of fire"—See Ezekiel 22.18–22 (cf. Is. 31.5–6, 8–9; Mal. 3.18, 4.1; Is. 30.33; 66.20, 23–24).

"The beach" is the border area between the sea and the land, which is to say, in the midst of the Gentiles and Jews.

Matthew 13.47–49 is similar to Matthew 25.31–36. The sheep are the good fishes and the goats are the bad fishes. The nations that fear God and treat kindly the pious Jews and Christians shall be those to be found in the millennial kingdom.

v.51 "Have ye understood all these things?"—The Lord asks this question because in speaking the mysteries of the kingdom of heaven He wants the disciples to understand thoroughly, whereas He wishes the blasphemers to be totally lost in not understanding His words (see Matt. 13.11–16). So that this question concludes the words found earlier in verses 11–16 of this chapter.

v.52 "Every scribe"—One who is familiar with the Old Testament. From this we are assured that the kingdom of heaven is not the Messianic kingdom, otherwise the scribe would have already been in the kingdom of heaven. A scribe to be made a disciple means a scribe who will have accepted the teaching of the mysteries of the kingdom of heaven (which points to the Christian faith today).

"A householder" is the scribe. A house has its boundary. The boundary is not the open air but is the chambers of a house (see S.S. 1.4).

"Things new and old"—Old is the Old Testament and new is the New Testament. When we speak, we bring out of our treasure both the Old and the New Testaments.

The Rejection of the Lord, 13.54–14.12

Two classes of people reject the Lord—the common people (the residents of Nazareth) and the ruling class (King Herod and his followers).

v.54 The people in the city of Nazareth acknowledge that the Lord has wisdom and performs mighty works. They even admire Him. But they do something wrong when they ask "Whence ... ?" They should know by now that the wisdom and mighty works of the Lord come from God. They should therefore not ask such a question.

v.55 Because of their doubt, the evil one injects some wrong thoughts into their mind. Through the sudden turn which this verse records, these people become hopeless.

v.56 The names of his sisters are not mentioned. These people know the Lord according to the flesh. They know His earthly father and mother, brothers and sisters. So they reject Him. How people everywhere love to see a touch of the mystic. If someone is so powerful, there must be something mysterious surrounding that person. But if everything is known about him, he becomes common in their eyes, since for them there is nothing special surrounding him. The people in Nazareth have the same weakness. They imagine that Christ ought to be rather enigmatic and aloof, someone quite different from themselves: "We know this man whence he is: but when the Christ cometh, no one knoweth whence he is" (John 7.27).

v.57 The Jews reject the Lord not only because of familiarity but also because of the fact that no prophet is honored in his own country.

v.58 How very sad are these words. Many hinder the mighty works of God through their unbelief. The mighty works of God are often limited by the lack of faith. God loves to perform His wonders in us, but our faith frequently proves to be inadequate. Our faith is like a waterpot, the mighty power of God is like a spring of water. Without a waterpot, we can have no water. Alas, our faith today is sometimes like a bamboo bucket which leaks away the power of God.

THE GOSPEL ACCORDING TO MATTHEW

Chapter 14

The Rejection of the Lord, 13.54–14.12 (Concl'd)

v.1 This part of the section shows how the ruler, King Herod, rejects the Lord. A "tetrarch" (meaning, chief or ruler of a fourth part) is a king under the Roman Emperor.

"Heard the report concerning Jesus"—Perhaps he did so through the preaching of the twelve disciples.

v.2 Herod is willing to concede the Lord to be John the Baptist, but not the Christ.

vv.3–4 Before the Twelve were sent out to preach, John was imprisoned by Herod because he spoke frankly to the king that it was not lawful for him to marry his brother's wife (see Mark 6.19). We should not be careless about sin.

v.5 Herod would have killed John but for his fear of the people. However, after having contacts with John, he is convinced that John is "a righteous and holy man" (Mark 6.20), for the preaching of John touches Herod's conscience. He is perplexed and afraid; and so he seeks to protect, as well as to listen to, John. But though His conscience is touched, he is not able to resist the influence of the enemy. Satan at that time hides behind the scenes in his fight against God's children. How often we have a conscience, yet we do not have the power not to sin.

v.6 "Birthday"—This is the only instance recorded in the New Testament where a birthday is celebrated (see Gen. 40.20, the only mentioning in the Old Testament of a birthday celebration). It would appear that sin can easily enter in in the course of man's extravagant pleasure.

Herodias is an adulterous woman. For her sake John is imprisoned.

People should not thrust their children into the limelight of the world. The daughter of Herodias should be a lesson to parents.

v.7 At the height of joy, people frequently lose control of themselves. Herod's oath is a good example.

v.8 An innocent girl, at the instigation of her mother, asks for the head of John on a platter. A girl who has received such an education as this would seem to be lost forever. She is destined to grow up a wicked woman. Parents are responsible for their children in matters such as the cinema, dancing, reading materials, and so forth.

v.9 "Grieved"—For Herod's conscience is awakened. "Of them that sat at meat with him"—Yet he would rather sin than lose face.

vv.10–11 This is to be taken literally.

v.12 This verse unveils one of the principles for Christian living. The disciples of John come quietly, without noise of publicity, to take up the corpse and bury him; and then they go to tell Jesus. The principle? To make no noise when unjustly treated, hide the evidence of one's own mistreatment, and tell the Lord Jesus. How differently we would react if we followed such a principle. Too often, when we are ill-treated, we broadcast the proof of our mistreatment.

The Feeding of the Five Thousand, 14.13-21

v.13 This second section tells of the death of the Lord for our sake as typified by the breaking and distributing of bread to the multitude. John 6.1-14 gives the same incident, and afterwards from John 6.26 onward the meaning of the distribution of bread is explained. This is not a picnic; on the contrary, this incident foretells in type the death of our Lord (see especially John 6.35,48,53-58).

vv.14-16 Compassion is the nature of the Lord. However much He may be rejected, His compassion never fails to come forth. The disciples want to send away the multitude—to send them away from the Lord. Sometimes we assume the same kind of tone. We believers ought not take an irresponsible attitude; instead, we should seek every opportunity to be responsible. How we must learn from the Lord Jesus in this respect. Do not be forced to make bricks under the lash of a whip. The Lord supplies men's need as well as preaches the word of life. He is here as a rich poor man.

"Give ye them to eat"—Believers should not be miserly. Let us not be poor rich people.

vv.17-18 Now why does the Lord want the disciples to give to the multitude to eat? Because the disciples do have something, however little they may have.

"Bring them hither to me"—The *least* thing, placed in the Lord's hands, becomes the *most*.

v.19 If the loaves are not in the Lord's hands, He cannot bless. After blessing, there must be the breaking. How people love the blessing but abhor the breaking. "Except a grain of wheat fall into the ground and die" (John 12.24). A grain has the possibility of *not* dying, if it resists going into the ground. How can the 5,000 men be filled if there is no breaking? And how can the Lord break the loaves if they are not given over to His hand? Whenever and wherever a person resists the Lord's breaking, he will have to be laid aside by the Lord. The Lord always takes our consecration for real, and so He starts to break us. Yet many there are who cry out for anguish upon the first or second hint of God's breaking work in them!

"Gave"—After being broken, these loaves must be given to the multitude. But to deliver to the multitude requires strength. Yet strength will be there if these believers yield themselves to be broken. Sometimes after consecration there will come extraordinary things, such as the losing of someone you love or the losing of wealth. This is an indication of breaking, for breaking will not occur until you are consecrated.

v.20 "And they all ate, and were filled"—Whenever the Lord gives, He always gives to satisfaction ("rivers of living water" is another example of this; see John 7.38).

"That which remained ... twelve baskets full"—Each time after consecration and use by the Lord there is always increase. This is a spiritual law. Yet frequently after work we feel the need of "spiritual repair"—and how wrong this is, for ours is the life of a trolley car and not that of a motor car. When our Lord is hungry, He gives from himself living water to the Samaritan woman, and still He is filled. Hence we need to learn to feed others; we should never be spiritually selfish.

"Twelve baskets full"—This points to eternal completeness. The effect of the death of Christ is eternally complete. (By contrast, the seven baskets full spoken of in chapter 15 signify the fullness of the children of Israel during the millennial kingdom.)

v.21 Why are the women not numbered? Because the married women are "one flesh" with the married men (see Gen.

2.24); the unmarried women (virgins) need to be hidden; and the children, not being of age, are not counted.

The Walking on the Water, 14.22–33

This third section implies, by its phraseology, some of the great truths in Scripture, such as Jesus' resurrection and ascension ("went up into the mountain"), His intercession ("to pray"), the Great Tribulation (the disciples left behind during "the fourth watch of the night"—which is the darkest period), the Lord's coming again ("he came to them"), and so forth.

v.22 "Boat" represents the church. The boat is in the sea; so also is the church now in the world.

v.23 "Went up into the mountain apart to pray"—This signifies the resurrection and ascension of our Lord, and His intercessory ministry for us before God.

v.24 "The wind was contrary"—This signifies the persecutions the church suffers in the world.

"He constrained the disciples to enter into the boat" (v.22) —The Lord permits us to face temptations in the world so that we may grow spiritually.

"And when even was come" (v.23)—"Even" or "evening" represents the time after the Lord has departed from this earth. For the Lord is the true light. After His departure, the world enters into darkness, and will not see light until the return of the Lord as the Morning Star and Sun of Righteousness. This is why in the sight of the Lord the church is a lampstand and the believers are the light of the world.

v.25 "In the fourth watch of the night"—This typifies the Great Tribulation. After the darkest time of the night, the dawn comes: "The morning cometh, and also the night" (Is. 21.12).

At the time of the Great Tribulation the Lord shall come to His disciples.

vv.26–27 Earlier we saw that people do not believe in the Lord because they consider Him as not being mysterious enough. Now, though, they are afraid because He is too mysterious. Even the disciples are afraid. The Lord immediately comforts them, however, thus revealing His love for them.

vv.28–31 This narrates the story of Peter walking upon the water. From this incident we may deduce several important principles:

(1) The call of the Lord comes through invitation, "Bid me come unto thee" (v.28). Believers should ask the Lord to invite them.

(2) Believers should imitate Peter in being special and in following the Lord first. Peter comes to the Lord earlier than do the rest of the disciples.

(3) "Bid me" shows the obedience of Peter.

(4) Though staying in the boat is shaky enough, Peter dares still further to venture forth.

(5) "And he said, Come" (v.29)—The Lord's word is a promise. Without the Lord's promise it would be a senseless adventure. Some people may accuse Peter of being fond of showing off; but the Lord, far from scolding him, encourages him to come. His promise shows His approval.

(6) People may think it is safer in the boat. There is no need to walk upon the water to follow the Lord. Yet we should realize that the life of a believer is a life of faith. It is easy to have and exercise faith within the framework of a corporate situation, but to have faith individually is hard. As a matter of fact faith is personal. Peter walks upon the water by faith. And this is recommended by the Lord.

(7) Seeking mere adventure is wrong, but believers ought to venture forth into the unknown on the basis of the word of God.

And such is an adventure of faith. It will work out to be experience. He who seeks only for security shall lack experience.

(8) In walking upon the water, Peter should not have looked at the strong wind. He has the word of the Lord; he therefore ought not look at the wind and the waves. In looking at these things he easily forgets the Lord's word. Without the word, one should never walk on the water in the first place, even if everything is calm. Since walking upon the water does not depend on the wind and the wave, one should never look at these matters. One should look only at the Lord. And then he will not look at them.

(9) How the Lord must have hoped that more would come down from the boat (the brothers and sisters in the church) and walk upon the water by faith. The comparison here is between the Christians walking upon the water and Christians staying in the boat.

(10) Whenever believers encounter the winds and storms of life, they should lay hold of the Lord's word. For the word of God is the sword of the Holy Spirit—the only offensive weapon at the believer's disposal.

(11) Sometimes the faith of a believer is weak; nonetheless, the love of Christ is so great that He will sustain him with grace.

(12) "Immediately" (v.31)—That is, just before sinking down.

(13) "O thou of little faith, wherefore didst thou doubt?" (v.31)—Doubt stems from little faith. First faith, then doubt. Without believing, there can be no doubting. Peter at least had faith; only, his faith was too little.

v.32 "And when they were gone up into the boat"—The "they" here are Peter and Christ. This must have been a most gratifying and joyous experience to Peter.

v.33 "And they that were in the boat worshipped him"—They could not help but worship.

A Type of the Millennial Kingdom, 14.34–36

This fourth section serves as a type of the future millennial kingdom when the Lord shall return to the land of Judea.

v.34 "Gennesaret" means the protectorate of the king. It therefore signifies the kingdom. The Lord Jesus has come to His millennial kingdom.

v.35 "And when the men of that place knew him"—They recognize that it is Jesus, for He is the Lord Christ who cannot be hidden. His love, compassion, holiness, righteousness, and so forth cannot be concealed. Will people recognize us as true Christians?

"And brought unto him all that were sick"—As the sick touch the Lord they are healed. How precious this is. Are all our prayers for healing answered? Not necessarily, for Paul was not healed of his affliction nor was Timothy's stomach trouble healed. Healing belongs to the millennial kingdom (Mal. 4.2).

v.36 "Touch"—Even touching the border of His garment is enough. How we need to touch the Lord in prayer. Alas, how many throng Him, but how few really touch Him!

Chapter 15

This chapter intimates to us the heart of God. Both Matthew and Mark have the same objective of causing people to know God's heart, that is to say, how much He loves the world that He gives His only begotten Son. The Lord Jesus does not openly declare that He is the Son of God, yet He hints that He is. Jesus has done many good things in the past, as recorded in the earlier chapters of this Gospel, but now He will do more in order to give people sufficient evidence to recognize Him as the Son of God.

The Tradition of the Elders, 15.1–20

v.1 The Pharisees are the pragmatists, while the scribes are the theologians. These two groups are usually incompatible, but now they join hands in questioning the Lord. This indicates the balanced influence of the Lord, otherwise these people would never conspire together.

Jerusalem is the religious center. But it is also the rebellious center: how our Lord weeps over this city. The Jerusalem of that day is like Christianity of our current day. In Matthew 2 we saw how Herod and the entire city of Jerusalem had been troubled at the news of the newborn king. They had not welcomed the Lord. And it is to be noticed later that during the last week before His crucifixion, the Lord will not be found staying in Jerusalem, but will spend those nights in a home in Bethany.

For in that house, unlike in Jerusalem, there is life, love, and true service.

v.2 Previously the Pharisees had questioned the Lord on the matter of violating divine commandment, and they failed in such questioning. Here they are seen asking about the matter of tradition. Tradition may be kept, but it should never be taken as being on an equality with the word of God. Unfortunately, people often mistake tradition as being God's word. Our Lord obviously knows the principles of good hygiene. Yet He purposely violates them as a means of challenging such bigotry.

v.3 Compare Mark 7.7. What the Lord contends is that no tradition can ever replace God's word. "In vain do they worship me, teaching as their doctrines the precepts of men" (Mark 7.8).

vv.4–6 When the tradition of men is supplementary to the word of God, the first will soon become more important than the second and make void the commandments of God.

v.5 "Given to God"—This phrase serves as the meaning for the word "Corban" which appears in chapter 7 of Mark's account of this incident. "Corban" is anything that is brought near to God—a gift or an offering. There are two kinds of offering: (1) a direct one (such as the putting of an offering into the offering box), and (2) a vow such as that of Jephthah (Judges 11.29–40): Jephthah's vow contradicted the divine commandment of "Thou shalt not kill" (Ex. 20.13), and other relevant divine injunctions (Lev. 18.21, Deut. 12.31). The Pharisees would rather keep Corban and thus make void the commandment of God. How frequently we declare: The Bible says thus and so, but ... This "but" according to the tradition of the elders precipitates all the confusion.

v.7 Hypocrites are not the really bad, but the false good. False good is worse than real bad.

v.8 All who advocate the authority of tradition honor God with their lips but their heart is far from Him.

v.9 If the heart is far from God, one's worship is in vain because God seeks for those who worship in spirit and in truth.

v.10 The Lord not only speaks to the scribes and the Pharisees, He also speaks to the multitude. He speaks to people today. And what He speaks concerns not merely the tradition of washing hands, but every other tradition.

v.11 Man's wickedness is within rather than without; hence there is no absolute need of washing the hands. Whatever comes from the heart defiles man.

v.12 The Pharisees resist the word because of their prejudice.

v.13 (1) The Lord acknowledges that tradition comes from men.
(2) One day all the traditions of men will be rooted up. Let us not wait till that day.
(3) What is not planted by God are the teachings of the Pharisees. May all our traditional teachings of man be rooted up today lest they come before the judgment seat of Christ.
(4) From this verse we can apprehend how necessary it is for us to uproot all heresies.

v.14 "Let them alone"—Our Lord is never in haste. Time will prove the truth or falsity of anything. How contrary, though, is fallen human nature. We are always in haste.

"The blind guide the blind"—People other than just the Pharisees were listening to the Lord that day: they too are blind, for the one who can follow a blind man must be blind himself. But one who sees will never follow the blind. The fanatic loves to listen to the fanatic; the confused, to the confused. The blind enjoys leading, the ignorant likes to teach, and the novice loves to preach. Who is he that launches out blindly? Only the blind. Hence the blind one is a most subjective person.

vv.15–20 The parable is that "if the blind guide the blind, both shall fall into a pit" (v.14). And the application of such a parable is on the washing of hands. The heart is the source of all evils. The tradition of the Pharisees encourages the people to wash their hands most clean and white. Yet such tradition neglects the matter of the defiled heart. There is therefore no need to go to Africa to find the heathen; they can be found in large numbers in England, America, China, and Japan.

The main points here are three: (1) how defiled the heart of man is, yet (2) how merciful is the heart of God, and (3) how necessary to have our hearts cleansed. Please note that whereas verses 15–20 speak of *man's* defiled heart, verses 21–28 speak of the heart of *God*. Without a knowledge of the human heart there can be no understanding of the heart of God. (As we shall soon see, verses 21–28 also speak of the heart of the Gentiles.)

The Canaanitish Woman, 15.21–28

v.21 "Withdrew"—Jesus wishes to leave these hypocrites and to go to the region of Tyre and Sidon, cities that are cursed of God. He had openly cursed them through the mouth of the prophets (see Is. 23, Joel 3.4). Hence our Lord would rather leave secret sinners and go to open sinners.

"The parts of"—Or the boundary thereof. Though we do not live in Tyre and Sidon, we are nonetheless within their borders.

v.22 "A Canaanitish woman"—She belongs to the race of the Canaanites, so she too is under a curse (see Gen. 9.25–26).

"Came out from those borders"—That is, she comes out of the place of curse.

"O Lord" is a cry for mercy. But "thou son of David" is a wrong cry, since the Son of David has nothing to do with a Canaanitish woman.

v.23 "But he answered her not a word"—His not answering her is not a refusal, but on the contrary is another expression of love; for as the Son of David, He has no part with the Gentiles. This woman therefore stands on an improper ground. In view of this, we too should be careful as to how we address the Lord in prayer.

"Send her away"—The disciples became impatient and asked the Lord to settle her request quickly.

v.24 "But unto the lost sheep of the house of Israel"— The work of the Lord while on earth is directed primarily toward the Jews. His openly expressed work towards the Gentiles only really begins in the house of Cornelius, after His resurrection and ascension. While on earth, therefore, the Lord's work for the Gentiles remained largely concealed. Even with respect to the house of Israel, He went only to the lost sheep (that is, to the remnant). Why does the Lord say this to her? To give this woman a handle to hold on to. Though He is sent to the house of Israel, it is nevertheless only to the lost sheep that He is sent. "The lost sheep" has a much wider scope. Is not this woman a lost sheep? May she not receive grace? If only she will acknowledge that she is a lost sheep. The Lord throws out to her a distant thought. His not answering her at first (v.23) is not a rejection; rather, a silent permission. Although He does not open His mouth at the beginning, His heart is aching with love to show her grace. Unless the woman stands on the ground of a sinner,

He is unable to answer her request. Let us see that the silent delay of God is not an outright rejection. His delay is not an indication of any indifference, He is instead waiting for us to come around.

After the Lord finally speaks that one word, He says no more. But how free is His love and how expectantly He waits. The appearance of outward distance does not mean repudiation.

v.25 The woman understands and lays hold of the Lord's word. She reasons within herself: I thought all the children of Israel were moral and good. How was I to know that He only goes to lost sheep? If this is true, then it is grace, and there is therefore no positional restriction. Though I am a cursed sinner, I am also a lost sheep who may receive grace.

The Lord Jesus, in this one word, thus lowers the entire nation of Israel to be at the same level as that of Tyre and Sidon. All are sinners. Now, therefore, she no longer cries out "Lord, thou son of David"; she merely cries "Lord"—for she at this moment understands the meaning of salvation.

v.26 "And he answered and said"—This is the first time the Lord answers her directly. What He had said before (v.24) was spoken directly to the disciples and only indirectly to the woman.

"Dogs"—The Lord compares the Jews to sheep and the Gentiles to dogs. Only the children of Israel are counted as sheep: They are the Lord's sheep made reference to in John 10. But He also has "other sheep" (John 10.16), the saved ones among the Gentiles. The Jews consider themselves to be sheep, hence the Lord says lost sheep. The Gentiles likewise claim to be sheep, yet the Lord says dogs. Sheep are cloven-footed (external cleanness) and chew the cud (internal cleanness)–see Leviticus 11.3. This woman reckons herself a sheep, but she is actually a dog. Even so, the Lord still gives her a word with which to lay hold.

v.27 "Yea, Lord"—She acknowledges that what the Lord has said is true and what she has said is wrong. In the Greek, there are two different words for "dog": (1) a wild dog, and (2) a domesticated dog. Here the term used is that for a domesticated dog. The Lord gives her the second of these two terms and she lays hold of it. In essence, this woman says, Though I am a dog, yet I am Your dog; and therefore I may eat of the crumbs that fall from Your table.

v.28 "O woman, great is thy faith"—The Lord calls her "woman" and commends her for her faith before He grants her request (such is the way of His reward—first praise, then gift). His heart is touched and He marvels at her faith. Let us always understand that God's delay or testing takes us through a school of faith. The longer the delay, the greater the faith. The salutation, Son of David, suggests a natural relationship that is not there. If anyone thinks his conduct to be fairly good and assumes thereby that he is all right, God will have to give him up. But if a person is willing to humble himself and stand on the ground of a dog, God will begin to bless. May we learn from this incident how to lay hold of God's word in prayer.

Many Miracles of Healing, 15.29–31

"And Jesus departed thence, and came nigh unto the sea of Galilee"—The Lord returns to the midst of the children of Israel. He first comes to the nation of Judah, then to the Gentiles, and finally back to the midst of the children of Israel. The Jews need to repent, the Gentiles must believe. This section typifies the beginning of the millennial kingdom. The Jews realize their illnesses, and hence they come to the Lord, and the Lord heals them (healing is a token of the power of the millennial kingdom). And thus, they glorify God through Christ (see v.31).

The Feeding of the Four Thousand, 15.32–39

What the woman in the earlier episode ate were crumbs, but now the Lord spreads the table which signifies the grace and abundance of the kingdom. There is no period when more people are saved than during the millennial kingdom. "Four" (thousand) flows out of "three", that is to say, flows out of the Creator; thus "four" represents the world (people). "Seven" (loaves) is a perfect number, while "seven baskets full" denotes abundance.

Another precious thought which can be gleaned from this passage is the fact that our Lord Jesus, like the crowd of four thousand men, has also had nothing to eat for three days. He knows how to stand on the same ground with His audience. Can we listen to the word of God and not feel hungry for three days? But on the third day the Lord multiplies the loaves for the multitude. As for himself, He fasted forty days and refused to turn the stones into bread. Hence for others we should have compassion, but for ourselves there must be discipline and self-denial.

"I would not send them away fasting"—There are today two different kinds of people: (1) those who are advocates of social service, doing nothing but social service; and (2) those who are champions of spiritual needs, supplying only spiritual nurture. Both are extremes. "Faith apart from works is dead," said the apostle James (2.26). Compassion is most natural, unless a person "shutteth up his compassion from him" (1 John 3.17). Hence every believer should do his best to render both material and spiritual help to his brethren and to others.

"Whence should we have so many loaves . . .?"—Those who say such words look only at the environment. The prime lesson of faith is to be rid of the "whence" in our thinking. No prayer of faith ever says "whence"; if God says so, that is enough.

The loaves given to the disciples for distribution represent resurrection. The loaves in the hands of the disciples originally can never multiply, but after being broken by the Lord, that which remains of the multiplied loaves after the feeding of four thousand men, besides the women and children present, fill up seven baskets. A life that has been dealt with by the cross is no longer natural but is supernatural and overabundant in supplying the needs of others.

THE GOSPEL ACCORDING TO MATTHEW

Chapter 16

The Pharisees and Sadducees—and the Leaven Thereof, 16.1–12

v.1 Here we find the Pharisees and the Sadducees form-
ing a new compromise between themselves. In the previous
chapter we saw how the Pharisees had joined hands with the
scribes, two groups that were not deadly against each other. But
in the present case, the two groups of the Pharisees and the Sadducees are normally great adversaries. Yet here, they are found
coming together to tempt the Lord because of their mutual unbelief. The unbelieving always play the same trick. In chapter 12
we saw that due to unbelief both the Pharisees and the scribes
asked for a sign. And here again, we have the Pharisees teaming
up with the Sadducees to ask for a sign once more. And why?
Because they are all Jews, and "the Jews," said Paul, "ask for
signs" (1 Cor. 1.22). They had asked for signs earlier (chapter
12) in order to satisfy their curiosity. But now they ask purely
for the sake of tempting the Lord. The Lord, though, keeps
strictly to His former decision without any change. Others may
seek for improvement, but the Lord is the same yesterday, today,
and forever (Heb. 13.8), for He is perfect and His thought
needs no alteration.

"Trying" is a word to signify a testing of the Lord. Such action is a sign of unbelief: unless you do something to convince

me, I will not believe. The world always wants to see God first before they will believe. Yet our Lord never performs miracles merely to pass the test of man. He does not intend to use miracles to attract the unbelieving. He of course can do wonders, but this is not something for men to govern or to ratify. In spiritual things, He is not subject to any authority other than the Father.

vv.2–3 "The heaven is red"—Since they talk about heaven, the Lord will also speak of heaven. He reprimands them for knowing "how to discern the face of the heaven" but not how "to discern the signs of the times" (v.3). He admits that they are scientists, even as are the unbelieving of today. In His view they only know the cause and effect of certain things but do not know the signs of the times. How adept people are in neglecting the signs of the times! What a pity they cannot discern the ever present signs! Their self-contentment (like many scientists today) makes them blind. To the Lord, the sign is already there, and hence He has no need to perform another one; for the sign of the times is the cross.

v.4 The sign of Jonah confirms the death and resurrection of the Lord. Just as Jonah had left his native land, so the Lord shall depart from this earth.

"Evil" speaks of personal character; "adulterous" signifies improper communication. Not just one person, but all mankind is corrupted. Hence, the Lord departed.

vv.5–6 "Take heed and beware of the leaven of the Pharisees and Sadducees"—Take care of the temptation of the Pharisees and Sadducees. These two groups are like leaven which has the possibility of leavening the disciples: leaven in the sense of saying but doing not (see 23.3), trying to reform others while they themselves refuse to be reformed. How careful we need to be in making friends. How easy it is to be leavened by the unbelieving and the ungodly. The Pharisees are the dead fundamentalists, while the Sadducees are the unbelieving modernists. The leaven here is our asking the Lord to perform something before believing. Thus this is temptation. The Lord warns us because we are susceptible to being leavened.

v.7 The disciples are perplexed. They mistake leaven for bread, and it is therefore a misapprehension of what Jesus meant. Such a misinterpretation of the word of the Lord is very common today. Such erroneous logic with respect to the Scriptures is quite prevalent in our time. Now such misunderstanding by the Twelve reveals their unbelief and foolishness. Even though they had forgotten to bring bread, would the Lord ever say such words in referring to bread? They forgot their experience of the multiplication of the loaves. A person's subjectivity can often lead him to misinterpretation.

vv.8–12 "And Jesus perceiving it"—Nothing is hidden from the Lord.

"O ye of little faith"—Little faith is not without some faith. Still, our Lord is dissatisfied with little faith.

"Why reason"—This is an expression of unbelief. If people misinterpret the Bible, it is always men's fault, never God's. The lesson to be learned from this short section is that in this age we must beware of the leavening influence of the Pharisees.

Peter's Great Confession, 16.13–20

It is not until this moment that the Lord now begins to reveal himself. Previously, His real person was only hinted at. Verse 21 which follows this passage really forms the center or pivot of the entire Gospel of Matthew.

Caesarea Philippi is named after Tetrarch Philip, the brother of Herod.

v.13 "The Son of man"—Why does the Lord style himself as the Son of man? Names in the Bible are very important. (In the Epistles, the names used for Jesus are mainly the Lord Jesus, Jesus Christ, and so forth because the work of salvation is already accomplished. In the Gospels, however, He is called the Son of God or the Son of man because the work of salvation is not yet finished. And in the book of Acts, He is called the servant of God until the events that took place in the house of Cornelius.)

The appellation, the Son of man, implies (1) He is being rejected, (2) He is glorified for our sake, and (3) He is a man. Here it applies especially to His being rejected.

v.14 Men concede that He is either John the Baptist who at that moment was the most recent servant of God, or else Elijah who was most zealous in religion, or else Jeremiah who was most pessimistic; but they will not acknowledge Him as the Christ. John had already testified that Jesus is the Son of God, yet men will only say that He is a prophet.

v.15 The Lord is asking us the same question today. How do you answer? A religious leader, a social worker, a philosopher, a revolutionist? Take note of the fact that Jesus is not satisfied with the title of prophet. Do you confess him as Christ?

vv.16–17 "Bar" means son. "Jonah" means dove. Combined, the surname of Simon means having the revelation of the Holy Spirit. Men are never able to judge Jesus aright because they do not have God's revelation and therefore judge by their own opinions. The Lord, in not being satisfied, puts the same question to His disciples. And Peter's answer is a proof of his being born anew (see 1 John 5.1; 4.15). Christ is the one upon whom the hope and plan of God will be accomplished. So what Peter says here is: "You are the only one who accomplishes God's hope and plan." The term "Christ" refers to His work, whereas the term "the Son of God" refers to His person and to

His personal glory. Our Lord possesses three different kinds of glory: (1) personal—the glory of being God in eternity, (2) individual—His glory as man on earth, and (3) moral—the glory of His righteous conduct on earth.

Simon is Peter's old name. "Bar-Jonah" means (as we have seen) son of the Holy Spirit, that is to say, one who is born of the Spirit. How blessed it is to confess the Lord Jesus as the Christ, for this is through the revelation of the Holy Spirit. We do not become Christians by reasoning but by revelation (Gal. 1.15–16).

God gives us revelation through four different means: (1) nature—such as through the heaven, sun, moon, stars, and so forth; (2) writing—the Holy Scriptures; (3) Jesus; and (4) the Holy Spirit. The revelation of the Holy Spirit is of utmost importance because without such unveiling none ultimately can be saved.

v.18 "Also"—One thing has just been said, now something else is being added.

"I will"—When the Lord utters these words it is evident that the church is not yet built.

"Peter . . . upon this rock"—In the Greek text "rock" is *petra*, a massive piece of rock; whereas "Peter" is *petros*, a stone. These two terms are therefore different. A foundation cannot be laid upon a *petros*, a small stone. No one ever builds a house on such a foundation. Peter is but a little stone, but the Lord Jesus is the *Petra*—the Rock (see 1 Peter 2.7–8). In confessing Christ, Peter becomes a small stone. Whoever confesses Christ is a small stone—that is to say, a living stone. The spiritual house (the church, the habitation of God) is made up of living stones. So that the rock is the Lord Jesus Christ whom Peter confesses. Had the rock been Peter, the church would have soon fallen into ruin since Peter was one who had quivered before a maid and had denied the Lord three times. Without this confession of Christ there can be no church (according to some ancient authorities, Philip baptized the eunuch after the latter had made the confession; see Acts 8.37 mg.).

"Church" in the Greek is *ecclesia*, the called-out assembly—those who have been called out and separated from the world. Consequently, every saved person is a saint who has been sanctified ("For if the blood of goats and bulls, and the ashes of a heifer sprinkling them that have been defiled, sanctify unto the cleanness of the flesh: how much more shall the blood of Christ, who through the eternal Spirit offered himself without blemish unto God, cleanse your conscience from dead works to serve the living God?"—Heb. 9.13-14).

"Gates of Hades"—Gates serve as entrance and exit. Neither Hades nor death can hold on to believers or the church, because the incorruptible life has already been manifested in them (see 2 Tim. 1.10).

The body of Christ is twofold: (1) the physical body of Christ through which is manifested the life of God; and (2) the corporate body of Christ—the church—with which Christ, after His resurrection and ascension, clothes himself on earth. Hence the church is where the Lord deposits His life today. This incorruptible life has come out of Hades. For the Lord has the authority to have His life enter in and exit out of Hades at will. Hades has no power to hold back this life. And what has been deposited in the believer is this very same life. For this reason, Hades cannot withhold us either. Believers too shall be resurrected first, because of their having this life. As to non-believers, though, their life will be detained by Hades after their death. Resurrection is the life which cannot be held back. However vicious the environment—trial, persecution, malice, murder, and so forth—and though we may be walled in on all sides, we have a life which can neither be withheld nor overcome by any environment.

v.19 This verse is easily misunderstood. "I will give unto thee the keys of the kingdom of heaven"—Are the keys given only to Peter? Does the binding refer to forgiveness of sins? The word keys is cast in plural number—is there then one for the Jews (as used on the day of Pentecost) and one for the Gentiles (as used in the house of Cornelius), as is explained in the Scofield Reference Bible? Obviously the keys cannot be changed in their purpose in the hands of different users.

Verse 18 speaks of the gates of Hades; this is in contrast to the door of the kingdom of heaven. The subject in verse 18 is the church while that of verse 19 is the kingdom of heaven. The church in verse 18 is built by the Lord himself ("I will build my church"). Yet the kingdom of heaven in verse 19 seems to be built by men. Hence the keys are not those of the church, rather they are the keys to the kingdom of heaven as the verse itself says. Otherwise, Peter could really be a pope.

The kingdom of heaven: (1) whereas, on the one hand, the church is built by none other than the Lord himself (through regeneration, life, the Holy Spirit, and revelation from above) and not by flesh and blood—on the other hand, the kingdom of heaven is the realm in which we are called to be disciples; (2) in the kingdom of heaven, God causes us to enjoy our privileges as disciples; and (3) in the kingdom of heaven we are also to perform our duties and fulfill our responsibilities as disciples.

Here the Lord is telling Peter, "You shall bring people into the kingdom of heaven"—so that the keys mentioned here suggest the first step in the procedure of entering the kingdom of heaven, the first few things which help people to enter through the door. Peter used them in the events recorded in the book of Acts: (1) He had the key of witnessing—his preaching on the day of Pentecost (2.14ff.); (2) he also had the key of baptizing —his exhorting the people to be baptized into Christ (2.38–41; see also Rom. 6.3) that they might be obedient to the Lord and His command. Thus in Matthew 28.19, we have Christ's command to His disciples to "make disciples of all the nations" (the use of the first key) and this to be followed by "baptizing them" (the use of the second key). He who is not baptized can be in the church, but not in the kingdom of heaven (see Matt. 21.31–32). It is the Lord who adds to the church day by day those who are being saved (Acts 2.47 mg.; 16.5). Preachers can only bring people into the kingdom of heaven. The kingdom of heaven in its outward appearance can be likened to *the outer precincts* of the house of God which is the church. In these outer precincts one may find the tares, but in the true church these tares never exist.

The keys are not only given to Peter but also given to us. For please note that in Matthew 18.18 the Lord is recorded as giving the same promise again, but there the pronoun is "ye"—not just Peter but all who are in the church (see Matt. 18.19,20 where the church is brought into view). So, we too have these keys. With these keys we have the authority to bind (close) as well as to loose (open).

Since the keys which Peter has denote preaching and baptizing, naturally our keys are the same. Peter receives the keys first only because he confesses first.

"Loose"—We begin to preach the gospel and to baptize. "Bind"—Because the keys are in our hands we have the authority not to preach or not to baptize.

In Matthew 28 those who receive the great commission are eleven *disciples*, not apostles (the latter are God's gift to the church). The emphasis is therefore on the kingdom of heaven. In the entire Bible there are two distinctive yet inseparable lines: namely, the church and the kingdom of heaven.

v.20 "They should tell no man that he was the Christ"— To some of the Jews, that is, to those who have blasphemed the Holy Spirit, the Lord as Christ is not to be mentioned. The Son of God is eternal, and Christ fulfills the plan of God. In the presence of the Jews who have rejected Him He is not to be mentioned as such. This also confirms the fact that since the moment of their blasphemy of the Holy Spirit as recorded in 12.24, these blaspheming Jews have been rejected by the Lord.

Jesus Foretells His Passion
and Underscores the Way of the Cross, 16.21–27

v.21 "From that time"—Since the time that Christ is confessed and the church is to be built. The death which our Lord reveals here is not atoning death, rather death through persecution and rejection. (According to the Scriptures, the death of the Lord has two aspects: atoning death, which, it should be noted, the evangelicals hold to reverently; and rejecting death, which the liberals maintain strongly). Many of the sufferings of our Lord are not of an atoning nature but are of a rejecting nature. The Lord prophesies of His death here only to the point of death through rejection. Later on, the same prophecy is repeated; but there the Lord speaks much more plainly of His death, thus indicating a great departure that constitutes another peak in the book of Matthew.

v.22 "And Peter took him"—Peter's old temperament bursts forth. He acts quickly without any deliberation. He tries to persuade Christ, though the latter never yields to human persuasion nor listens to man's teaching. Peter's advice flows out of his affection, just as we frequently persuade our loved ones not to suffer. Undisciplined thought is dangerous, but undisciplined emotion is even more dangerous. Peter's act is prompted by his undisciplined emotion. Outwardly it appears well, yet actually it hinders God's will; and therefore it is greatly abhorred by the Lord. Do we not also say "Be it far from thee" when we try to dissuade our loved ones from going the narrow way? Is not this similar to Peter's hindering the Lord Jesus?

v.23 The Lord does not overlook Peter's fault, nor does He accept Peter's good will. He turns around, which action shows that Peter must have tried to take hold of the Lord from behind Him. Whatever is said behind one's back is usually wrong.

"Get thee behind me"—How strange this may sound, since Peter is actually behind Him already. The real meaning here is in not giving Peter any chance to speak further. Whoever thinks of teaching or helping the Lord must be wrong, for the Lord is perfect in everything. [Two other instances of Jesus' followers trying to teach the Lord: (1) "Thou seest the multitude thronging thee . . ."—Mark 5.31; and (2) "They have no wine . . . Woman, what have I to do with thee?"—John 2.3–4.] This is the moral glory of our Lord.

Peter has just confessed the Lord, yet he immediately thereafter falls into the trap of Satan and is being used by the enemy. (Recall how after the victory of Jericho there came the defeat at Ai.) We should be doubly careful after any victory. That which hinders people from going to the cross comes invariably from Satan. "Get thee behind me"—for you are a stumbling block, blocking people from going on. The Lord considers Peter's hindering as being of Satan. All who mind the things of men have thinking which comes from Satan. How very close Satan is to the mind of men.

v.24 "Come after me"—If the cross is here taken to mean with atoning character, how can we ever follow? Can *we* possibly atone for sins? The high priest of old alone could enter the Holiest of all. Hence atonement is solely the work of the Lord (who is our High Priest). But the cross, as we have mentioned, speaks not only of atonement but also of sufferings—such as rejections, inquisitions, persecutions, beatings, and so forth. The Lord calls us to suffer, not to atone. Following the Lord is different from believing the Lord. Believing puts a person in the church, following puts him in the kingdom. It is highly dangerous to believe and not to follow. "Follow me" is the Lord's minimum demand as well as the cheapest price to pay.

"Let him deny himself"—Denying the self is to follow the Lord. Deny one's own mind and seek to satisfy the will of God. Denying the self is for the sake of taking up one's cross. "Any man" is a disciple. The cross is of two kinds: (1) that of atoning death—the cross of Christ, see John 11.50–52; and (2) that of sufferings. Every believer has his own cross as ordained of God. The cross which the Lord arranges for each believer is different. Yet though the ways be different, they all nonetheless are the cross. The cross signifies being stricken, a being stricken on the way. After we are saved we must go this way which God has foreordained. May the "strike" of God come upon us. The Lord is teaching us through Peter. He reprimands His disciple for minding the things of men, which essentially is being insubordinate to the "strike" of God. Denying the self is the only condition for following the Lord. Denying the self is repudiating one's own idea. Taking up the cross means to endure the suffering that flows out of such repudiation. To follow the Lord is to go His way in obedience.

v.25 "Life" in the Greek text is actually "soul"—To save one's soul today is to lose it in the future. To lose it in this age is to save it in the age to come. Soul includes mind, will, emotions. Saving the soul means to gratify one's mind, will, and emotions in this age. It is not to deny the self. But losing the soul in this age does mean to deny the self. It is the very opposite of saving the soul. It is equivalent to a sacrificing of oneself for the Lord. Losing the soul in the future is to lose the satisfaction and joy which are in the kingdom. Like the wicked one-talent servant, there will be weeping and gnashing of teeth during the time of the kingdom. The wicked servant wants to enjoy himself in this world. He refuses to labor; and instead of using his napkin to wipe away his sweat, he uses it to wrap up the single talent he has. To lose one's soul in the future is to suffer shame during the kingdom age, though he still retains eternal life. Finding the soul in the future is to receive the glory and satisfaction of the kingdom.

v.26 What shall a man be profited if he gain the whole

world with all its wealth and pomp and ease and forfeit the glory of the kingdom of heaven? What thing can he give in exchange for his soul? The Lord considers the saving of the soul in this age as sheer foolishness. Here is the spiritual law of exchange.

v.27 "The Son of man"—Hereafter this is what the Lord mainly calls himself, which implies the thought of suffering.

"Then" proves that the "deeds" to be judged are those pertaining to the saving of the soul or to the losing of the soul for Christ's sake. Deed is the basis for *reward*, not for eternal life. So that at the coming of the Lord, what will happen can be simply diagrammed as follow:

In order to know whether one will be rewarded in the future, he has no need to wait till he stands before the judgment seat: he will know if he but examines his own deeds. If he loses his soul today, he is sure to gain or find it in the future. If he gains or keeps it today, he is sure to lose it in the future.

v.28 This verse plainly connects and introduces what is to follow in the succeeding chapter, which will be taken up next.

Sundry Notes on Chapter 16

1. God is most patient. Even though the world says He is nonexistent, He is not in the least anxious but continues to hide himself as He sees fit.

2. How many of today's preachers are conducting themselves like actors! Homiletics as often taught in the classroom teaches people how to perform.

3. Foolishness and unbelief are twin brothers.

4. We who spread the gospel are foreign missionaries, for we do not belong to this world.

5. The verdict which the high priest of that day pronounced upon the Lord Jesus was most unjust (see Matt. 26.63ff.). He asked the Lord if He were the Christ, and the Lord answered yes. The high priest ought then to have examined the claim to find out if indeed it were true or false before he passed down his judgment. Instead, as soon as he heard the Lord's answer he tore his garments, and immediately he and the rest of the Sanhedrin sentenced the Lord to death for committing the presumed sin of blasphemy.

6. In reading the Bible we should not seek for spiritual knowledge alone. As God's servants, our foremost desire is to know the demands of the Lord.

THE GOSPEL ACCORDING TO MATTHEW

Chapter 17

The Transfiguration on the Mount, 16.28–17.8

16.28 The "some of them" spoken of in this verse from the previous chapter are Peter, James and John now specifically mentioned here in chapter 17.

"His kingdom" is the kingdom of the Son of man. The kingdom of God means eternity, whereas the kingdom of the Son of man signifies the heavenly part of the millennial kingdom (see Matt. 13.41 and Ps. 8; in Rev. 3.21 there are two thrones: we have part in the throne of the Son of man. It should be noted, incidentally, that the earthly part of the millennial kingdom is represented by the nation of Israel as the center of all nations.).

"In his kingdom" speaks of the glory of the millennium. In the preceding passage we are exhorted to deny ourselves. Why? Because in the losing of our soul we shall gain it. When will this be manifested? At the time of His coming (16.27). And verse 28 is used to explain His coming. On three occasions Peter, James and John are seen alone with the Lord—in the house of Jairus, on the holy mountain of transfiguration, and in the garden of Gethsemane. The scene before us now (which is the second of these three occasions) is a preview of the beauty of the kingdom of heaven. It appears for a while, then is withdrawn. "We did not follow cunningly devised fables, when we made known unto you the power and coming of our Lord Jesus Christ," Peter testified, "but we were eye-witnesses of his majesty . when we were with him in the holy mount" (2 Peter 1.16,18). This proves that what appears is truly the coming of the kingdom of the Son of man.

"Shall in no wise taste of death, till they see"—These words are spoken by the Lord because these three disciples are to see the kingdom beforehand.

v.1 "And after six days"—Toil and conflict are all over. (Luke 9.28 says "about eight days"; this is because in his reckoning Luke includes additionally the day on which Jesus spoke these words. Matthew, writing a book of doctrine or teaching, is stricter in his reckoning).

"A high mountain"—We are not told the name of the mountain. It suffices us to know that it is a holy mountain (2 Peter 1.18).

Peter, James and John are all ministers of God's word.

"Apart" in the Greek original means "privately"; great revelations are received in private. It is only in secret that we have God's manifestation and receive His communication.

v.2 "And he was transfigured"—Such transfiguration is possible as the Son of man. It is impossible with the Son of God. Not that He is transfigured from the Son of man to the Son of God; only that as the Son of man He is transfigured from lowliness, suffering and rejection to glory and honor of the kingdom. It is advisable to take up the cross for such glory. This proves how wrong Peter's word—"far be it from thee, Lord"; instead, it encourages us to suffer and to bear the cross.

"His face did shine as the sun"—Matthew alone notices the face, even the glorious face of the King. The sun is also a type of the kingdom, and therefore it conveys the idea of glory.

v.3 "Moses and Elijah"—Varied are the ways the three Gospels record these two men. In Mark, it is "Elijah and Moses"—for Mark speaks of servanthood, and so Moses, being the servant of God, is listed lower. Luke initially identifies them merely as "two men"—for he deals preeminently with manhood. But Matthew immediately identifies them as "Moses and Elijah": the one representing the law, the other representing the prophets. The law and the prophets, as symbolized by these two men, have spoken much concerning the Lord for centuries past, and not just once on this present occasion. For the law tells us how the Lord will be a sacrifice for sin, and the prophets prophesy how He is to be King and receive glory. The law shows His suffering while the prophets depict His glory.

"Talking with him"—That is, these two men are conversing with the Lord as to how He is to fulfill the law and the prophets. Luke gives the answer in his account: "And spake of his decease which he was about to accomplish in Jerusalem" (9.31).

v.4 Peter speaks again, and once more he shows his ignorance. He can only do fishing (as on the day of Pentecost and in the house of Cornelius), not make tents (as was Paul's ministry in building God's true tabernacle, the church). Even so, it does indicate that Peter knows and recognizes the glorious delight of the kingdom of heaven, and hence he does not wish to leave the mountain.

"I will make here three tabernacles"—What a mistake Peter has made:

(1) for thinking that one can enjoy the glory of the kingdom of heaven without the need of losing one's soul and bearing the cross (that is, without ever going down the mountain again to suffer; for as we soon learn, there are demons down below). How many others have the same idea! When they receive some blessing from God, they cease to strive for growth. They become lazy. They reject suffering and seek only for blessing.

(2) for imagining that now is the millennial kingdom. Many are the "Peter-type" believers who fancy they can enjoy the blessing of the kingdom of heaven today.

(3) and for conjecturing that Moses and Elijah can stand on

the same level with the Lord. On earth our Lord is truly humble and lowly, yet in the kingdom of heaven He is the highest. Even though Moses and Elijah are honorable among men, they cannot stand parallel with the Lord—for the Father loves supremely the Son to whom every knee shall bow (see Phil. 2.9–11; see also Is. 45.23, Rom. 14.11). Moses indeed comes back from the dead and Elijah most surely is raptured, but they cannot be on an equality with Christ.

The Lord gives no answer to Peter. His silent response is the best reply.

v.5 "While he was yet speaking"—God interrupts Peter's words of nonsense. He does not want Peter to speak any further, and so He says, "Hear ye him"!

"A bright cloud"—the same as in the Holiest of all (cf. Ex. 40.34). God has come to the holy mountain (cf. Ex. 24.16).

"A voice"—the same as coming from the mercy seat upon the ark (see Ex. 25.22).

"This is my beloved Son"—Such words thus lift Him above Moses and Elijah. Grace far surpasses the law and the prophets. Why is this same declaration, uttered by God earlier, repeated here? Let us see that at His baptism, the death and resurrection of the Lord is being exemplified; here, what is in view is His determination to go to the cross (for He resists Peter's objection). Today God delights in those who obey and bear the cross. Whoever pleases Him receives the kingdom.

"Hear ye him"—Do not speak vainly, just listen. Many can talk, but they are not able to hear. Hear what? Whatever the Lord says, especially His words about denying the self and taking up the cross (for this, see earlier on Matt. 16.24–27). Hear Him—the Lord Jesus and no longer Moses and Elijah.

v.6 "Sore afraid"—Who is not afraid when God appears!

v.7 "Be not afraid"—This occurs 365 times in the Bible;

one can be appropriated for each day of the year. Every day can be blessed "now"; for this is still the dispensation of Grace.

v.8 "They saw no one, save Jesus only"—The law and the prophets, the glory of the Son of man, the overshadowing of a bright cloud and the Voice, as well as the companions: all have passed away: Jesus alone remains. May we see Jesus only.

vv.1–8 Hence to recapitulate this section: here we have the kingdom of heaven as represented by the various ones who were present at the holy mount, namely:

(1) Christ is glorified as King;

(2) Moses represents believers who have died and are resurrected (1 Cor. 15.52, 1 Thess. 4.13–17);

(3) Elijah represents those who are alive and are raptured (1 Cor. 15.51b-52, 1 Thess. 4.13–17);

(4) Peter, James and John represent the children of Israel who are not transformed but are as people in the kingdom (see Is. 11.10–12); and

(5) the multitude down the mountain represent the nations (again, see Is. 11.10–12).

Judging from verses 1–8, we can gather that people change after death but not beyond recognition. They still bear their former likeness. The three disciples easily recognize Moses and Elijah, and so is the rich man who has died able to recognize Abraham immediately (see Luke 16.22–24).

Conversation on the Descent, 17.9–13

v.9 "Tell the vision to no man"—Why? Since the Lord is already rejected, it makes no sense attempting by means of His glory to draw the unbelievers further. When people are still in doubt, there remains a place for persuasion. But to those who will not believe, attraction is of no help. On the other hand, the three disciples have special ministries to fulfill, and hence they do need to be specially strengthened by such an experience.

v.10 The three disciples ask because they have just seen Elijah. They have a fresh image in their mind. They wonder if the manifestation on the mount is a fulfillment of prophecy (see Mal. 4.5).

v.11 According to the determinate will of God, Elijah did indeed come. If people are willing to accept the testimony of John the Baptist, the latter becomes Elijah—yet not in the sense of Elijah coming back to life but in the sense of John having the "spirit and power of Elijah" (Luke 1.17).

v.12 Unfortunately people did not accept the witness of John, but treated him despitefully. Thus, they shall not see Elijah today. If they treated the forerunner badly, they will show the Son of man the same ill-treatment. If Elijah is rejected, the Messiah will also be rejected. For this reason, the glory as seen on the mountain must be covered. This age is unfit to witness such a testimony. Did not our Lord say, "A disciple is not above his teacher, nor a servant above his Lord" (Matt. 10.24)? If the Messiah is being rejected, Elijah too shall be rejected. And again He says, "He that rejecteth you rejecteth me" (Luke 10.16). What is the use of Elijah if they will not have the Messiah?

v.13 Even though the Lord does not mention the name of John, the disciples know He means John the Baptist. Sometimes the Bible may not speak openly; even so, we need to understand the mind of the Lord.

The Demoniac Boy Healed, 17.14–18

This section reveals to us how the Lord feels toward man's unbelief.

vv.14–15 "A man"—He is one of the remnant.

"Into the fire . . . into the water"—Water is cold, fire is hot. Such a demon causes a possessed person to be both chilled and burning. Many demons are of this kind.

v.16 The disciples cannot cure the epileptic. They think casting out demons is easy, and they have had experience in this area. But in spiritual things, we cannot act on supposition. If there is not the real power present, we will unavoidably fail. They tried, but they failed. They cannot cure the tortured one.

v.17 Here we see the agony which an unbelieving heart gives to the Lord. "How long shall I bear with you?"—The word "bear" tells of untold sufferings. Unbelief is worse than any scolding or beating. How long shall the Lord bear it? Being in the world, He suffered long. He is compelled to endure, and there therefore comes forth such an utterance.

"Faithless" is towards the Lord while "perverse" is towards ourselves.

"Bring him hither to me"—Neither the parent (or parents), nor the child himself, nor these disciples can do anything in the situation. The Lord alone is able. How must the father of the child be comforted by this word. How precious and how consoling. Yet why not go to the Lord Jesus in the first place?

v.18 "Rebuked"—Rebuke the demon for he should not torment the child. And after the rebuke must come the command. In casting out a demon, prayer alone is not enough. There must be both rebuke and command. We so often dare only to pray but dare not to rebuke. To pray is to receive authority and power from God. But after we have received such authority and power, we must use it in rebuking and commanding the demon to come out. The demon knows the Lord Jesus. When the man asked for healing, he had diagnosed his child as being epileptic. But when the Lord healed, He had diagnosed the situation differently, for He rebuked a demon. Hence when we pray for healing, we need to have discernment to perceive whether the cause is natural or supernatural. People involved in the boy's plight said it was merely an illness, yet the Lord declared it to be demon-caused. And when the demon went out, the illness was cured. So that the real source of this particular sickness was the demon.

If you pray for the sick and you have faith, God will certainly heal him. In case the sick one is not healed, you need to discern immediately if there is a supernatural cause involved.

The Power of Faith, 17.19–21

The three verses in this section may be called the textbook in the Scriptures on the matter of casting out demons.

v.19 The disciples, having failed to cure the lad, now come to the Lord secretly, for they are afraid of losing face before the people.

v.20 "Because of your little faith"—Or their unbelief. Such unbelief, we must be careful to notice, comes from believers; therefore it does not refer to not believing the Lord Jesus as Savior. Since the mentioning of the "mustard seed" is metaphorical in character, the mountain must also be metaphorical. The latter speaks of conclusive and deeply rooted difficulties. Although a mountain is most stable, faith has removed many mountains, many difficulties. Unlike wandering stars, mountains sit steadfastly where they are. Matters such as unbelieving children and unemployment are like mountains. Yet faith can remove such mountains and deal with all kinds of difficulties. Why, then, turn first to other people for help?

v.21 mg. "But this kind goeth not out save by prayer and fasting"—Faith is different from prayer and fasting. The Lord shows us here the prayer after faith. We often say that after having faith there is no need to pray again, for all that is required is praise; for if more prayers are offered, faith will be shaken. This certainly is true with regard to asking God. But as towards demons, it is not so. There must be incessant prayer after faith is given. Having received the faith for casting out demons, we should then ask further for its execution. In Luke 18 the widow perseveres in prayer, asking for revenge on her adversary. The adversary, of course, is Satan, whom we must attack by means of prayer throughout our life. Having had faith, there needs to be prayer and fasting. These two are attitudes as well as acts of conduct. On that particular day, the Lord did not appear to have been praying and fasting, yet He could cast out the demon. This proves that He must have prayed and fasted. Furthermore, He doubtless always had the attitude of prayer and fasting—facets of attitude which signified dependence on God and self-denial. So that aside from such conduct, there must also be such an attitude. Every believer is required to have a long preparation.

"This kind"—The strongest kind of demons. The demonic world has both its powerful and less powerful ones. With the small demons, singing hymns and uplifting the Bible is sufficient to drive them away. Nevertheless, we should never underestimate them, but then neither should we overestimate them. Jessie Penn-Lewis once said that to despise evil spirits is reason for injury, while an exaltation of evil spirits causes the loss of our own dignity. We ought always to remember the word in 1 John: "Ye are of God, my little children, and have overcome them: because greater is he that is in you than he that is in the world" (4.4). We should also acknowledge that we are helpless in ourselves, and that therefore we must give ourselves to prayer and fasting.

The essential conditions for casting out demons are (1) Faith—believing that the Lord's name has been exalted by God above every name, that in the name of Jesus Christ every knee shall bow, of things in heaven and things on earth and things under the earth (Phil. 2.9–10, Eph. 1.20–22, Heb. 1.2–4). Every demon knows Philippians 2.9 and 10. Let us ourselves firmly believe in Philippians 2.9 and 10. Sometimes simply declaring the Lord Jesus is quite sufficient because He is the emblem of victory, power, and authority. We declare that Jesus is Lord or that Jesus is Victor.

(2) Boldness—if we are fearful, we either have no faith or have little faith. Since the name of Jesus is already high exalted, we ought to maintain our dignity. Remember well the word of 1 John 4.4, and we will not be defeated but the demon will surely be cast out.

(3) Patience—the demons are skillfull in delaying tactics. Do not doubt as to whether the name of the Lord is effective. If the demon tries to linger for 100 days, let us be determined to stay on for 101 days. For please be aware that "Beelzebub" means king of the flies: the demons are like flies: they go and come again: they themselves are very patient.

The Passion Foretold a Second Time, 17.22-23

v.22 For the second time our Lord announces He will be killed. This instance, however, is different from the first time He announces His death (see Matt. 16.21). On the first occasion, the Lord declares it is the Jews—"the elders and chief priests and scribes"—who will reject Him. Here in the second instance, it is the Gentiles—"the hands of men"—who shall reject Him. He will be delivered over to the Gentiles (represented in the person of Pilate) by the Jews.

v.23 "And they were exceeding sorry"—This is because the disciples fail to see the cross as the symbol of victory. First shame, then glory. First suffering, then the throne. We too worry about the narrow way of the cross.

The Temple Tax, 17.24-27

Originally tribute was "atonement money" (see **Ex.**

30.13–16; cf. 2 Chron. 24.6). It is half a shekel, usually paid at the time of enrollment, but later it was collected for the expense of the temple. Everyone, whether rich or poor, must pay the tribute money. The tax collector considered the Lord to be an unusual person. Hence, he first asked Peter about it.

vv.24–27 Peter says "Yea"—his impulsive temperament is again set loose. The Lord, being the Son of God, has no need to pay tribute. Yet neither does Peter need to pay. For the Lord not only is himself free, but He sets others free as well (see John 8.36).

"Cause . . . to stumble"—As a matter of principle, anything which touches the person, the holiness, and work of God allows no compromise; there can therefore be no accommodation in such areas, even if it should cause anyone "to stumble" or be offended. For other matters which are minor, however, we should imitate the Lord here so as not to offend anybody. Here the Lord exhibits great wisdom. He is gentle but not weak, humble but not hesitant. How often in many things He makes ground for other people.

There is another lesson to be learned here. Believers today should not abuse the title of the sons of God. This will be in full display in the kingdom age, but not in this present age. Do not oppress others, but rather be willing to be oppressed if necessary. Today is the time for paying tribute.

"Go thou to the sea, and cast a hook"—The Lord exhibits gentleness and grace on the one hand, and manifests authority and honor on the other.

"For me and thee"—This is the order. Why not use "us"? Because the Lord can never stand on the same level with us. He is the Firstborn and the only begotten Son; whereas we are but sons. By hiding His glory the Lord pays tribute; in grace He pays tribute for Peter. He can certainly supply our every need.

THE GOSPEL ACCORDING TO MATTHEW

Chapter 18

The Question of Rank, 18.1–4

v.1 "In that hour"—This phrase is connected to the matter of obtaining the temple tax mentioned immediately before in the preceding chapter. The incident of Peter fishing for the shekel shows how the Lord hides His own glory and manifests His grace. Hence the first section in chapter 18 teaches us how believers today should imitate the Lord in concealing themselves and exhibiting grace. They should deny their rights.

"Who then is greatest in the kingdom of heaven?"—Several times the disciples have asked this question. It really appears to be an insoluble problem among them; for even during the night of the Lord's betrayal the disciples will be found quarreling over this same matter. Yet the Lord's disciples of today are no better in this particular respect.

What is the background for their contending? (1) Nine disciples had been left behind in the plain (17.1), (2) Peter was called *petros*—meaning "a stone" (16.18), (3) the keys of the kingdom of heaven were given to Peter (16.19), (4) the Lord then paid tribute money for Peter (17.27), and so forth. Now every person desires to be great, nobody loves to be small. In his own field, each person endeavors to have an impressive development: he dreams of greatness.

v.2 "He called . . . a little child, and set him in the midst of them"—The Lord concretely demonstrates His points as well as speaks forth in parables. By setting the little child in the midst of the disciples He is able tangibly to draw a comparison between the two parties. A single glance at the little child will tell the observer his height, weight, age, experience, and so forth. There is not even the need to inquire. A quick look will do.

v.3 "Except ye turn"—"Turn" is regenerative in meaning, signifying a new beginning of life. "Become" is not an acting like a child, but becoming a child. It is not a being childish. He who pretends to be a child is no child at all. Everyone who enters this world must pass through a period of childhood. Similarly, all who enter the kingdom of heaven must go through a kind of childhood. The kingdom of heaven presents three different aspects: (1) the sphere of Christianity or Christendom, (2) the church, and (3) the millennial kingdom. What is referred to here is the second of these aspects.

Now it does not say here that ordinary children can enter the kingdom of heaven. The passage reads, "become as little children"—and an ordinary child is therefore used here merely to demonstrate a principle. Otherwise, Nicodemus cannot be born anew. Those who are not born again cannot understand what happens to someone at regeneration. The word "as" speaks of selflessness, dependence, and humility.

v.4 Verse 3 solves the question of entry, while verse 4 resolves the matter of greatness. If having been born again one can keep himself always humble as a little child, this man is the greatest in the kingdom of heaven. Unfortunately, many forsake this condition. Though they are but children, they act like grownups (see 1 Cor. 3.1). To "become as little children" is the one condition for entering the kingdom of heaven, and *to hold on to* this condition becomes the very basis for subsequent greatness.

In paying the tribute money, our Lord exhibits a child-like

humility. This does not suggest that believers must not grow in knowledge nor instruct or help other people. For the humility shown here relates to the matter of attitude. We should have a humble attitude. A little child does not look at himself, nor does he possess a competitive heart (the worst that happens to a believer is to become competitive in spiritual things). Paul acknowledges himself as being the least of the apostles (1 Cor. 15.9)—and this is not determined through comparison. He would even rather be separated from Christ if necessary, for the sake of his kinsmen's salvation (Rom. 9.3). All this reflects how selfless he is. He does not look at himself at all. He is one of the best children in the kingdom, for as he runs the race, he casts no glance at Peter or John. He simply stretches forward for the prize from on high. Humility is having no pride, not a having no ability to preach or lead a revival campaign. Only he who humbles himself as a little child has no pride at all. And the one who humbles himself shall be exalted (Luke 18.14).

Concerning Stumbling Blocks, 18.5–14

v.5 "In my name" reflects a deeper thought than the phrase "for my sake" (see, for example, 16.25). He who is as a little child is a humble person in whose life is the glory and love of Christ. Therefore, whoever receives him receives Christ. Let us love all the saints as well as love Christ (see Phile. 5).

v.6 In dealing with people, believers either receive such little ones or cause them to stumble. Causing people to stumble spiritually is more serious than doing people physical harm. "Stumble" means a shaking of people's faith in Christ or a giving people an occasion to oppose God. In paying the tribute money, Christ on the one hand exhibits His humility and on the other hand causes no one to stumble. In order not to cause any stumbling to others, it requires us to be humble and to take a lower place.

v.7 The occasions of stumbling are plenteous in this world. Woe to those who stumble others. This is especially true in relation to Christians—for though they do not therefore lose eternal life, they shall nonetheless suffer much loss in the millennial kingdom.

v.8 How to avoid stumbling? By first taking care of oneself. If a person himself does not fall, he will not cause other people to stumble. Yet if he himself falls, people will follow him in falling (for example, in case you yourself gamble, others too will gamble, or else they will for this very reason despise Christ). Should the activity of your hand or the movement of your foot cause you to stumble, you ought to pay the greatest price of cutting it off and casting it away—else, if you allow it to stay you will stumble others. The one who holds on to any stumbling action will himself "be cast into the eternal fire"; yet please note that although the fire here is described as being eternal, this is not our eternal portion. The emphasis in this passage is on what *kind* of fire, not on how a person shall be burned.

v.9 "Eye" points to the lust of eyes: to lust after a woman whom a man looks at (see Matt. 5.27–30). It is better to pay the cost and cast it away. Stumbling involves two things: (1) he despises other people, and (2) he himself falls. To avoid any stumbling, let us be careful not to despise other people.

v.10 "Despise not"—Treasure the souls of others.
"Little ones"—Those who seem to have no value materially or physically.
"Angels"—They are ministering spirits (Heb. 1.14). They ascend and descend upon that spiritual ladder that Jacob saw in his vision at Bethel (see Gen. 28.11ff.; cf. John 1.51). They carry prayers upward and bring blessings downward. Do not let our angels stand idle because of our lack of prayers. Because of

the Holy Spirit indwelling us in this present age, the ministration of the angels has already been greatly curtailed.

v.11 mg. Many authorities in their versions have not only "in heaven their angels do always behold the face of my Father who is in heaven" but also "for the Son of man came to save that which was lost"—and for these two reasons, therefore, none of the little ones can be despised.

vv.12–13 This parable is the same as the one recorded in Luke 15.1–7. The only difference between these two Gospel accounts lies in their intent. Whereas the parable in Luke speaks to sinners of the reality of salvation, here in Matthew it declares to believers the compassion in salvation.

"Any man" refers especially to the Lord Jesus.

"One of them"—Any human sheep who has gone astray.

"Doth he not leave the ninety and nine, and go unto the mountains, and seek that which goeth astray?"—The Lord is unwilling to lose even one. Sheep are rather foolish. When they go astray, they cannot find their way back (see Is. 53.6). The 99 sheep are suppositional; they do not refer to the righteous, since in the world no one is righteous. The Lord himself goes after the lost sheep; He has not entrusted this task to angels. For the Good Shepherd is willing to lay down His life for His sheep.

v.14 Since the heart of the Father is not willing to lose one of these little ones, how can any of us cause others to stumble and to be lost? God finds joy in saving souls. Believers on earth may not enjoy the pleasures of this world, yet they can certainly find joy in saving souls. Because the Lord is not willing to lose a little sheep and because God finds pleasure in saving souls, we should never offend other people. But what if other people offend *us?* How should we then cope with the situation? This we see in verse 15.

Our Duty towards Offenders, 18.15–20

v.15 We should still maintain the heart attitude of saving the lost sheep. In this verse our Lord is not correcting the brother who is at fault, rather is He correcting the brother who is not at fault. For we are prone to make mistakes when we attempt to show another his fault. In any given situation it is easier to deal with the righteous person than with the one at fault. How very easy for us to adopt an inappropriate attitude in dealing with an improper situation on the part of others. The failure of Moses is a good case in point: when the children of Israel were at fault, Moses dealt with them with highly inappropriate words. Let us never fall into wrong ourselves because other people are wrong.

"Between thee and him alone"—Nobody else is to be present. This is for the sake of covering evil.

"Show him his fault"—Here it is neither to show off your own excellence nor to reprimand him for his fault. Showing a person his fault is to be done in the spirit of humility, and such a one who does it in this way is deemed to be the greatest in the kingdom of heaven. But in case you scold him—considering yourself as better than he—you are boasting like a Pharisee.

"Thou hast gained thy brother"—This is the aim, trying in love to restore a brother.

v.16–17 If he refuses to hear you, he is still not to be given up. Every means must be used, such as the witness of two or three and the church, before he can "be unto thee as" (1) "the Gentile"—one with whom you cannot fellowship, and (2) "the publican"—one who is disdained. (Yet this class of people are not to be excommunicated from the church, because their sin is mainly that of a stubborn will. But those who commit the sins listed in 1 Corinthians 5.11 should be excommunicated.)

v.18 The purport of this verse is the same as that of

16.19. It is what may be called borrowed forgiveness. God binds or looses through the church or Peter.

"Ye" is plural in number, and therefore has reference to the church (as represented by all the disciples). When people ask for baptism or the breaking of bread, the church has the authority to decide. However, let us not be hard-hearted, since there will also be binding and loosening in heaven. Let binding and loosening be done under the authority of the Holy Spirit (see John 20.22–23). For if it is executed merely according to personal opinion, it will result in total failure. Who has this authority? The Roman Catholic Church? The Pope? No.

v.19 "Again" follows the preceding verse but adds some new meaning to it. This principle of binding or loosening applies not only to dealing with brethren but also to prayer.

"Two" is the least of plural numbers. Yet such plurality is adequate.

This verse applies specifically to corporate prayer. Such corporate prayer is of two kinds: (1) loosening—of God's power, gifts, the door for God's word, pains, burdens of sin, and so forth; (2) binding—of Satan, the wicked, unexpected woes, and so on.

"Shall agree on earth as touching anything that they shall ask"—Agree as in a symphony. Such prayer of one accord is very difficult. For example, in praying for a sick person, A may ask God for healing, B may maintain neutrality by asking for God's will to be done, and C may ask God's discipline against the sick person. This fully indicates that they do not agree. To be harmonious, all must have the same mind and the same opinion.

v.20 "For"—How precious is the reason for making the binding and loosening possible.

"Gathered together"—These two words do not necessarily refer to a prayer meeting.

"In my name"—No one can meet except he is drawn by the

love of Christ. We are like iron, and the Lord is the magnet. The magnet seeks for iron. The life of Christ in His body constrains us to gather together in His name. The Lord does not want us to gather in any other name or names. When a woman is married, she takes on no other name than that of her husband. But how many names other than Christ's have today's Christians taken up! Where is the man who permits his wife to be named after another man? Likewise, the Lord will not have us named after any other name but His own. Not to gather in the name of the Lord is reckoned as being rebellious. Gathering in His name and then adding on other names is considered as being adulterous.

(The church in view in verses 18–20 is the church local, which is the miniature of the church universal spoken of in Ephesians 5.23 and Matthew 16.18.)

Christians stand in the position of a bride—even the bride of Christ; therefore they need to keep themselves chaste. Our Lord praised the church at Philadelphia because they did not deny His name; instead, they kept the word of His patience. Is it not strange that many Christians do not seem to mind any insult to the Christian faith, but do mind very much an insult to a denomination? They can stand indignity against Christ, but not an affront against their particular denomination.

Discourse on the Kingdom Law of Forgiveness, 18.21–35

v.21 The passage above defines the relationship between any offense and the church. Here it presents the relationship of sin with the kingdom of heaven. Peter raises this matter because the Lord had spoken of forgiveness in the preceding passage. Or he may raise it on the basis of what the Lord had said as recorded in Luke 17: "Take heed to yourselves: if thy brother sin, rebuke him; and if he repent, forgive him. And if he sin against thee seven times in the day, and seven times turn again to thee, saying, I repent; thou shalt forgive him" (vv.3–4). Peter deemed seven times to be most forbearing. (For note, incidentally, that during this time two famous rabbis had ruled that forgiving three times was quite sufficient. And hence seven times would be more than double the rabbinic decision of Peter's day.)

v.22 "I say not unto thee"—Such an utterance fully manifests the dignity of the Lord. "Seventy times seven" may indicate no limit. Yet even if it means a literal 70 × 7, it would still be quite sufficient, as the following equation will demonstrate: 7 (completeness) × 7 (completeness) × 10 (human completeness) = 490 (completeness of completeness).

v.23 "A certain king" is God.

"His servants" are the saved believers. Some take these servants to be unsaved sinners, but such an interpretation is impossible because (1) they are called servants; (2) they have direct dealing with God; (3) "the servant" of verse 24ff. alludes to Peter, for he asks the question "How often shall my brother sin against me, and I [a saved person] forgive him [another saved brother]?"; and (4) verse 35 says, "So shall also my heavenly Father do unto you [the saved ones] ..."

"Make a reckoning"—God will never forget or be confused. What a believer in his daily life owes God, God will reckon one day. The time of reckoning must be in this age: God may allow a person to be seriously ill or to encounter great dangers. Sometimes His discipline can be quite severe.

Some suggest that the time of reckoning is in the age to come, that is, at the judgment seat of Christ (2 Cor. 5.10; see also 1 Cor. 3.10–15). But this is impossible because (1) at the judgment seat of Christ, there will be no more grace but all righteousness, and therefore the Lord will not be moved with compassion; (2) in the kingdom it is absolutely impossible to take a fellow servant by the throat and to cast him into prison; and (3) verses 32–34 refer to the age to come at the judgment seat of Christ and hence the teaching in verse 35 which follows is that if one does not forgive his brother in this present age, the heavenly

Father will deal with him in the coming age in accordance with the manner outlined in verses 32–34.

v.24 "Ten thousand talents"—Whether of gold or silver, it is nonetheless a tremendous amount, which the servant can never repay (a talent is equal to 1152 ounces of gold or of silver). What a believer owes God in his daily life probably far exceeds symbolically even this colossal amount.

v.25 "And his wife, and children, and all that he had"— Not that the king really wants to sell this man, his wife and children, and all his things. It simply indicates that God will deprive him of everything.

v.26 Four elements are included here: (1) repentance ("fell down"), (2) humility ("worshipped"), (3) an asking for mercy ("have patience"), and (4) a making a vow of consecration ("will pay").

v.27 "Being moved with compassion"—The lord in the parable, but even more so our God in heaven, is moved with compassion not because the servant is willing to pay back, but because of the latter's repentance and humility and pleading for mercy. He knows very well that the servant is not able to repay, and so he forgives him the debt. "Released . . . . forgave"—These verbs describe actions which happen in this age. If these actions can happen in the age to come, the Lord's righteousness will be compromised. Today God not only releases but also forgives all our debt. The grace of God always surpasses human expectation.

v.28 "Went out"—That is to say, after the time of his personal reckoning or chastening, this servant went out from the presence of his lord. "One of his fellow-servants" is also one of the king's servants (a saved person).

"Owed . . . . a hundred shilling"—A small amount.

"Laid hold on him"—Though the first servant in the parable has repented, he nevertheless has no indelible impression of the mercy shown him. He momentarily forgets and resorts to violence. This proves that his former repentance grew out of desperation, not out of despair of repayment. Though he is temporarily humble, his repentance has left only shallow marks upon him. Soon he forgets the amazing grace of the Lord. Did not David likewise rashly judge the rich man in Nathan's parable?

v.29 In spite of the minuteness of the debt, his fellow-servant exhibits a repentance, humility, pleading, and vow similar to that of the first servant.

v.30 "And he would not"—He will not accept the same kind of pleading from his fellow-servant because he does not recall his own pleading and forgiveness.

"Cast him into prison"—Settle it by law, unmindful of grace. Though such action is legally righteous, even so, righteousness should never be applied in this case since the first servant had just received grace himself. Had he never before obtained grace, he might be quite lawful in casting his fellow-servant into prison. But now, after receiving grace the righteous act is clearly to be gracious to others.

v.31 The prayer and cry of the saints ascend to God.

v.32 This verse may refer to this age, and if so, God calls the servant home; or it may refer to the age to come, that is, a standing before God's judgment in the future.

v.33 The Lord reprimands the servant for forgetting the grace he had formerly received. This word is the focal teaching of the parable.

v.34 This cannot be read as God taking back His word concerning His initial grace towards redeemed sinners; but God's subsequent grace, as illustrated in this instance, must be withdrawn by God in order to maintain His righteousness.

"Pay all that was due"—After the thousand years of discipline come to an end.

v.35 Verses 21 and 22 introduce the subject, verses 23–34 give the parable, and verse 35 draws the conclusion. This parable is used to teach people today.

"From your hearts"—Often we forgive on the face, by our lips, or even through action, but we do not forgive from the heart. The Lord, though, stresses the heart. If a believer fails to forgive others, he is in danger of being cast into prison till every penny is paid. How can we not forgive? How can we not ask for forgiveness? No believer should have any brother or sister towards whom he will not nod the head or speak, or with whom he will not correspond.

THE GOSPEL ACCORDING TO MATTHEW

Chapter 19

vv.1-2 Each time after He has instructed people, the Lord usually performs some works such as healing the sick, casting out demons, and so forth. In this particular instance, He heals the sick.

Concerning Divorce, 19.3-12

v.3 This verse inaugurates a new problem: the kingdom of heaven and man's natural relationships.

"For every cause"—The Jews at that time advocated divorce at will. (By comparison, in China there were seven conditions for divorce, but among the Jews of Jesus' day there were probably seventy times seven reasons for divorce—even unsavory cooking might be a cause for such action!) The Pharisees liked the idea of divorce, yet they had some uncertainty about it too. Therefore, they asked the Lord this question.

v.4 "He who made them from the beginning made them male and female"—Three points may be deduced from this statement: (1) that marriage is instituted by God since He made both male and female; (2) that monogamy is God's will for He made only one Adam and one Eve; and (3) that God dislikes divorce, since in answering that God made one Adam and one Eve, the Lord implies that this is not a question of law but a matter of origin.

v.5 Although the relationship between parents and children is most intimate, there is another relationship—that between husband and wife—which is even closer. If the relationship of parents to children is almost unbreakable, how much more inseparable must be the relationship of husband and wife!

v.6 "One flesh"—Due to this fact of man and woman becoming one flesh, women are usually not numbered in Biblical accounts. The husband and the wife are one number in the sight of God. "So that they are . . . one flesh"; therefore "let not man put [such union] asunder"—and this is the final decision.

v.7 Most naturally the Pharisees proceeded to quote from the law of Moses. They presume that if they bring out Moses they can overturn the Lord. They assume the word of the Lord to be in conflict with Moses.

"Why then did Moses command"—Actually Moses did not *command,* he only *permitted* ("suffered"). The Lord alone can discern the difference.

v.8 Moses allowed the children of Israel to do a certain thing because of the hardness of their heart. But such is not God's original will. Hence the law cannot regenerate people, neither does it make any distinction between the regenerate and the unregenerate, nor can it make anyone perfect (Heb. 7.19).

v.9 The one and only proper cause for divorce is fornication. According to the law of the nations, there are all kinds of legal divorce. But before God, only one reason is acceptable. Let us note that the Bible does not put too much emphasis on the engagement or marriage ceremony. The real beginning of a marriage is the voluntary (not forced) sexual relationship, for according to 1 Corinthians 6.16 the two partners shall become one body, one flesh. Such physical relationship in marriage is most holy, because it is established by God. Irrespective of law, society, custom, and so forth, the fact remains that if there is a physical relationship, the two become one flesh. For this reason, in the Old Testament period, if a man should break the virginity of a woman, he must marry her—because physical union is one of the chief factors in marriage. Now fornication is an act which destroys the union of two as one flesh. And hence divorce simply confirms the broken union before God. We may therefore conclude that (1) fornication destroys the union before God, and (2) except for fornication no divorce is allowed. We believers ought to follow God's will, not the fashion of this age or man's law.

"And he that marrieth her when she is put away committeth adultery"—If the woman is put away because of fornication, then marrying her will be committing adultery. If a man married a divorced woman before he is saved, all are under the precious blood: there should be no more putting away. Or if a believer has a wife who has committed fornication, according to law and the word of the Lord he is allowed to put her away; yet if the wife repents, he can forgive her according to the grace of the Lord (John 8.3–11).

v.10 The disciples, too, had secretly endorsed this concept of divorce at will. So they said, "It is not expedient to marry"; but this is also contrary to God's original will.

v.11 "Receive"—It is a matter of capacity. None can be forced not to marry. Just as coercing people to be divorced is sin, so forcing people not to marry is likewise a sin. For not all men receive the gift of remaining single.

"But they to whom it is given"—The Lord discloses on the one hand God's original will and on the other hand, God's gift to certain people for celibacy.

v.12 To whom is the gift of celibacy given? Three classes of people are cited: (1) those who were born eunuchs—a physiological situation; (2) those who have been made eunuchs by men—a circumstantial situation; and (3) those who have made themselves eunuchs for the kingdom of heaven's sake—a spiritual situation. Paul is an example of the latter category. For the sake of God's work some people do not marry. Those who thus make themselves eunuchs for the sake of the kingdom of heaven have their special place in the kingdom (see Rev. 14.4). And in order to avoid any misunderstanding, our Lord purposely adds: "He that is able to receive it, let him receive it" (v.12b).

Jesus Receives Little Children, 19.13–15

v.13 The teaching of these verses is that there is no such idea as a person being too great to do too small a thing. The disciples assume that the Lord, being the Rabbi of rabbis, ought not do such a small thing. Simultaneously they themselves are irritated by this interruption and wish to demonstrate their exalted position as disciples.

v.14 "Suffer the little children . . . to come unto me"— The lessons to be learned by this passage are: (1) that no great person can refrain from doing the smallest thing, hence brethren should learn to sweep the floor, wash the windows, or do other menial tasks; (2) that in the kingdom of heaven people are like little children, yet not in the literal sense of being so, but in the spiritual sense of being innocent, humble, and dependent as are little children; (3) that the little children also possess a soul and spirit and are therefore equally precious before God; and (4) that God's love is able to be manifested in the smallest of matters.

v.15 "And departed thence"—Opportunity is not always available, because the Lord *will* leave. If people miss the opportunity to receive grace, there is no way to regain such a missed chance. How tragic this must be! In view of this, we should believe at the time of salvation. Though the door of grace is still open today, it will definitely be closed one day. Do not pass by the opportunity when it presents itself. For on each occasion that the Lord departed a certain place, there invariably were many sick and sinful people left behind. The same is true today.

The Peril of Earthly Riches and the Reward of the Heavenly Kingdom, 19.16–20.16

This rather lengthy passage is quite difficult to explain.

v.16 "One"—In other Gospels we are told that he is a ruler of the Jews (Luke 18.18, for example).

"Teacher"—Such a way of addressing the Lord is certainly an exemplary trait. It shows that this young man has heard of the Lord and has sought him for a long time.

"What good thing shall I do, that I may have eternal life?"— He already possesses considerable knowledge concerning spiritual things: (1) that eternal life is a must, (2) that he does not have this eternal life, (3) that doing a good thing may gain for him this eternal life, but (4) that he does not know what this good thing is which he must do to obtain eternal life. Notice that he does not ask if there *is* eternal life, nor does he think only of obtaining the pleasures of this age and not those of the age to come.

v.17 The Lord answers the young man according to the latter's background and status. Neither does He tacitly acknowledge here that doing some good thing will obtain eternal life (for to one who believes that doing a good thing is the way to eternal life, the most natural answer would be to say, Why not do good? But this is not the reply given by the Lord.).

"One there is who is good"—The Lord helps the young man to know himself. Only one is good (God), and there is none else.

"Keep the commandments"—for "he that doeth them shall

live in them" (Gal. 3.12). Unfortunately there is no one who
keeps the commandments and thus may be justified before God.
If one stumbles on the smallest point of the law, he is guilty of
all the laws (James 2.10). Law was originally a ministration of
the Lord God, yet it has become the ministration of death; so
says Paul (2 Cor. 3.7–9). Just as the dumb cannot ask how to
sing hymns to please God, nor can the cripple ask how to dance
so as to be welcomed, even so, no man is able to ask how to do
good so as to gain eternal life. Nevertheless, sinners today keep
on asking this question.

vv.18–19 The young man asks *which* of the commandments, because he already understands that there are so many.
Now what the Lord then mentions all belong to the second tablet
of law, since the fifth through the tenth commandments define
the duties before men while the first through the fourth in the
first tablet deal with the responsibilities before God. The Jews
considered themselves as having strictly kept the first tablet; consequently, the Lord asks the young man about the contents of the
second one.

v.20 "All these things have I observed"—By raising these
commandments the Lord hopes that the young man will come to
know himself truly and thereby answer, No. Yet he replies that
he has kept all these things.

v.21 How audacious is the spirit of this young man! He
accounts himself capable of doing all good things. And so the
Lord now points out one good thing which he is incapable of
doing—to sell all he has and give to the poor. He may not object
to *selling* all that he has, but to *give away* all is impossible. And
furthermore, to then follow the Lord—that is to say, to live a life
of wandering without any permanent place of rest—is *absolutely*
impossible.

v.22 "He went away sorrowful"—This proves that the young man is unable to do good. He can neither keep the Ten Commandments nor give to the poor, thus loving his neighbors as himself. When God gave the law He knew no man could keep it. It was given so that man (after he had sinned) might know himself as a sinner (see Rom. 3.20). How sad that this young man would rather forfeit eternal life and retain the pleasures of this world. He is therefore a perishing soul.

v.23 The Lord is now speaking to the disciples. He turns to another subject—the reward of the kingdom of heaven. The seed of this idea is actually sown in the Lord's words of verse 21. Since "eternal life", "the kingdom of heaven", "the kingdom of God" and "be saved" are all bound up together, this parable appears difficult to explain. Yet if we are clear on two different lines it will not be hard to understand after all. The two distinct lines of thought are (1) the pursuit of the young man is toward eternal life, and (2) by using this incident of the young man as teaching material, the Lord explains to His disciples the reward of the kingdom of heaven. Verse 21 actually contains a word pertaining to the kingdom. Going further than just dealing with the matter of initial salvation, the Lord points the young man to the truth of the kingdom: to "have treasure in heaven" denotes the abundance in the kingdom.

v.24 "Needle's eye"—Some commentators interpret this to refer to the small door in a Jewish city gate: a camel loaded down with wealth has great difficulty in getting through such a door. Hence the idea here is not that the rich man cannot enter the kingdom of God, but that it is difficult for him to enter in because sometimes our Lord will require him to forsake his wealth. Not impossible, only difficult. The definition of "a rich man" is one who is unwilling to give up to God the things which he loves. Under this definition it is quite possible to behold "a rich man" of only five or ten dollars.

"The kingdom of God"—The preceding verse is worded "the kingdom of heaven": How then is one to explain this? Well, the kingdom of heaven has three different meanings: (1) Christendom, (2) the church, and (3) the millennial kingdom. The kingdom of God also has three distinct interpretations, which are (1) a spiritual experience (see Luke 14.15), (2) the millennial kingdom, and (3) eternity. The kingdom of heaven in verse 23 has reference to the millennial kingdom and not to the church because the condition for entering the church and the kingdom is different from each other. Lest people might misunderstand, verse 24 records the Lord as using the term the kingdom of God. Hence, both the kingdom of heaven and the kingdom of God share together this meaning of the millennial kingdom.

v.25 "Astonished exceedingly"—The disciples misunderstand the Lord, for He shifts from the question of eternal life to the matter of reward. If it is so difficult for a rich man to enter the kingdom, how, they ask the Lord, can anyone be saved?

v.26 "And Jesus looking upon them"—The eyes too may speak.

"With God all things are possible"—To answer the question asked by the disciples, the Lord returns to the matter of salvation which is possible with God. God alone can change the greedy heart of a person. He is able to raise up a Saul of Tarsus, a Barnabas, a Levi, a Zacchaeus, those of Caesar's household (Phil. 4.22) and even the steward of Herod's house. The rich young ruler had said he was able but actually he was not, for God alone is able.

v.27 The question of Peter has the flavor of (1) self-righteousness, and (2) a bargaining spirit. In answering him the Lord reveals two sentiments. First, He sympathizes with Peter's understanding of good works as being the basis of kingdom reward. But second, He disapproves of Peter's strong self-righteousness and bargaining spirit. So that in verses 28–30 He is found encouraging Peter and building up his knowledge, whereas immediately following this in 20.1-16 He is found chiding Peter for his bargaining spirit.

v.28 "Ye who have followed me"—Those who emulate Christ in going the narrow way, taking up the cross with patience and humility.

"In the regeneration"—This word "regeneration" is used twice in the Bible: once in Titus 3.5 where it points to personal recovery—which is a being born again, and here in this verse 28 where it refers to the recovery of the world—the consequence of which is the millennium (see also Rom. 8.19–23 and Is. 11. 6–9). From Adam until Moses sin was in the world (Rom. 12.14), and from Moses until the Lord Jesus sin reigned (see Rom. 5.12–14, 21). All who are born again in this age are delivered from the power of sin, but not delivered from the presence of sin. Likewise in the regeneration of the world, first comes the deliverance from the power of sin (for Satan is bound for a thousand years—the period of the millennial kingdom—which is done by the Lord and not through any social reform done by men), and then shall come the new heaven and the new earth with deliverance from the presence of sin.

v.29 Mark's Gospel has "now in this time" and "in the world to come" (10.30). Matthew makes no such distinction in his account.

"Hundredfold" does not mean having a hundred fathers, rather it refers to a hundredfold joy as compared to the pain of leaving relatives and possessions behind.

"Eternal life" here points to eternal life in the kingdom. For eternal life is seen in three stages: (1) in this age—"hath eternal life" (see John 5.24); (2) in the millennial kingdom—that is, in the age to come (see Mark 10.30 and Luke 18.30); and (3) in eternity (see Rom. 2.5–7).

v.30 "Many . . . last" and "many . . . first"—These
words refer to rewards of greater or lesser kind and degree,
which can serve as a good warning to Peter for his self-righteousness.

Chapter 20

The Peril of Earthly Riches and the Reward
of the Heavenly Kingdom, 19.16–20.16 (Concl'd)

By reading the context carefully we can easily see that 19.30 has a vital connection with this chapter (as we have said before, the division of the Bible text into chapters is not Spirit-given but made arbitrary by man): for please notice that verse 30 of chapter 19 is similar to verse 16 of this present chapter. As regards Peter's earlier question, we mentioned that the Lord has two things to concern himself with: (1) to sympathize and encourage Peter and the other disciples by saying that everyone who leaves all for the Lord shall be rewarded; and (2) to correct in Peter an improper attitude which manifested itself as self-righteousness and a bargaining spirit, whereby one labors for the sake of reward and not because of his loving the Lord. As we already indicated in the previous chapter, 19.28–30 deals with the first item, and again 19.30, together with 20.1–16, deals with the second—namely, Peter's attitude. God is sovereign, and He is not bound by any law. So that this parable stresses the sovereignty of God, with the implication, therefore, that reward is according to grace. Now some view this parable as having reference to the matter of salvation. But this is impossible since salvation is accomplished by the Lord and not obtained through our works.

vv.1–16 "A man that was a householder"—This parable together with the one at the end of chapter 18 dealing with the unmerciful servant are most difficult to explain. We can only seek for their teachings but cannot expound their details. For instance, in the present parable we can explain the man that was the householder as God, yet God never hires anybody. And what is the meaning of a shilling a day? And who as laborers dare to murmur before God?

The householder, as we have said, is God. As to the first group in the morning, God comes to an agreement with them on their wages. With respect to the second group hired about the third hour, God says that "whatsoever is right I will give you" (v.4)—here there is no settled upon agreement. To the third and fourth groups, at about the sixth and the ninth hours respectively, He again does the same thing—there is no agreement. But to the fifth group who came at about the eleventh hour, He has not even mentioned any reward. Just here is the key—that there is no *legal* discussion. "Early in the morning" may represent the days of youth. "A day" means a lifetime. "About the third hour" has reference to those people who have stood idly by since early morning but are not called until then; that is to say, people who begin to do God's work at thirty years of age. And the additional laborers who come into the vineyard at later hours can refer to such who are forty or more and begin to serve God.

"And when even was come, ... pay them their hire"—The householder instructs his steward to begin with the latecomers, those who came in about the eleventh hour; otherwise, had it been the reverse order, those who worked earlier would neither have known the wages of the last laborers hired nor murmured about it. Nor would the Lord have been able to teach us this parable that at the time of rewarding there will yet be grace. Let us see that if He gives less than what is right, that would be unrighteous. But if He rewards the latecomers with the same amount as the earlier ones, that is His sovereignty. (It is as though He is saying to Peter: Do not be self-important and self-righteous, for you want to be ahead of everybody. In rewarding I will not owe you anything. Yes, you will be given the throne, but

God has the prerogative to give the same reward to those who work less and sacrifice less.) By this the Lord destroys the legalistic and commercial concept in Peter, who seems to have forgotten completely God's grace and sovereignty. Even though God will not use His sovereign power to do an unrighteous thing, He certainly can use this prerogative to dispense grace. He who overstresses reward tends to forget the Lord's love. And because of this characteristic in Peter, after His resurrection the Lord asked this disciple three times, "Lovest thou me?"—which was then followed by the command to work: "Feed my sheep" (see John 21.15–17).

In some versions (for example, the Authorized), verse 16 has "for many be called, but few chosen"; if so, then the connotations of 19.30 and 20.16 are slightly different. The "many" in 19.30 is broader and more general, and perhaps Peter is included therein. "The last" in 20.16 is more specific, since it must refer to those who were called to the vineyard about the eleventh hour. The laborers who would complain evidently forget the word which is found in Romans 9.14–24. Yet how grateful must be those who begin working about the eleventh hour and receive a shilling each.

Hence the teaching of the Lord here is: a person should always think of himself as having commenced working at about the eleventh hour, forgetting what he has left behind for the Lord's sake; and thus shall he receive the one shilling with contentment and gratitude. Or else he will only think about the sacrifice he has made so that when he receives his reward of one shilling he will be discontented and will fall backward.

The Passion Foretold the Third Time, 20.17–19

This is the third time our Lord Jesus reveals beforehand His own death. From this we know that His is not a martyr's death. For martyrdom is accidental, whereas our Lord knows how He is going to die. What he says includes two parts: (1) the chief priests and scribes—the religious part—and thus being judged and condemned by the Jews; (2) the Gentiles—the political part —and thereby being crucified by the Gentiles. And we know that all this was fulfilled. First the Lord Jesus was condemned by the Jews, and then He was delivered to Pilate. The Jews accused Him in the council as being blasphemous and before Pilate as being rebellious. The Jews are the instigators while the Gentiles are the executors.

The Ambition of James and John, 20.20–28

v.20 The mother of the two sons of Zebedee is deeply moved by what she has heard concerning reward, the throne, and the hard conditions of denying self and taking up the cross. She comes personally to the Lord to ask a favor. Her mentality is that her sons must not only have thrones but even the highest thrones! How Christians today also aspire to be the greatest. She reasons that since the Lord has borrowed her boat, net, and food, she certainly will not be refused in her request.

v.21 "What wouldest thou?"—She has asked but fails to tell the Lord what she asks for.

"One on thy right hand and one on thy left hand"—She reckons that if *her* sons receive glory, she also will be honored. This is bringing the natural to the kingdom, as though the kingdom of heaven is similar to the natural kingdoms of the earth.

vv.22–23 She thinks she knows what she asks for, but the Lord says to the sons: "Ye know not what ye ask"—yet the sons of Zebedee answer with one accord, "We are able"; but they still did not understand, for when the Lord suffered, all the disciples fled away.

"Cup" speaks of obedience to the will of the Father.

"Baptism" (see the parallel passage in Mark 10.38) points to the death of the cross.

The incident of Jesus' drinking the "cup" happened in the garden of Gethsemane, and his "baptism" came on the cross (see Luke 12.50). The cup signifies an offering of oneself in obedience; the baptism typifies death. Mark mentions baptism because the Lord is portrayed in his Gospel as the servant, and death is included in His servant's work. Matthew, however, omits the mentioning of baptism since in his Gospel the Lord is continually presented as the King. Matthew only speaks of the cup, which pointedly unveils Jesus' heart of obedience.

"Is not mine to give"—Position in the kingdom is not obtained through family relationship and petitioning prayer. It is not given as favoritism, nor is it gotten at will. It is "prepared"— the seat is prepared for whoever fulfills the conditions. For anyone to think that because he is saved he will inherit the kingdom is just like the two sons of Zebedee.

vv.24–25 "And when the ten heard it"—The disciples are now split into two parties, the two and the ten. The ten consider the two as too carnal, too unspiritual, too proud, and too discontented. Why are the two not satisfied with what the Lord gives but become so selfish as to care only for themselves and not their fellow-disciples? The ten, therefore, regard themselves as giving vent to righteous wrath. Actually, they too are selfish and proud (as Luke's account indicates, 22.24–27), otherwise they would not quarrel. Hence the two parties are not any different except in their utterance and intention. The ten may actually have mourned for not having had such a mother to plead for them!

"But Jesus called them unto him"—The Lord knows them, so He calls them together to tell them of three things:

(1) The church is not like the nations which have their rulers and great ones. For "all ye are brethren" (Matt. 23.8). It is not only unscriptural but also a violation of the command of the Lord to have popes, bishops, pastors, and elders as a religious hierarchy. To rule and to teach people spiritually is permissible, but to rule over people positionally is absolutely forbidden. The

bishops, elders, pastors, teachers, and so forth in the Bible are spiritually instituted. Today, however, a most carnal pastor may be ruling over a most spiritual carpenter, and people seek for the positions of elders and deacons for the sake of extending their personal influence in the church. We should faithfully serve the Lord and seek to please Him only. It is sinful to entertain the thought of gaining a higher position through service.

vv.26–27 And (2) a "minister" is a free man; but a "servant" (or "bondservant" in the Greek text) is a bondslave. "Great" is to be great among the great. "First" is to be the greatest in a group. The "great" must be a minister (the tone is lighter), while the "first" needs to be a bondslave (the tone is much heavier). The position in the kingdom is exactly opposite to the place of today. We wish to be great and first in this world, but the Lord calls us to be great and first in the age to come. How we today covet the reward but are unwilling to pay its cost. Spiritual greatness is in spiritual humbleness and suffering. We are able to be humble before God, yet we find it almost impossible to be humble before men.

v.28 And finally, (3) "the Son of man came"—He condescends from the highest to the lowest. He empties himself and takes the form of a bondslave. He comes not only to minister to men, but also to be Savior to the many.

Two Blind Men Healed at Jericho, 20.29–34

v.29 Jericho is a cursed city. The Lord, however, brings blessing to it by His coming.

v.30 "Two blind men"—The other synoptic Gospels record but one man. There are actually two, so Matthew especially documents it. They testify that Jesus is the Son of David, that is, He is to be King. "Two" is the number of witnessing.

These two blind men testify to the purpose of God. Though our Lord is rejected, yet He is to be King. This incident is a prelude to the entry into Jerusalem.

v.31 "They cried out the more"—The more they are rebuked, the louder they cry. Spiritually speaking, the more they are forbidden to testify, the louder God enables them to testify.

vv.32–33 "What will ye that I should do unto you?"— Our prayer needs to have a definite objective. "Lord, that our eyes may be opened"—The reason why prayer at the time of a crisis is usually answered is because we ask in specific terms.

v.34 Many after having their eyes opened go away to enjoy the scenery that had once been deprived them. Many after receiving blessing seek for pleasure. But these followed the Lord.

THE GOSPEL ACCORDING TO MATTHEW

Chapter 21

The Kingly Yet Humble Entry into Jerusalem, 21.1–11

v.1 "Drew nigh unto Jerusalem"—The place where God's prophets are slain.

"Bethphage" means "the house of unripened figs"—Jerusalem was originally the place of kings, yet the King of kings is now rejected because of unripened figs.

v.2 The other synoptic Gospels mention only the colt, but Matthew reports an ass and a colt. There is a typological reason involved.

v.3 "The Lord hath need of them"—In His capacity as the Creator, the Lord lays claim to them since the entire creation belongs to Him. Commentators usually take the ass to be representative of the Gentiles and the colt, the Jews. Actually the reverse is the truth: the ass represents the Jews and the colt, the Gentiles. Now from Mark's account (11.7) we see that the Lord rode upon the colt, with the ass no doubt following, thus signifying that the Lord has His hand upon the Gentiles and that the Jews are following. It is most difficult to ride a colt; even an ass expert is not able to do it. Spiritually speaking, before anyone is saved he is truly like a colt. But when he is saved the Lord can ride on such a colt. The horse speaks of war, while the ass speaks of peace. In the instance now before us, the Lord comes as the Prince of Peace riding a colt—that is to say, a young ass ("a colt the foal of an ass"—Matt. 21.5); at His second coming, though, He will ride on a militant white horse.

v.4 This is a fulfillment of a prophecy by the prophet Zechariah (see Zech. 9.9).

v.5 In the prophecy of Zechariah are to be found such words as "just" and "salvation"—terms which Matthew omits. The reason for such omission is that whereas justice and salvation in the Old Testament point specifically to the kingdom, here Matthew is only interested in showing that the Lord is King even though He is rejected.

vv.6–9 We previously mentioned how the incident of Jesus opening the eyes of the blind as recorded in the preceding chapter serves as a prelude to what we find in this chapter. For now the multitudes are heard to shout forth the same thing as did the blind men of Jericho, namely—Hosanna to the Son of David.

Many commentators consider this incident as our Lord's last offering of himself to the Jews. This, however, cannot be correct; because as early as the time of chapter 13, the Jews have already been rejected by Him. Otherwise, why should the Lord while now at Jerusalem spend his nights at Bethany (see 21.17; cf. also Mark 11.11–12,19). It is because Jerusalem has become a rejected entity.

v.9 "Hosanna" originally meant "Save, we pray thee"— It later turned out to be an expression of praise. Here is the One who has power and is therefore worthy of our praise.

vv.10–11 How sad that on the road they call Him the Son of David, but here in the city they call Him the prophet Jesus from Nazareth of Galilee. And not long hence they will also crucify Him.

"All the city was stirred"—This is parallel to the situation in chapter 2. Everything is fine on the road, but the situation changes drastically after entering the city.

Jesus Cleanses the Temple Again, Heals the Sick,
and Accepts the Children's Praise, 21.12–17

vv.12–13 For the second time the temple is cleansed. The first cleansing came at the commencement of the Lord's work (see John 2). But now it happens at the closing of His work. On the first occasion the Lord cleansed the temple in His capacity as the Son of God, for He then declared, "my Father's house"; here He cleanses in the position of the Son of David as King. For the Lord Jesus to be King, He must first have a pure worship. Though money-changing and sacrifice-selling seem to facilitate the worship of God, our Lord nevertheless looks upon these as unclean activities. He has no need for intermediaries. These people hang out the "shingle-signs" of assistance but actually seek gain for themselves. They profess to make things convenient for the temple, yet everything is run on a commercial basis.

"A den of robbers"—To open a store on the street is business, but to have a stall in the temple is robbery. The Lord shows us that the temple must be kept pure.

v.14 First the cleansing—the maintaining of purity; then the healing—the overflowing of grace. The sick here interestingly enough are not the leprous, but the blind and the lame. It is the restoration of sight and strength that will cause people to know and to do His will.

vv.15–16 The shout of "Hosanna!" earlier on the road was a case of heartless praise by the multitudes. It was done in a moment of enthusiasm. Here, only a few children are left to praise Him. It is evident that the priests are envious, for they are moved with indignation after they have seen so many wonderful things. They themselves cannot praise because they are not children.

v.17 "To Bethany"—The Lord spends the seven last nights in Bethany. Doubtless He must be in the house of Martha and Mary, and He had no need to notify them beforehand. Should not the Lord have the same convenience with all of us? In Jerusalem He can find no dwelling place; but in Bethany He always has a place available for himself. For here is a home in which are life and service. Bethany is a real home full of grace, love, and song.

Jesus Curses a Fruitless Fig Tree and Gives a Principle of Prayer, 21.18–22

v.18 "Returned to the city"—From Bethany to Jerusalem. "He hungered"—There is something He misses, something with which He is not satisfied.

v.19 "A fig tree"—This represents the Jews. Vine, fig tree, and olive tree—these all are representative of Israel (just as the plum blossom, for example, is the national flower of China).

Mark's account says "it was not the season of figs" (11.13). It may appear that the Lord should not have cursed it. However, we are told that the fig tree in Judea has two gatherings. When the tree is covered with leaves, it bears *early* ripened figs; the later ripened fruits will follow some time afterwards. And hence this is why the Lord comes to the tree to find figs; otherwise, He would never have done this. Mark's observation concerning the season of figs had reference to the second and therefore greater ingathering of figs. Our Lord therefore justifiably curses the fig tree because it deceives people by its luxuriant foliage. It puts up a good appearance. The same is true with man. Leaves point to man's own righteousness, a righteousness with which Adam himself attempted to cover his own nakedness. But fruit is that which really satisfies God, fruits which the Jews of Jesus' day had not produced.

"By the way side"—This is indicative of the same location as "the way side" mentioned in Matthew 13. It is in close proximity to Satan.

vv.20–21 "If ye have faith"—When the Lord speaks, He has faith in His own word. We believe in the promise of God, in His word.

"Sea" signifies "the Gentiles" while "this mountain" has reference to the children of Israel.

"Be thou taken up and cast into the sea"—The metaphor may be applied to the scattering of the children of Israel among the nations until they seem as though they have almost disappeared.

Looking at this verse as indicative of a principle of prayer, let me say that we sometimes need to speak to the mountain—for "mountain" speaks also of an obstacle or a persisting difficulty (just as, conversely, "plain" stands for prosperity). When our prayer produces sufficient faith and constraint, we should speak directly to the problem. In casting out demons, for example, we not only pray to God but after having faith we also rebuke the demon.

v.22 This is one of the greatest promises. "Believing" is all which is required.

Jesus' Authority Challenged, 21.23–27

v.23 Having seen the wonderful things done by the Lord (see verse 15), the chief priests and the elders ask these two questions. As a matter of fact, these are but a single question, since by understanding the one you will know the other.

v.24–27 "I also will ask you"—Believers may learn from

the Lord here. When they too are asked unnecessary questions, they can ask back just as the Lord did. The question our Lord asks is most meaningful, for John the Baptist was His forerunner. These same questioners had inquired of John before as to whether he was the Christ, and John had given them his testimony. So that if the question about John were solved, their question about our Lord would likewise be solved. Yet how slippery they are. They neither believe nor answer the question.

"We know not"—This is a lie. The truth is that they will not reply honestly, for they would lose face if they did.

"Neither tell I you"—Concerning the matter of authority, the Lord does not say here that He does not know or that He cannot tell. We know He is all-powerful and all-wise. He therefore cannot tell a lie. Hence the principle here is (1) to ask back, or (2) to not tell.

Three Parables of Warning: (1) The Two Sons, 21.28–32

vv.28–30 This parable depicts the position of the Pharisees, the scribes, the elders, and the priests. The phrase "two sons" stands for all the children of Israel, since they are all chosen in the flesh (today only those who are saved are brothers; in John 8 the Jews are reckoned as the devil's children). Now the first son in the parable represents the publicans and the harlots. They are recognized sinners, yet they repent and become obedient. The second son represents the Pharisees and so forth. They are obedient only in words, such as praying on street-corners and wearing broad phylacteries while leaving undone the weightier matters of the law. And so the Lord asks His interrogators to decide which of the two sons in the parable actually did the will of their father, symbolizing of course the will of the heavenly Father.

vv.31–32 "The way of righteousness" is also the way of peace. John had exhorted the Pharisees once; the faith of the publicans and the harlots all about them should have encouraged them again, yet they would not believe.

"The kingdom of God"—Why did the Lord not say the kingdom of heaven? Because the emphasis here is on spiritual reality.

"Go . . . before you"—This is a Greek expression which means that the publicans and harlots have entered while the Pharisees have not, not in the more common sense of it meaning that some enter in ahead of others.

Three Parables of Warning:
(2) The Wicked Husbandmen, 21.33–46

vv.33–40 "A man that was a householder"—This parable of a householder cannot be explained on the *human* level because (1) God never goes away to another country, and (2) God knows beforehand that the Jews will kill the Lord.

"A householder" typifies God. "Vineyard" speaks of the boundary of Israel. "Hedge" signifies protection (see Job 1.10). A "winepress' is that which gladdens man's heart. And "tower" is a watchtower by which people see and know what is coming.

"Let it out"—The vineyard is neither sold nor given as a gift. It is rented out, and hence God still holds the ownership. The land of Israel is let out to the Jews for them to manage.

"When the season of the fruits drew near"—This shows how expectant God is. Even before the coming of the Lord (the "my son" in the parable), He is already so expecting.

"His servants"—A reference to the prophets sent before Christ. They were all persecuted and some even killed.

"His son" points to the Lord Jesus. "They will reverence my son"—This is spoken according to human logic. So far as God is concerned, the Lord does not stumble into death at the hands of fate; He instead comes with the express foreknowledge and purpose to die after He has emptied himself and taken the form of a bondslave.

"This is the heir"—Again this is spoken according to human

reasoning. For in actuality the scribes and Pharisees have refused to accept the Lord as the heir.

"The husbandmen" typify the Pharisees, the scribes, the chief priests, and so forth.

v.41 They themselves give the verdict. It was partially fulfilled in 70 A.D. at the destruction of Jerusalem by the Roman general Titus, but will be completely fulfilled during the Great Tribulation. For have they not answered and said, "His blood be on us, and on our children" (Matt. 27.25)?

"Other husbandmen" point to the other Jews who believe and who are in the kingdom.

v.42 "The builders" are the scribes, the Pharisees, and the priests.

"The stone . . . the head of the corner" is the Lord Jesus.

"Marvellous in our eyes"—The Jews who are related to the Lord in the flesh will not believe in Him, while they of the nations do believe. The cornerstone also speaks of resurrection (see Ps. 118.22–23, Acts 4.11).

"Did ye never read in the scriptures?"—Just ask yourselves.

v.43 "The kingdom of God"—Again, the emphasis is on spiritual reality, since only spiritual experience can be taken away.

v.44 To the Jews the Lord is a stumbling block. They fall on Him because they do not see earthly splendor and the outward dignity of a king in Him (see Is. 8.14–15, Rom. 9.32–33, 1 Cor. 1.23, 1 Peter 2.8). But to the church He is the Rock, and the Head Stone of the corner (1 Cor. 3.11, Eph. 2.20–22, 1 Peter 2.4–5). To the nations He is the Stone that smites (Dan. 2.34,44–45). Hence the first part of verse 44 points to the Jews, and the second part points to the Gentiles or the nations. The Jews are stumbled at Him today, for even now many still call Him the son of a carpenter, a deceiver, and so forth. And the nations will be scattered as dust at the coming of the kingdom.

vv.45–46 Those who do not believe are always in fear. Christians are bold because they are not afraid of being despised or mocked. The fearful dare not believe in the Lord, thus facing eternal death.

Chapter 22

Three Parables of Warning: (3) The King's
Marriage Feast for His Son, 22.1–14

v.1 "And Jesus answered and spake again in parables
unto them"—Again, this parable of a certain king cannot be
fully explained in *human* terms because (1) it is impossible that
the servants will be killed, (2) the king cannot be so democratic
as to gather in people from the highways for his son's wedding
feast, and (3) the king will not send his armies to destroy murderers.

This parable follows immediately upon the preceding one.
The previous parable shows how the Gentiles are accepted (yet
not every Gentile is saved) after God has rejected the Jews. The
parable here discloses how the Jews are rejected because they
first reject the Lord.

v.2 "The kingdom of heaven"—It does not say the church
but the kingdom of heaven, for it is the domain of the kingdom of
heaven that is here presented. In the church, the whole body of
believers are saved; whereas in the outward sphere of the kingdom of heaven there are still those unsaved in it. (Please note
that the parable in Luke 14.15–24 focuses on the gospel. It is not
the same parable as the one given here.)

"Marriage" speaks of a covenant relationship. "Feast" denotes God's prior prepared abundance.

There is no mentioning of the bride because this parable does not deal with the purpose of God.

v.3 "His servants"—The disciples of John the Baptist and of the Lord.

"Call them that were bidden"—This points to the children of Israel. God sends His servants to invite the children of Israel to come and enjoy His abundance. Such is the mission of the disciples of John and of the Twelve and the Seventy sent out by the Lord.

"They would not come"—They do not believe the testimony given by these disciples.

v.4 "Other servants"—The apostles and the disciples on the day of Pentecost and afterwards. The apostles and the disciples testified to the Jews for the second time on the day of Pentecost. They bore witness in Jerusalem but failed to go even to neighboring Samaria. So God allowed persecution to come upon them that they might be scattered to the nations. Paul began his ministry in the same manner. He first went to the Jews in the Dispersion, and after they rejected the Lord he declared that he would go to the Gentiles.

Verse 3 gives the invitation; verse 4 tells that oxen and fatlings are killed, and all things are now ready—that is to say, the Lord Jesus has already died and is resurrected.

vv.5–6 "But they made light of it"—This depicts exactly the situation on the day of Pentecost. Even though 3,000 and later 5,000 in Jerusalem were saved, yet they were but a little flock compared to the great multitudes gathered in that city. According to the Jewish historian Josephus, on the day when Christ was crucified there were gathered together three million people in Jerusalem.

"Farm" speaks of agriculture; "merchandise" signifies commerce. "The rest" are those who are neither engaged in agriculture or commerce—people such as the priests, the scribes, the Pharisees, the Sadducees, and so forth.

"Treated them shamefully, and killed them"—They killed Stephen and James, and they imprisoned the other apostles. These verses are thus completely fulfilled.

v.7 "But the king was wroth; and he sent his armies, and destroyed those murderers"—This was literally fulfilled in 70 A.D. when Titus destroyed Jerusalem and blood flowed in the streets.

v.8 "They that were bidden were not worthy"—Those that were bidden were obviously the Jews, but simply because they have rejected the invitation does not mean that the abundance of God is going to be wasted. He will give it to others.

v.9 Those who are called have been bidden before, but we Gentiles are saved as though by accident: "As many as ye shall find"—and this is grace. All who believe have eternal life.

v.10 "Both bad and good"—God's calling today ignores the question of a good or bad historical background. The abundance of the gospel has no respect of former good or bad, because the ultimate purpose of the gospel is to glorify God's Son.

v.11 "To behold the guests"—This happens at the judgment seat of Christ.

"Wedding-garment"—In Oriental countries, the wedding garments are not prepared by the guests but provided by the host. The wedding garment is Christ, our robe of righteousness. We need to be clothed with Christ (cf. Rom. 13.14, Gal. 3.27). God has covered us with "the robe of righteousness" (Is. 61.10). God has provided the wedding garment for us, but the man in the parable thinks his own garment good enough (self-righteousness). He refuses to take off his own garment and change to another one. He will not trust in Christ as his righteousness.

v.12 "And he saith unto him"—The Lord does not ask why we beat people, told lies, or violated the law several days before. He merely asks us why we did not put on the wedding garment. No question on past history, He only asks if there is Christ our righteousness present upon us.

"And he was speechless"—This proves that the man knowingly does it, because he could not offer any reply. It really does not matter if one is poor, because the king has already made provision. If anyone considers himself unworthy, the king has the wedding garment ready for him. What there needs to be a concern for is any unwillingness to take off the old and put on the new.

v.13 Whoever does not trust in Christ as righteousness will be cast into outer darkness.

v.14 Many are included in the domain of the kingdom of heaven, but few are the chosen.

Three Captious Questions: (1) Tribute to Caesar?

v.15 What follows are records of how the Jews tempt the Lord Jesus. If they cannot ensnare Him in His conduct, they will try to trap Him in His talk. Today people do the same thing.

v.16 The Pharisees and the Herodians (the latter being Jewish "quislings" or traitors to their country) are deadly enemies, yet they join forces in tempting the Lord.

"Their disciples"—Only *blind* scholars will come under the tutorship of blind masters.

"Thou art true, and teachest the way of God in truth"—

They first flatter the Lord to insure that He will continue to speak the truth and not lie so that they can ensnare Him in His talk, for they measure the Lord according to their own deceitful selves.

"Carest not for any one"—Which means You, Jesus, will speak the truth to us Pharisees and Herodians regardless of Caesar.

"Thou regardest not the person of men" has the same effect as "carest not for any one"—Even before Pilate, the Lord speaks the truth.

v.17 "What thinkest thou?"—Not what is reasonable nor what is lawful, but what is His opinion. Only thus can they ensnare Him in His talk.

"Is it lawful . . . or not"—Both aspects of the question are snares: the one will make Him a traitor to Israel, the other, a rebel to Rome.

v.18 "Why make ye trial of me, ye hypocrites?"—The Lord discloses right away their hypocritical scheme.

v.19 "Show me the tribute money"—Gold and silver the Lord has not. So, He asks them to show Him one of the coins. Only those who pay tribute to Caesar have Caesar's money. The Lord has none.

vv.20–21 There is not only wisdom but also instruction in our Lord's answer. (1) Believers should not interfere with politics. Render to Caesar the things which are Caesar's. (2) Yet they should pay tribute, because the things of Caesar's should be rendered to Caesar. As to the believers themselves, they are God's. (3) The Jewish nation was destroyed because they had not rendered to God the things that are God's. Instead, they went after idols. Hence God punished them.

v.22 "And when they heard it, they marvelled"—Who will not marvel at such wisdom? If any reader is not amazed, he is worse than the Jews.

Three Captious Questions: (2) Is There a Resurrection?

v.23 As soon as the two parties leave, the Sadducees enter upon the scene. It is like rotary warfare. These Sadducees really believe that there is no resurrection (after people die, they are just annihilated), nor are there angels. How people even today conceive imaginary problems to harass others, just like these Sadducees of old!

vv.24–28 "Now there were with us ... "—This is a fabricated story.

v.29 "Ye do err"—This is our Lord's verdict. "Not knowing the scriptures"—That is to say, they have no spiritual knowledge. "Nor the power of God"—They have no spiritual experience. These form the basis of human error. It behooves us believers to have both knowledge and experience.

vv.30–32 "For in the resurrection"—The Lord not only affirms the fact of resurrection but also explains that God is the God of the living, not of the dead. What He means is this: "You say that a person is annihilated after death; yet if this is so, then on the occasion of Moses witnessing the burning bush, Jehovah would have introduced himself as the God of the dead, the God of the annihilated. This could never have encouraged Moses. The logic is that if He is the God of Abraham and Abraham is a dead person, then this will make Him to be the God of the dead. But He is *not* the God of the dead, and therefore Abraham though dead will yet become alive. So too will Isaac and Jacob be resurrected." For the description about resurrection, see 1 Corinthians 15.50–57.

v.33 The word "astonished" speaks of defeat. They are amazed that such a difficult question has been answered.

Three Captious Questions:
(3) Which Is the Great Commandment?

vv.34–35 "Gathered themselves together"—The Pharisees reassemble and put forward one of their own, a lawyer, who is so confident of his own eloquence that he believes he will not yield to the gifted elocution of the Lord.

v.36 "Which is the great commandment in the law?"—Yet in actual fact all commandments are equally essential, and therefore you cannot honor one and despise another.

vv.37–38 "The great and the first"—This is so because this commandment includes all the other commandments. If any one of these other commandments is violated, it automatically breaches the "all" in loving God.

v.39 "Neighbor"—All the people aside from one's own self. This points to the Lord Jesus. See the parable (in Luke 10.30ff.) of the man going down to Jericho who fell among thieves and was helped by the Samaritan who is the man's neighbor (the Lord Jesus).*

v.40 These two commandments include all of them: the first one includes all the commandments which are in relation to God; and the second one, all those pertaining to man. For remember that the Ten Commandments are divided into two

---

*For further insight into the parable of the Good Samaritan from this point of view, see Mr. Nee's book, *Ye Search the Scriptures* (New York, Christian Fellowship Publishers, 1974), pp. 68–69. Translated from the Chinese.—*Translator*

parts—those relating to God and those relating to men.

The Lord's Unanswerable Question, 22.41–46

v.41 "Jesus asked them a question"—You have asked Me enough questions; now let Me ask you one.

v.42 "What think ye"—This is in apposition to that question in verse 17 which the Pharisees put to Him. Yet the Lord does not ask a difficult question here. Even a three-year-old child can answer it.

v.43 "Call him Lord"—The Lord Jesus does not deny what the Pharisees have just answered, that the Christ is the Son of David; yet He proceeds to bring out the other aspect.

vv.44–45 "The Lord said unto my Lord"—The first "Lord" is Jehovah, the second is the Messiah. Our Lord wants us to understand that according to the Spirit, He is David's Lord. The Pharisees only know the Christ as the Son of David, just as today's modernists know Him only in this way. Praise God, He is also David's Lord.

v.46 "No one was able to answer him a word"—They do not answer because they would not answer.

THE GOSPEL ACCORDING TO MATTHEW

Chapter 23

This is one of the easiest chapters in Matthew's Gospel because it has only teaching, no doctrine.

The Jewish Multitude Warned Against Pharisaism, 23.1–12

v.1 "To the multitudes and to his disciples"—In speaking, our Lord usually does not mix up the multitudes and His disciples. Here, though, He speaks to them together. This is due to the fact that the teaching to follow is directed especially to the Jewish people in general, and His disciples are naturally placed in that position too.

v.2 "Sit on Moses' seat"—According to Jewish history, many significant changes have come since the time of Moses: wicked kings, the Captivity, the destruction, and so forth. As a result, people no longer knew or kept the law of Moses. The zealous among them stepped forth to lead the people back to the ancient law. These were the forefathers of the Pharisees and the scribes. In the beginning they sat on the seat of Moses both in name and in practice. They performed as well as taught the law. Generation after generation this tradition continued till by the time of the Lord Jesus there came to be nothing left but a name. Even so, our Lord did not deny that the Pharisees did sit on Moses' seat in name.

v.3 "These do and observe"—To the Jews, before the death of the Christ they must keep the law. Only after His death is the law terminated. For this reason, then, the Lord enjoins the Jews and His disciples to keep the law.

The principle which underlies this verse is of great importance. The concepts toward the law in today's church are of two opposite kinds: (1) People are saved by grace and not by keeping the law; but to attain sanctification we must keep the law. (2) Again, people are saved by grace and not by keeping the law; and hence we need not keep the law after we are saved, though we do keep the commandment of grace. The latter concept is correct. The gist of the Letter to the Romans is that no sinner can be justified by the works of the law; while the theme of the Letter to the Galatians is that no saved person can be sanctified by works of the law. These two letters have sufficiently proven that neither justification nor sanctification comes by the works of the law. According to the teaching of Romans 7, if a person still keeps the law after he is saved he is reckoned an adulterer. For by keeping it, it indicates that the law has not died. In such a situation, then, how can he be married to Christ and not commit adultery? Accordingly, we must die to the law so that we may receive eternal life through Christ Jesus.

"For they say, and do not"—This contrasts sharply with the Lord Jesus, "who was a prophet mighty in deed and word before God and all the people" (Luke 24.19). How sad today that many preachers, like the Pharisees of old, can say but cannot do.

v.4 "They bind heavy burdens and grievous to be borne, and lay them on men's shoulders"—Based upon the existing law, the Pharisees create laws outside of the law of Moses and lay them on people's shoulders, yet they themselves do not keep what they teach. At the beginning, the forefathers of the Pharisees had ruled that whoever offended Moses' law must be punished but that the one who violated their own law could be forgiven. But gradually these two laws assumed equal status, so that whoever gave offence to either of these laws would be punished. And finally, it developed that whoever offended the law of Moses might be forgiven, but that the one who might violate the law of the Pharisees must be severely punished. The Pharisees of Jesus' day had come to view the law which they had established as representing the essence of the law of Moses, and therefore of greater importance. The matter of "Corban" was a typical example (see Mark 7.11–13).

Today's disciplines and creeds assume the same rule: keep what is easy to keep, but what is not able to be kept is something that is only applicable to the Jews for them to keep—that is to say, take what in the Bible is possible to follow as being for the Gentiles but all which is difficult apply to the Jews or relate it to the millennial kingdom. We certainly have learned from the Pharisees. Yet is this right or wrong?

v.5 "To be seen of men"—Here the Lord unveils their real motive: to be seen of men. How dangerous this is. In the areas of giving and preaching sometimes these serve as masks to show how zealous and spiritual people are.

"Make broad their phylacteries"—These are strips of parchment on which are written words of Scripture and placed in cases of calfskin and bound on the forehead and arm (see Deut. 6.8, 11.18).

"Enlarge the borders of their garments"—This has reference to the cord of blue used as a fringe of the garment on which are also inscribed passages of Scripture.

v.6 These actions reflect their pride before men.

v.7 "To be called of men, Rabbi"—Modern men have this same problem, for they too like to be acknowledged as teachers of other people. On the whole, the Lord reveals to us the

Pharisees' motive and design. Oftentimes we are zealous in good works but we need to inquire for what reason we are doing them.

v.8 From the idea of being called Rabbi, our Lord turns to instruct us: "Be not ye called"—Believers are equal on earth. There should not be one above the other. To call people pastors in the church is but a metamorphosis of this ancient idea of calling people Rabbis. Elders and deacons are offices, not class distinctions. Sacerdotalism is a falling away into the old position of the Pharisees.

v.9 "Call no man your father"—This does not mean the father at home; it has reference to a so-called father in the church (anyone who has authority), such as "the Fathers" in the Roman Catholic system.

"For one is your Father, even he who is in heaven"—This proves that the "father" immediately mentioned before has reference to *religious* fathers. Unfortunately, during the second century there had already arisen these so-called church fathers, all of whom were merely disciples to the early apostles.

v.10 "Master" is less honorable than Rabbi. It is also a religious title. We may call people mister so-and-so, but not master alone. The Lord charges us to call one another brothers and sisters.

v.11 This is the second time the matter of "greatest" is being touched upon (see Matt. 20.26–27 above). How exceedingly important is this principle, that true greatness lies not in fame, position, or name—but in service.

v.12 The way of the cross is in humility. Humility is voluntary. It is the absence of vainglory, not the result of being despised.

Scribes and Pharisees Indicted: The
Seven Woes, 23.13–36

There are altogether seven woes, since some authorities insert a verse 14 that reads: "Woe unto you, scribes and Pharisees, hypocrites! for ye devour widows' houses, even while for a pretense ye make long prayers: therefore ye shall receive greater condemnation" (cf. Mark 12.40 and Luke 20.47). Hence the first to the fourth woes belong to one class, and the fifth through the seventh belong to another.

v.13 "Woe unto you, scribes and Pharisees, hypocrites!" —Not woe to the sinners, the harlots, and the publicans. Not woe to the Sadducees the agnostics, nor woe to the Herodians the quislings. Because everybody among the populace, even women and children, knows who they are. But the scribes and the Pharisees are respected as being big brothers, as being the sure recipients of reward and blessing. Consequently, the Lord makes a special effort to uncover their true situation.

"Ye shut the kingdom of heaven against men"—The use of the term the kingdom of heaven here denotes the spiritual realm of the kingdom, that is to say, the true church—a body of believers. But these Pharisees and scribes hinder people from believing in the Lord Jesus. Their unrighteous deeds stumble people; their erroneous teachings lead people astray.

v.15 They convert the Gentiles to Judaism, and call them proselytes (the Greek meaning: "to come to"). They are most zealous in declaring that the Gentiles who worship idols will perish, so that they should instead worship the only true God— the God who created the heaven and the earth. Yet after these Gentiles become proselytes, nothing is done to build them up. Added to their original evil (of having at one time worshiped idols) is the evil of the Pharisees, and thus they become twofold more sons of hell than the Pharisees themselves.

vv.16–17 Here is a law which they have added, namely, that the gold of the temple is greater than the temple itself. They consider gold to be greater because it is worth a considerable amount.

vv.18–19 Likewise, the Pharisees regard a gift laid upon the altar as being greater than the altar itself. But the Lord deems both the temple and the altar to be greater, because they sanctify the gold and the gift. Here He also teaches us on sanctification. Sanctification is not the eradication of the root of sin such as is the pulling out of an aching tooth. What can you pull out of gold and gift? Sanctification means a being set apart for God. There are gold and gift everywhere, but only those which are set apart for God are sanctified, and therefore not to be touched by anyone. In like manner, the sanctification of a believer is a being separated from among men. It has two aspects: (1) the temple, which signifies an abiding in Christ, just as the gold in the temple—by it being there—is sanctified (note that the temple speaks of Christ—see Matt. 12.6, John 2.21); and (2) the altar, which denotes consecration—that is to say, the presenting of oneself to the Lord after he is saved and thus being set apart for His use.

vv.20–22 These words prove the falsehood and absurdity of the laws of the Pharisees.

vv.23–24 The following three woes deal with the Pharisees' manner of life.

"Tithe"—One tenth. When they weigh the mint and anise and cummin, they use the most sensitive balance so as to prevent any error, even of one milligram. They keep the rituals of the law, but they have no desire to keep the law's weightier matters such as justice and mercy and faith. They strain out the tiny little gnats in their food, yet they swallow the camel without a blink of the eye!

vv.25–26 What is mentioned above concerns the habit of the Pharisees to avoid the weightier matters of the law while keeping its lesser matters. The woe pronounced here deals with their seeking outward appearance.

"Extortion"—Exercising one's own lust to suppress other people. "Excess"—Indulging in one's own lust to the full.

vv.27–28 "Sepulchres" are where the dead dwell.

"Whited" to beautify the graves; that is, using outward paint to cover inward death.

vv.29–30 They love to erect monuments. They concede that their fathers were wrong in killing the prophets. The unbelieving Jews of today are no different, for they say if Christ were living at this present time, they would never crucify Him.

vv.31–32 Their boasting merely proves that they are the sons of those who killed the prophets.

"Fill ye up then the measure of your fathers"—They will soon kill the Lord and later kill His disciples.

v.33 Here the Lord indeed manifests the fact that He does not regard the person of men, because He now severely bhides them as serpents, the offspring of vipers (Satan himself is called the "old serpent"). They call God their Father and consider themselves children of Abraham (see John 8.41,39), not knowing that they actually are "children of the devil" (1 John 3.10, cf. John 8.44a). Our Lord then speaks of hell here, and preachers today ought to speak of hell too. God is not a doting patron.

v.34 The Lord prophesies how the saints will suffer persecution and martyrdom.

"Shall ye . . ."—This refers to the future. They will not only whitewash sepulchres and set up monuments but also dig graves.

vv.35–36 "Abel" was the first one murdered. The "Zachariah" here mentioned is not the Zechariah told of in 2 Chronicles 24.20–21 who was the son of Jehoiada the priest, since that would be too early timewise. No, he was the prophet Zechariah the son of Berechiah (see Zech. 1.1). "Barachiah" and "Berechiah" have the same sound, with only a slight difference in the Greek and Hebrew spellings. This prophet Zechariah was a post-Captivity prophet. He was one who was killed in the temple after its restoration.

"This generation"—This means from that day when Jesus spoke, even up to this present age. The time-span is very broad in scope—it covers the Gentiles as well as the Jews.

Jesus' Lament over Jerusalem, 23.37–39

"O Jerusalem, Jerusalem, that killeth . . ."—Jerusalem habitually killed the prophets and stoned those who were sent by God.

"Your house"—No longer does the Lord say "my Father's house" or "my house" but "your house"; for the Jews have been rejected.

"Till ye shall say"—They will bless the Lord in the millennial kingdom after the Great Tribulation. In the meantime, the wild olive branch (the Gentiles) is being grafted into the good olive tree (see Rom. 11.13–24).

The Great Tribulation will mark the end of the dispensation of grace. Each dispensation has a similar conclusion to it: the dispensation of Innocence was concluded by the flood; the dispensation of Human Government, by the confusion of tongues; that of Promise, by the going down to Egypt; that of Law, by the Babylonian Captivity; and the dispensation of Grace, as we have noted, will be terminated by the Great Tribulation; while that of the Kingdom will be ended by the old heaven and the old earth being consumed by fire.

(Rapture)

In order to understand Matthew 24 and 25, it is essential to have a clear knowledge of the subject of rapture. For it is one of the most important matters in this last hour. Unfortunately it is greatly misunderstood by many.

Rapture is the same as the word "receive" found in John 14.1–3. It does not signify the idea of "climbing up" to heaven but of the Lord receiving us to heaven. Hence rapture is a specific term used to denote His receiving us at His soon return.

There are different views on rapture among believers. Some say (1) that the whole body of the saved will be raptured before the Great Tribulation; others believe (2) that the whole body of the saved must go through the Great Tribulation before they are raptured; while still others feel (3) that a part of the saved will be raptured before the Great Tribulation and a part of them will be raptured after the Great Tribulation. There are mainly these three schools of interpretation on the subject; yet merely because any one of them is different from the one you hold to does not give you any warrant to denounce the different view as heresy. It is wrong to withhold fellowship simply for this reason.

Well-known believers are found in all three schools. Of the first school mentioned, names can be cited such as J. N. Darby, William Kelly (C. H. Spurgeon once said that Kelly's brain was as large as the universe), R. A. Torrey (who later changed to a post-tribulation rapture view), Phillips Brooks, James Gray, Arno C. Gaebelein, J. A. Seiss, C. I. Scofield, and so forth.

Of the second school, there could be listed such names as George Muller (who first believed in pre-tribulation rapture), A. J. Gordon of Boston, A. B. Simpson, W. J. Erdman, W. G. Moorehead, Henry Frost of Canada, James Wright, Benjamin Newton, and so on.

And as to the third school, we have names such as Hudson Taylor, Robert Chapman, Robert Govett (Spurgeon praised his writings as having light a century ahead of his time and as being full of gold), G. H. Pember, D. M. Panton (the "prince of prophecy") and others.

None of the three schools can completely ignore the others, yet only one is correct. Let us therefore examine them with fairness, having the attitude of a judge and not that of a lawyer.

I. Reasons given by the first school—that is to say, by the adherents of a pre-tribulation rapture—are presented in the following paragraphs.

A. 1 Thessalonians 1.10 "The wrath to come"—This is the Great Tribulation. Since the Lord Jesus will deliver us from the wrath to come, we must be raptured *before* the Great Tribulation. Also, 1 Thessalonians 5.9 "For God appointed us not unto wrath"—Once again this "wrath" has reference to the Great Tribulation.

Let me say, though, that such an interpretation of "wrath" here as being the Great Tribulation is incorrect. How do we know that this wrath must necessarily be the wrath in the Great Tribulation? And even if it were granted that it is, such an interpretation of this word "wrath" would still be unreasonable because the Great Tribulation, on the one hand, is God's punishment and wrath coming upon the unbelievers, and on the other hand is Satan's attack and wrath descending on the believers. When Satan assaults the believers, the latter enter into the experience of the Great Tribulation but do not come under the wrath of God.

B. Jeremiah 30.6–7 "The time of Jacob's trouble"—The Great Tribulation is only for the Jews, not for the Gentiles or for the church. Since the church is not the Jews, we therefore will not go through the Great Tribulation. See also Daniel 12.1.

If there were only these two passages in the entire Bible which speak of the Great Tribulation, then the Great Tribulation would indeed be exclusively for the Jews. But we can read other passages in the Bible, such as Revelation 3 which speaks of "the hour of trial, that hour which is to come upon the whole world, to try them that dwell upon the earth" (v.10). The prophecies of Jeremiah and Daniel were directed toward the Jews, and hence they used such words as "Jacob" and "thy people" quite logically.

C. Revelation 4.1–4 Interpreters of this first school consider Revelation 2 and 3 as depicting the age of the church; 4.1 as referring to the rapture of the church; 4.4 (with the 24 elders) as representing the glorified church after the rapture; and chapters 5 and 6 as having reference to the beginning of the Great Tribulation.

But 4.1 is not spoken to the whole church. It is only spoken to John. "Come up hither" is an accomplished fact in the personal experience of John on the isle of Patmos. Otherwise, Philip's experience as recorded in Acts 8.29 might also be taken as signifying the rapture of the whole church.

As regards the 24 elders, it is rather absurd to deem them as signifying the glorified church, for the following reasons:

(1) 24 is not the number of the church; only seven or multiples of seven are, such as the seven churches in Asia.

(2) Nowhere in the Scriptures does "elder" ever represent the church. There are elders in the church and among the Jews,

but not all believers are elders. God first created the angels, then He chose the Jews, and finally gave grace to the church. How can the church bear the title of elders?

(3) In Revelation 4 and 5 we learn that the elders sit on thrones with crowns of gold on their heads, whereas Christ is standing there. Can the church receive glory before Christ is glorified? Thrones and crowns are symbols of kingship.

(4) The elders are clothed with white garments. Some suggest that these garments speak of Christ our righteousness for His blood has washed them white. Yet nowhere in the Scriptures is there mention made that the garments of the elders are washed with the blood. *Our* robes need to be washed with blood because we have sinned; but the 24 elders have never sinned.

(5) The elders never experience redemption. In chapter 4 we observe that they sing the song of creation. And we see in chapter 5 that though they sing the song of redemption, they sing not of themselves but of men who are purchased by the blood of the Lamb. "And madest them to be..."(v.10)—The word "them" here refers to the church. Now if it is the church who sings, would she use "them"?

(6) Revelation 4 deals with the universe and not with the church, the nations, or the Jews. And hence we may say that these are the elders of the universe. The church is not an elder of the universe.

(7) Revelation 5.8. The church cannot bring people's prayers to God.

(8) Revelation 7.13 If John also represents the church, it would then be the church asking the church.

(9) John calls one of the elders "My lord" (7.14), thus indicating that his position is lower than the elders. If the 24 elders represent the church, then John who is among the first in the church, should be the elder of the elders.

(10) The number 24 should be taken literally, not symbolically. Since one of the elders speaks to John, how can one twenty-fourth of the church talk to John? The number is fixed, and

hence the elders are fixed. These 24 elders are archangels who rule the universe. Even under Satan in his domain there are principalities and authorities.

D. 1 Thessalonians 4.16–17 Do not these verses speak of rapture? Obviously they do, yet they do not specify what time. They deal with the *fact* of rapture, not with the *time* of rapture. Thus, they.can not be used to prove pre-tribulation rapture.

E. 1 Corinthians 15.50–52 Whether dead or living, all will be raptured. Yet, again, it presents the fact of rapture without specifying a time sequence that would indicate a pre-tribulation rapture. On the contrary, it can be used to prove a post-tribulation rapture. "At the last trump" is a descriptive phrase that is equal to the seventh trumpet cited in Revelation 11.15. Some people advance the theory that according to Roman custom the trumpets are sounded three times. But the Holy Spirit follows no Roman law.

F. Luke 21.36 The Lord distinctly promises that the church may escape the Great Tribulation and "stand before the Son of man" —This no doubt refers to rapture. Nevertheless, there is a condition involved. Not for all who are simply born again, but for those born-again ones who watch and pray. "That ye may prevail"—If you watch and pray, you may prevail. Hence the promise is given to those who do these things. Does everyone in the whole church watch and pray? Let us pay attention to this.

G. Revelation 3.10 This is reckoned as being the strongest argument, yet it too is a promise with a condition. It therefore cannot be taken as evidence for the pre-tribulation rapture of the entire church. What is meant by "the word of my patience"? Today people revile Him and curse Him, but the Lord neither punishes them nor smites them with lightning and thunder.

Such is the patience of Christ in this age. Today we are patient together with Christ. We do not resist. But does every Christian keep the word of His patience in this manner? If so, the whole church would indeed be raptured. If this verse can be used indiscriminately to prove the rapture of the whole church before the Great Tribulation, then people can with equal justification forget the condition "whosoever believeth on him" and erroneously claim that all men are saved.

Furthermore, the promise of the Lord here is addressed to the church in Philadelphia, not to the whole church. If the church in Philadelphia can represent the whole church, then we may surmise that the entire church will be raptured before the Great Tribulation. Yet at that time there were actually these seven churches in Asia Minor, and the promise of the Lord was given to but one of these seven. Accordingly, the church in Philadelphia cannot represent the complete church; or else the overcomers in the other six churches mentioned will not be raptured.

II. This first school has not only no scriptural evidence but bases too much of its arguments merely on assumptions. For such a weighty problem like rapture, it should certainly not be decided on mere assumptions. Its assumptions are as follows.

A. Revelation 1–3 speaks of the church. After chapter 3 the church is no longer mentioned, so that she must have already been raptured by the time of chapter 4ff. (in the kingdom age, all will be righteousness and majesty; there will not be the patience of Christ). If chapters 1–3 refer to this age, chapters 4–19 will be the time of the Great Tribulation, in which the church has no part. This kind of argument is called the argument from silence.

However, we cannot say that from chapters 4 through 19 the church is never touched upon. Even though the word "church" is not used, many other descriptions employed do indeed fit the church, such as "didst purchase unto God with thy blood men of every tribe, and tongue, and people, and nation" (5.10), "the saints" (17.6), and "the armies which are in heaven" (19.14). Unquestionably the word "church" is not used, but who can say that those in view in the above examples do not belong to the church?

Furthermore, "the things which must shortly come to pass" (including the Great Tribulation) are shown to "his servants" (22.6), and "these things" (including the Great Tribulation) are testified "for the churches" (22.16). These things will not be written if they are not relevant to the church and to the believers.

B. After the church is raptured, there will still be very many on earth who shall be saved. These are the saints who come out of the Great Tribulation (see Rev. 7.9–17). They are saved during the Great Tribulation. There is a weakness in such assumptions by this first school which it must recognize; otherwise its adherents will be unable to round out their theory.

Let us understand, however, that the "great multitude, which no man could number" (7.9) must exceed the number of 200 millions ("twice ten thousand times ten thousand") which is the biggest among many numbers cited in the book of Revelation (9.16). Taking today's population at about 2 billions,* there will still be 1.5 billions after one fourth are killed (Rev. 6.8). Such a numberless multitude who "come out of the great tribulation" mentioned in the Revelation 7 passage must therefore have reference to those overcoming saints who come out of the great tribulation experienced by all believers throughout the twenty centuries of church history.

C. Before the Great Tribulation, the Holy Spirit returns to heaven. Since the church is with the Holy Spirit, it may be

---

*That is, in the early 1930's; but the world population for 1976 was estimated at about 4.3 billions.—*Translator*

assumed that the whole church is raptured before the Great Tribulation. The basis for this assumption is 2 Thessalonians 2.6–7 where the phrase "one that restraineth" is made to refer to the Holy Spirit.

Yet "one that restraineth" cannot be the Holy Spirit, for the subsequent clause—"until he be taken out of the way"—is not the proper terminology to be used in speaking about the Holy Spirit. The Third Person of the Trinity has many different names, such as the Spirit, the Spirit of glory, the Spirit of revelation, etc; and the word "Spirit" is usually present—and even though in one instance the word "Comforter" is used alone, yet from the next clause which follows ("even the Spirit of truth") it is evident that this has clear reference to the Holy Spirit (John 14.16–17). Never do the Scriptures say the Holy Spirit is "he that restrains"; moreover, how can the Holy Spirit be said to "be taken out of the way"? Furthermore, where does the Bible announce that the Holy Spirit is absent during the Great Tribulation? And how can there be the so-called believers of the Great Tribulation if the Holy Spirit is not present? For no one is saved without the Holy Spirit. He who is born of the Spirit is spirit.

Moreover, this matter of the Holy Spirit's presence during the Great Tribulation is clearly shown in Revelation 5: "and seven eyes, which are the seven Spirits of God, sent forth into all the earth" (v.6). The time of the Great Tribulation is the time of the latter rain (see Acts 2.15–21, Joel 2.28–31). The prophecy of Joel was not completely fulfilled on the day of Pentecost. For on that day there were no "wonders in the heaven and in the earth: blood, and fire, and pillars of smoke"; nor was "the sun . . . turned into darkness, and the moon into blood" (Joel 2.30–31). All of these five wonders will be fulfilled around and in the time of the Great Tribulation: blood (first trumpet), fire (first and second trumpets), smoke (fifth trumpet), sun and moon (sixth seal). Pentecost is only a miniature, a foretaste. Peter does not say: "It is fulfilled"; he merely says that "this is that" (Acts 2.16). As a matter of fact, the Holy Spirit is going to do greater work during the time of the Great Tribulation. If there will not be the Holy Spirit present, how can the saints ever endure during the Great Tribulation?

D. The disciples in the four Gospels are Jews. It is to them, that is to say, to the Jews, that the Lord exhorts to watch and pray. Since we Christians will be raptured anyway, there is no need for us to be exhorted to watch and pray. We go to the Epistles for our inspiration.

However, the disciples are Christians, and they too are in the church. Are not the disciples called Christians (Acts 11.26; cf. Matt. 28.19)?

E. Adherents of this first school of interpretation do not regard much of the four Gospels and the Acts as written for Gentile believers. C. I. Scofield, for example, maintained that the so-called Sermon on the Mount is exclusively for the Jews.

They forget, though, the words in Matthew 28.20 ("teaching them to observe all things whatsoever I commanded you") and in John 14.26 ("and bring to your remembrance all that I said unto you"). They base all their teachings on the words of the apostle Paul, whereas they should remember what Paul himself said in Colossians 3: "Let the word of Christ dwell in you richly" (v.16).

F. "This gospel of the kingdom shall be preached in the whole world . . .; and then shall the end come" (Matt. 24.14). They suggest that the gospel of the kingdom is different from the gospel of grace and that the gospel of the kingdom is only preached during the time when the Lord was on earth and immediately before the Great Tribulation. Since we are saved by the gospel of grace, it is their contention that the gospel of grace need not be preached to the whole world before we are raptured. Thus, the gospel of the kingdom will only be preached again ten or twenty years before the Tribulation.

Yet the gospel of the kingdom is the gospel of the kingdom of God, and the gospel of grace is the gospel of the grace of God. According to Acts 20.24–25, "the gospel of the grace of God" spoken of in verse 24 is none other than "the preaching" of "the kingdom" mentioned in verse 25. Also, please note from Acts 1 that the Lord after His resurrection spoke to the disciples "the things concerning the kingdom of God" (v.3).

　　　G. They view the work of Christ on earth as fulfilling the ministry towards the circumcised, thus showing a definite Jewish background; and therefore whatever is commanded in the Gospels is not for us Christians but is for the Jews.

Let me say in response, however, that the dispensation of Grace also begins with Christ. Please read the following passages: (1) Matthew 11.13–14 and Luke 16.16—where the phrase "from that time" in Luke means from the time of Christ; (2) Acts 10.36–37 and 13.25–27— where we see that "the word of this salvation" (13.26) begins to be preached at the time of John the Baptist; (3) Mark 1.1–15 and John 1.1–15—from which we learn that "the gospel of Jesus Christ" (Mark 1.1) commences with John the Baptist; (4) Luke 4.17–21—which verses describe the gospel of grace in a number of ways and concludes by recording the Lord Jesus as saying: "Today hath this scripture been fulfilled" (v.21); (5) John 4.23—wherein the phrase "and now is" indicates that during the dispensation of Grace those who worship God worship Him in spirit and truth (whereas under the dispensation of Law, men apprehended God in the flesh and according to rituals); and (6) John 5.24–25— which verses tell us that what is included in the phrase "and now is" is the gospel of grace.

　　　III. The Bible has sufficient evidence to prove that the church passes through the Great Tribulation. The following are some of the evidences.

A. 2 Thessalonians 2.1–9. Please read this passage very carefully. Verse 1 gives the topic of this passage—namely, the coming of Christ and rapture. Since the rapture spoken of here is a being gathered in the air, there is already a hint as to its being after tribulation. In verse 2, the word "spirit" signifies another spirit, not the Holy Spirit; the term "word" means rumor; "us" refers to Paul, Silvanus and Timothy; and "the day of the Lord" is the day of the coming of Christ and rapture. In those days there were people who deluded the Thessalonian believers by saying that the day of the Lord had already come and that they had been left behind. Yet verse 3 shows that this day will not arrive until after the following two signs: (1) that before rapture, there will appear the man of sin, the son of perdition, who is the Antichrist; and (2) that there will first come the falling away, which is apostasy. When will the man of sin be revealed? It will naturally be at the Great Tribulation. So that rapture will be after this Tribulation. At least part of the church must go through the Great Tribulation.

B. 1 Corinthians 15.50–55; 1 Thessalonians 4.16–17. The first passage dwells on resurrection and change; the second deals with resurrection and rapture. These two are parallel passages. All students of the Bible agree that the events in both passages happen at the same time. Is there any intimation as to the actual time for these events? Indeed, there is. "At the last trump" indicates that the time must be after the Tribulation. The first school of interpretation insists that the blowing of the last trumpet occurs before the Tribulation, but its adherents have not a single Scripture verse to support their view. The last trumpet is sounded after the Tribulation; it is the last of the seven trumpets mentioned in the book of Revelation. How absurd it would be if after the *last* trumpet had been sounded there would still remain seven more trumpets to be heard! It would be like having had the *last* son born, only to be followed by seven more sons.

Someone contends that the "trump" here is the trump of the church, not that of the Tribulation. Where, then, is there recorded in the Scriptures anything said about the *first* trump of the church? Still others say that Paul merely borrows from the Roman military custom, that as soon as the last trumpet is blown the entire army marches away. Yet the Scriptures have not adopted this Roman military practice. This "trump" is the trump of God, not of the church. Without a doubt it is the last of the seven trumpets cited in the book of Revelation. Furthermore, according to Revelation 10.7, at the sounding of the seventh trumpet the mystery of God is finished—which mystery is the church.

C. Other evidences are these:

(1) Matthew 24.3, 13.40, 28.20: "the end of the world"—The word "world" is *aion* in Greek, which means "age"—that is to say, the end of this age. Chronologically, the Great Tribulation falls in this age. If rapture is to occur before the Tribulation, there will be a gap of three years and a half.

(2) 1 Corinthians 15.25; cf. Acts 2.35: "till he hath put all his enemies under his feet"—This is factual after the Tribulation.

(3) 1 Timothy 6.14: "that thou keep the commandment, without spot, without reproach, until the appearing of our Lord Jesus Christ"— The appearing of the Lord Jesus Christ will occur after the Tribulation. If He is to come to the air before the Tribulation, would there be any need for waiting, watching, and keeping?

IV. Though there are evidences in the Bible on a posttribulation rapture of believers, this still does not imply that the *whole* body of believers will be raptured after the Tribulation. And hence this second school of interpretation has its errors too. For the Bible clearly indicates to us that some believers are raptured before the Tribulation. Here are some of the reasons for this view.

A. Were the *entire* body of believers to be raptured after the Tribulation, there would again be no need for us to watch and wait and be prepared. Knowing that the Lord would not come before the end of the three and a half years' period, we could live evilly up to three years five months and twenty-nine days. Yet such a concept violates the very principle of the Scriptures.

B. Were *all* of us believers to be raptured after the Great Tribulation, then our waiting would not be a waiting for Christ but for the Antichrist, since the latter must come first.

C. The church would lose her hope— "Looking for the blessed hope and appearing of the glory of the great God and our Savior Jesus Christ" (Titus 2.13)—for included in this hope is the blessing of escaping the Tribulation.

D. The second school of interpretation does not accept the idea of a secret rapture; yet its followers forget the word, "Behold, I come as a thief" (Rev. 16.15). A thief comes secretly, is never preceded by a band, and always steals the best.

E. This second school views the twelve disciples as being purely Christians in direct contrast with the view of the first school which considers these twelve as being merely Jews. As a matter of fact, however, these twelve disciples are Christians as well as representatives of the Jewish remnant. For example, in Matthew 10.5–6 and 23.3 we see that all have a Jewish background, a fact which is thus inapplicable to Christians.

F. There is a failure in this second school to distinguish between rapture and the appearing of the Lord. There is a difference between Christ coming *for* the saints and Christ coming *with* the saints. That which Enoch prophesied, as recorded in Jude, points to the coming of the Lord "with his holy myriads" (see Jude 14–15 mg.) when His feet step down on the Mount of Olives. So does the prophecy which is given in Revelation: "Behold, he cometh with the clouds; and every eye shall see him, and they that pierced him; and all the tribes of the earth shall mourn over him. Even so, Amen" (1.7). In taking the historical view, the second school of interpretation regards that part of Revelation up to chapter 17 as having already been fulfilled, with only the part from chapter 17 onward waiting to be fulfilled. (This is exactly opposite to the futuristic view taken by the first school of interpretation which deems only chapters 1–3 as having already been fulfilled, with the rest remaining to be so.) If the book of Revelation only records primarily things of the past, then how can the average child of God ever understand it? It would require doctors of philosophy and learned historians to comprehend it! Furthermore, it would no longer be revelation either!

V. As we have come to see, the first school lacks scriptural evidences while the second school, though it possesses many proofs, nevertheless has many errors too. What, then, does the Bible actually teach? Let us consider the following observations.

A. Revelation 3.10 "The hour of trial, that hour which is to come upon the whole world"—This is the Great Tribulation. This verse tells us that a certain class of people may escape the Great Tribulation, even those who keep the word of the patience of Christ. Instantly it tears apart the arguments of the second school of interpretation as well as those of the first. Although Philadelphia represents the true church in the dispensation of Grace, it is nonetheless only one of the seven local churches in Asia at that time. Thus it shows that only a relatively small number of people (one seventh) may be raptured before the

Tribulation. Furthermore, pre-tribulation rapture is not based purely on our being born again as children of God, but is dependent on one other condition, which is, our keeping the word of the patience of Christ. Do all believers today keep the word of the patience of Christ? Obviously not. It is therefore evident that not the *whole* body of believers will be raptured before the Tribulation.

The second school contends, however, that this passage of Scripture does not refer to pre-tribulation rapture, for it speaks of keeping— that God will "keep" them safely through the Great Tribulation: just as, for example, when an entire house is caught on fire, one room may be left untouched; or for example, when the land of Egypt came under the plague, the land of Goshen where the children of Israel dwelt in Egypt went unscathed (see Ex. 9.26, 10.23). Such an explanation is erroneous because (1) the "keeping" in view here is not a keeping *through* but a keeping *from*. In the Greek text, after the word "keep" in this verse there is the word *ek* which means "out of" (as in the word *ekklesia* which means "the called out ones"). Here, therefore, *ek* signifies a being kept out of the Tribulation. And (2) "Because thou didst keep the word of my patience, I also will keep thee from the hour of trial" (3.10a)—As we have seen, the trial which is to come upon the whole world is the Great Tribulation; but notice that it is not a keeping from the *trial* but a keeping from the *hour* of the trial. In order to be kept out of the hour of trial, we must *leave the world.* There are only two ways for God to keep us out: death and rapture. And hence part of the living will be raptured before the Tribulation.

B. Luke 21.36 also proves that not the entire church but only a part of it will be raptured before the Tribulation. The accounts of Luke 21 and Matthew 24 are quite alike, except that Matthew stresses more the coming of Christ and the Tribulation while Luke focuses more on the destruction of Jerusalem and the Tribulation. Hence there is the famous question asked in

Matthew (24.3), and there are also more parables recorded in Matthew's account than in Luke's. In 70 A.D. Jerusalem experienced a terrible destruction, and at the end she will experience a great tribulation. The record in Luke can be outlined as follows: 21.8-9 —the things before the end; 10-19—believers will suffer; 20-28—how Jerusalem will be destroyed (verse 28 seems to suggest that the saints will all pass through the Tribulation); 29-33 —a parable guaranteeing the certainty of these things to come; and 34-36—Were it not for this passage, it might be inferred that the whole body of believers would surely be raptured after the Tribulation: yet verse 34 has a change in tone from the preceding verses, verse 35 shows that the things mentioned earlier concern the whole inhabited world, and verse 36 presents the condition for escaping the Great Tribulation— which is to watch and pray.

How are believers to escape all these coming things and to stand before the Son of man? Naturally by being raptured. Death is not a blessing: we do not pray and expect death. The condition here for rapture is to watch and pray. Hence here, not all the regenerated may be raptured. Pray always. What to pray for? Pray that we may escape all these things which shall come to pass. "That ye may prevail" (or, "ye may be accounted worthy" AV). It is not a question of grace, but rather a matter of worthiness. How about worthiness? God cannot receive you to the place where you have no desire to go. Some people may consider heaven as too tasteless a place in which to live as may be indicated by these words: "Lest haply your hearts be overcharged with surfeiting, and drunkenness, and cares of this life" (v.34). If a balloon is tied, it cannot ascend. In sum, Luke 21.36 shatters the arguments of both the first and second schools of interpretation.

The second school may still raise other arguments, such as (1) that rapture is not dependent on conduct—yet in reply it should be asked whether anyone thinks a carnal believer lying on a bed of fornication will be raptured? Or (2) that the phrase "all these things" does not refer to the Great Tribulation but to the surfeiting, drunkenness, and cares of this life cited in verse 34. In reply, it should be noted that verse 36 reads, "all these things *that shall come to pass*"—whereas "surfeiting, and drunkenness, and cares of this life" pertain to the things *which are present now*. And therefore, "watch ye" means to not be deceived by such activities.

C. Other proofs as follows:

(1) By reading Matthew 24.42 together with 1 Thessalonians 5.2,4, it is evident *that there are at least two raptures:* for note that the first passage suggests rapture before the Tribulation because one must be watchful since he does not know when his Lord will come; while the second passage suggests rapture after the Tribulation because one knows when the day of the Lord shall come.

(2) The places to be raptured towards are also different. Whereas Revelation 7.15 mentions to "the throne of God" and Luke 21.36 mentions "to stand before the Son of man", 1 Thessalonians 4.17 says that it is to "the air"— Such distinctions would thus indicate that the entire body of believers is not raptured all at one time.

(3) Mark 13 states, "But of that day or that hour knoweth no one, not even the angels in heaven, neither the Son, but the Father" (v.32). So that the day of the coming of Christ is unknown. But 1 Thessalonians 4 declares that "the Lord himself shall descend from heaven, with a shout, with the voice of the archangel, and with the trump of God" (v.16). From this second passage we know that the appearing of Christ is after the sounding of the seventh trumpet. And hence the first passage relates to pre-tribulation rapture while the second relates to post-tribulation rapture.

VI. Questions raised against separate rapture, and answers thereto, are submitted below.

A. Some people say that the rapture of the church cannot be divided because the body of Christ cannot be divided. It should be noted in reply, however, that the body is a figure of speech which signifies one life. If the body is taken literally, then there is already division today because the Lord is now in heaven, Paul has already died, we remain living on earth, and some believers are yet to be born.

B. Others object that rapture is part of redemption, that since redemption is according to grace, rapture cannot be based on the concept of worthiness. In reply, it needs to be pointed out that while the act of changing (see 1 Cor. 15.51–52) is indeed according to grace, the act of being taken (rapture) is according to works.

C. Some observers ask, Is it not rather cruel to take away hope from the church? To which we must answer that in the Scriptures there is no such false hope given; and therefore it is better to alert people to this fact.

D. 1 Corinthians 15.23, say some, only mentions "they that are Christ's" and that nothing is said about works. But let us be aware that this verse does not speak of rapture, it speaks of resurrection.

E. Since the dead will not go through the Great Tribulation, would it not be unfair to the living for them to go through it? Will not the righteous God be unjust in this regard? In response, let me say that we do need to be concerned; for during the millennium each and every believer (including all believers who died prior to the Great Tribulation) will receive, as a consequence of appearing before Christ's judgment seat, the things done in the body while alive, according to what he has done whether it be good or bad (2 Cor. 5.10).

F. Since in 1 Corinthians 15.50–52 ("We all shall not

sleep, but we shall all be changed") "all" is the word used, surely this signifies the whole body. Yes, the "all" here does indeed refer to the entire body, but it does not have reference *to the same time.* For example, we all will die, but certainly not all of us will do so in one day.

G. There is a distinction made in the Bible between wheat and tares, some say, but no difference made between wheat and wheat; consequently, all wheat must be raptured. In reply, it should be noted that the times of ripening for wheat are not the same. Thus there are the firstfruits and the later harvest.

H. Some argue that according to 1 Thessalonians 4.15, the living "shall in no wise precede them who are fallen asleep" —The dead are resurrected at the seventh trumpet; and so timewise, rapture occurs after the Tribulation. Now if there is a first rapture, it will have to take place before the resurrection of the dead. But since this verse distinctly says "shall in no wise", how then can rapture take place twice? Let me say in reply that it is most precious and significant to find in both verse 15 and verse 17 the qualifying clauses "we that are alive, that are left"—Now to be alive is obviously to be left on earth; why, then, is there this apparent unnecessary repetition? Because it implies that there are people who though alive yet have already gone ahead (that is, raptured) and therefore are no longer left on earth. Would Paul enlist himself among this class of people who are alive and are left? Not at all. He uses the word "we" only because he is speaking at that moment of writing. And the proof of this is that since Paul no longer lives today, he cannot be numbered among those who are left on earth.

Our summary conclusion to all this is that the third school of interpretation seems to be the correct one—that is to say, that one group of believers will be raptured before the Tribulation while another group of believers will go through the Tribulation and be raptured afterwards.

THE GOSPEL ACCORDING TO MATTHEW

Chapters 24 and 25

How To Divide Jesus' Great End-Time Prophecy

Having gained an understanding of rapture, we will now proceed with Matthew 24 and 25. These two chapters deal with prophecies concerning (1) the Jews, (2) the church, and (3) the Gentiles. Aside from what is found in the book of Revelation, these two chapters contain the most significant prophecies for our present age. Whereas the book of Revelation gives details, the Gospel of Matthew treats only of principles. These two chapters are not easy to read. A hundred years ago* few seemed to pay any attention to them. Since 1828,** however, people have begun to study them carefully. Due to a difference in background, various students of the Bible advocate different interpretations on these chapters. In general, there are three varied schools of thought: (a) that all which is prophesied here pertains to the church, as advocated by Benjamin Newton; (b) that all in these chapters is related to the Jews, as championed by John Nelson Darby and C. I. Scofield; and (c) that some of the material in these two chapters concerns the church, as we maintain. The reason for such differences lies in one's understanding of

---

* It should be noted that the author gave these readings in the early 1930's.—*Translator*

** For the significance of this date, see footnote at 13.31–32 above.—*Translator*

who or what the disciples stand for: whether (a) the disciples represent the church; (b) the disciples symbolize the Jews; or (c) the disciples signify the Jewish remnant as well as the pillars of the church.

How to divide these two chapters is of utmost importance, else we will be confused by the first two schools.

Let us retrace our steps and once again review the background for these two chapters, as furnished for the reader of this Gospel in chapters 21 to 23. As recorded in 21.43 the Lord prophesies that the kingdom of God will be taken away from the Jews. In 22.21 we see that He charges the Jews to be submissive to the Gentile power. And in 23 we observe Him chiding the Pharisees. The "house" in 23.38 is the same as the "temple" in 24.1. There it should be stated as "my Father's house"—but it has come to be termed "your house". All this indicates that the Lord has clearly rejected the children of Israel. Such, then, is the background.

Before the Lord are two classes of people: (1) the rejected Jews, and (2) a nation that can bear fruits (21.43). In this connection, therefore, the disciples may represent (a) the Jewish remnant, and (b) the called out ones. Accordingly, we have a combination of the Jews and the church. It is highly important for us to find out which section relates to the Jews and which relates to the church. In our view (and in the view of others too, such as D. M. Panton who felt that 24.31 is a distinctive line of demarcation), 24.1–31 pertains to the Jews, while 24.32–25.46 pertains to the church. This division is based on internal as well as external evidences, as follows.

A. 24.1–31 concerns the Jews, since everything here is *literally* interpreted; but 24.32–25.46 concerns the church since everything there is *spiritually* interpreted. For example, "winter" in verse 20 is literal since it is in actual fact a difficult thing to flee in the winter ("sabbath" too is literal); "summer" in verse 32, however, is to be spiritually interpreted since it points to the soon coming of the kingdom (while the "fig tree" refers to the nation of Israel). Or as another example, in verse 26 "the inner chambers" must be interpreted literally, whereas in verse 43 "the house" is to be interpreted spiritually. Hence what concerns the Jews is to be literally interpreted; but what concerns the church is to be spiritually interpreted (see Matt. 13.11–13).

B. The part *before* 24.31 is full of Jewish background, as is made clear by the usage of such terms as "the holy place" (v.15), "in Judea" (v.16), and "sabbath" (v.20); but the part *after* 24.31 is plainly without any localized restriction in its terminology.

C. The things mentioned before 24.31 are physical in nature, whereas all those things mentioned afterwards are moral in character. For instance, the nations, the mothers with children, and the children mentioned in the first part are all physical or literal in meaning; yet the virgins, the servants and the householder, and the goats and the sheep cited in chapter 25 have moral implications about them. In addition, "go ... forth" in 24.26 and "went forth" in 25.1 are different in character, with the former being literal and the latter being moral in their implications.

D. Before 24.31 there is no moral demand included; what is required is to flee. But after 24.31 there are moral demands presented, such as watch, be ready, and so forth—which actions are the responsibilities of the saints at the end time.

E. Since the Jews are still expecting the Messiah, there are false Christs being mentioned before 24.31; but there is no word

about false Christs after 24.31, because the latter part is addressed to the church.

To sum up, then, Matthew 24.4–31 speaks to the Jews;
Matthew 24.32–25.30 speaks to the church; and Matthew
25.31–46 speaks to the church about the Gentiles. Perhaps an
outline of this would be helpful, as follows:

MATTHEW 24.4–31

Item	Verses	Prophecies	
1	4–6	Rumors of wars—Signs	
2	7–8	Wars, famines, earthquakes	
3	9–13	Persecution—Tribulation	
4	14	Preaching of the gospel of the kingdom	
5	15–22	Great Tribulation	Great Tribulation Is Come
6	23–28	False Christs, false prophets	
7	29–31	Change in celestial phenomena	

MATTHEW 24.32–25.46

Item	Verses	Prophecies		
1	24.32–35	Fig tree—Sign of end time	Signs	
2	36–42	The Days of Noah—*Parousia*		
3	43–44	Master of the house *vs.* thief	The Process of *Parousia*	Outward
4	45–51	Two kinds of servants		
5	25. 1–13	Ten virgins		Inward
6	14–30	Three servants		
7	31–46	Sheep and goats—The end		

Introduction: the Disciples' Threefold Question, 24.1–3

v. 1 When the disciples look back at the temple, they feel
glorious about it. No other nation on earth has such a holy place.
The stones at the outside are ground so smoothly that they are

exquisitely beautiful. The vessels of fine gold in the house glitter brightly and are of exceeding worth.

v.2 "See ye not all these things?"—Do not the "these things" here point to the huge stones and the golden vessels? For the Lord knows their mind well.

"Verily I say unto you . . . that shall not be thrown down"— What men see are the outward and the temporary, but the Lord with His spiritual insight sees through the visible. In the eyes of men today how very beautiful is the world and how civilized it is in material things. Yet by seeing with the spiritual eye of the Lord, man can recognize the fact that the earth with all its material objects will eventually be burned. Why then should we believers still mind the things of earth? Then too, typologically speaking, the holy temple may represent the church. How much of today's church remains only in name but has lost her reality. She maintains her services just like the temple of old.

Why does the Lord ask the question of the disciples and give the kind of response that He does? His very asking indicates that unless His disciples adopt the same attitude as He has, they will not be able to understand prophecy. People who are occupied with the world will not think of prophecy. The disciples are unable to obtain the light of prophecy through reading because they are blinded by the light emitted by the world. They do not know that, however good the world is, the day shall come when all will be consumed by fire.

Why does the Lord say here that such a beautiful temple will be left desolate to the children of Israel? Simply because the glory of the temple is not in gold, silver and treasures, but in the presence of the Lord. If the Lord is gone, what use is the temple with its gold and treasures of the world? And hence these things ought not be left behind for us to contemplate. Let us, as God's temple, be careful as to whether we have the presence of God or are merely maintaining an outward appearance.

"There shall not be left here one stone upon another, that shall not be thrown down"—In 70 A.D. this was fulfilled literally. The Roman soldiers under General Titus broke into Jerusalem, burned the temple, and scraped off all the gold which overlaid the stones by turning them over after the gold had melted into crevices between the stones.

v.3 "He sat on the mount of Olives"—The Gospel according to Matthew mentions "mountain" eight times, and each time it is connected with something special. Especially on two of these occasions we find that there is some similarity in the situation—namely, those of 5.1 and 24.3. On the mountain mentioned in 5.1 (even though it is not specifically named), the Lord declares the law of the kingdom of heaven, lays down the prerequisites for entering the kingdom, and unveils the fact of co-reigning with Him in the future. On the Mount of Olives (24.3) we shall notice that He concentrates on prophecies such as those concerning rapture, tribulation, and judgment.

Why speak on the mountain? Since the hearers must needs climb the mountain, this signifies the paying of a cost. All who are not willing to pay the cost cannot be expected to understand prophecy. The reason people do not like to listen to prophecy or deny the fact of the second coming is because they are unwilling to climb the mountain and pay the cost. There is quietness on the mountain, so too was there quietness on the isle on which John received the contents of the book of Revelation. The clamorous are not fit for studying prophecy.

The question of the disciples is threefold: (1) When shall these things be? (2) What shall be the sign of Your coming? and (3) What shall be the sign of the end of the world? These three should not be mixed up. In answering the disciples, our Lord replies one by one in three different parts. Regarding the answer to the first question, both Mark and Luke record it in great detail. Since Matthew's treatment is of a much broader scope, his record of this first question should be supplemented by Mark's and Luke's accounts in this particular area. Neither Mark nor Luke, however, treat directly the Lord's answers to the two other questions of the disciples, though there is no lack of teaching on their part concerning them. This is simply because Luke's primary objective, for example, is not rapture.

The Disciples' First Question

As to the first question ("When shall these things be?"), what are the "these things"? Since the phrase "these things" is cast in the plural number, there must be other matters in view besides the destruction of the holy temple. By looking into the background given in Matthew 23 (for we need again to remember that the division of the Bible into chapters and verses is not inspired), we will discern six things: (a) that the children of Israel are to be filled up with the sinful measure of their fathers (23.32); (b) that the Lord will send to them prophets and wise men and scribes (23.34), noticing as we do that the prophets spoken of here are not those of the Old Testament period since our Lord says "some of them shall ye kill and crucify" whereas in the Old Testament time there was no crucifixion; (c) that the Lord will avenge himself on the wicked children of Israel (23.35–36); (d) that the holy temple shall be destroyed (24.2); (e) that the house of Israel will look forward to the coming of the Lord and say, "Blessed is he that cometh in the name of the Lord" (23.39); and (f) that the Lord will gather the children of Israel as a hen gathers her chickens under her wings (23.37).

Since the disciples ask about these six things, the answers our Lord gives must likewise include all six of them. This we can see in chapter 24: (a) the children of Israel will be filled with the iniquity of their fathers (24.10–12); (b) the "you" in 24.9 are those who are sent by the Lord; (c) as a result of what the children of Israel will do to the prophets, the Lord will avenge himself on them with tribulation (24.21–22); (d) the holy temple will be defiled and destroyed as spoken of by Daniel (24.15); (e) the children of Israel shall expect the coming of the Lord (24.30)—for note that the phrase "all the tribes of the earth" refers to the twelve tribes of Israel; and (f) the Lord shall gather together His elect (24.31).

The Disciples' Second Question

Concerning the second coming ("What shall be the sign of thy coming?"), we need to distinguish three Greek words (1) *parousia*, (2) *apokalupsis*, and (3) *epiphaneia*.

The term used by the disciples in asking the Lord about His "coming" is the Greek word *parousia* which should be translated "presence"—it is used in the Scriptures 24 times. Besides the seven times wherein it applies to man (1 Cor. 16.17; 2 Cor. 7.6, 7; 10.10; Phil. 1.26, 2.12; and 2 Thess. 2.9), the remaining 17 occasions refer to the Lord (Matt. 24.3, 27, 37, 39; 1 Cor. 15.23; 1 Thess. 2.19, 3.13, 4.15, 5.23; 2 Thess. 2.1,8; James 5.7,8; 2 Peter 1.16; 3.4,12; and 1 John 2.28).

The word *apokalupsis* (meaning "uncovering" or "revelation") appears in the Scriptures in the following places: 1 Peter 1.7,13; 4.13; 1 Corinthians 1.7; and 2 Thessalonians 1.7. "Revelation" is given to help people to understand.

The term *epiphaneia* (meaning "appearing") is used in the Bible in: 1 Timothy 6.14; 2 Timothy 1.10, 4.1,8; Titus 2.13; and 2 Thessalonians 2.8 where this Greek term is translated as "manifestation" in English. The "appearing" is for the purpose of causing people to see.

The word "coming" in Matthew 24.3 is *parousia* ("presence"). Why does the Holy Spirit choose to use this particular term? Possibly because this matter of our Lord's coming is a rather complicated event and the Greek term *parousia* carries within its meaning a very broad scope.

The *parousia* (or "presence") of the Lord commences with the first rapture to the throne. "Be patient therefore, brethren, until the *parousia* of the Lord" (James 5.7). "Be ye also patient; establish your hearts: for the *parousia* of the Lord is at hand" (5.8). As we have noted earlier, all who have kept the word of the patience of Christ shall participate in the first rapture (Rev. 3.10).

Look further at 2 Peter 3.4, where the question raised is: "Where is the promise of his *parousia?*"

Then 1 Thessalonians speaks (1) of a standing before the Lord Jesus Christ at His *parousia* (2.19), (2) of the time of the *parousia* of the Lord with all His saints (3.13), (3) of how we shall all be caught up and meet the Lord in the air at His *parousia* (4.15–17), and (4) of having our spirit and soul and body preserved entire without blame at the *parousia* of our Lord Jesus Christ (5.23).

What are the things which transpire during the time of *parousia?* All who are Christ's shall be resurrected (1 Cor. 15.23). The *parousia* of the Lord is where the believers will gather together with Him (2 Thess. 2.1). In His *parousia,* He will deal with the Antichrist (2 Thess. 2.8). The lawless one will also have his own *parousia* (2 Thess. 2.9). If we abide in Christ we may have boldness and not be ashamed before Him at His *parousia* (1 John 2.28).

We deduce from these Scripture passages that *parousia* includes the throne and the air. Time-wise, it begins with the first rapture and ends with the appearing of Christ and His saints on earth. Thus *parousia* actually stands between the church and the kingdom. It comprises (1) the first rapture to the throne, (2) tribulation and the Great Tribulation, (3) the Lord descending to the air, (4) the general rapture of believers to the air, and (5) the appearing of Christ with His saints on earth. Perhaps the following diagram and the explanatory text which follows can make it clearer.

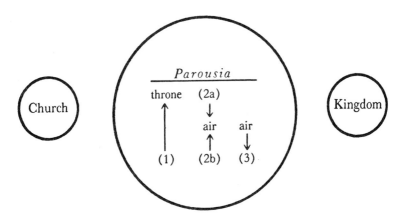

During *parousia* there are three periods which coincide with three locations: (see large center circle above): At the beginning of *parousia* (1) the overcoming believers are raptured to the throne (Matt. 24.37, 40–41). After some time (2a) the Lord descends from heaven to the air (1 Thess. 4.15–17, 1 Cor. 15.23)—(please remember that the throne is presently in heaven —Rev. 4.1–2). Meanwhile (2b) the dead in Christ shall rise, and those believers who are alive and left on the earth from the previous rapture (to the throne) shall, together with the risen dead in Christ, be caught up to the air. There they shall experience *parousia* with the Lord. And finally, *parousia* ends (3) with the appearing of the Lord with His saints from the air to the earth. He will bring to nought the Antichrist by the exploded glory of His *parousia* (2 Thess. 2.8–9).

What should be the attitude of believers toward *parousia?* Wait patiently (James 5.7–8); have the heart established unblamable in holiness (1 Thess. 3.13); and have one's spirit, soul, and body preserved entire without blame (1 Thess. 5.23).

What will happen to the believers in *parousia?* Each man's work shall be judged (1 Thess. 2.19, 1 John 2.28, 1 Cor. 3.12, 15).

The type of *parousia* is seen in 2 Peter 1.16,18.

Since *parousia* stands at the center of the entire body of truth concerning the end and the kingdom, it is essential to understand *parousia* thoroughly.

There are, as we have seen, two other words connected with *parousia:* (1) *apokalupsis*—that is to say, the Lord "reveals" himself by uncovering the veil around Him, and (2) *epiphaneia* —that after the curtain is raised you may see the Lord who has "appeared".

Many people assume that the appearing of the Lord will have to wait until He comes to earth. But this is a wrong concept. For *apokalupsis* and *epiphaneia* are also related to the church. True, the Lord shall appear so as to be seen by the world; even so, He also appears to the church. For *parousia* includes both *apokalupsis* and *epiphaneia*. If we have the *parousia* ("presence") of the Lord, we certainly have His *apokalupsis* (that is to say, He "reveals" himself to us) as well as His *epiphaneia* (that is, He is "seen" by us). As we wait for His *parousia,* we are also waiting for His *apokalupsis* and *epiphaneia*— to know and to see the Lord. We do not wait for His coming to earth. Though we do have the presence of the Lord today, this is spiritual and is by faith. We look forward to that day when we shall see Him face to face.

In the Greek text there is another word connected with the coming of the Lord which is worth noticing. That word is *erchomai*—which means "to come" and is therefore a verb. Now as we have seen, *parousia* is a noun and means "presence"—but since it is a matter of presence, it must involve at least two persons: for this reason, rapture is included in *parousia*. But in saying the Lord "comes" (*erchomai*), it does not include the rapture of the believers.

This word *erchomai* (or its variant) is used seven times in Matthew 24 and at least six times in Matthew 25 (24.5, 30, 39, 42, 43, 44, 46; 25.10, 11, 19, 31, 36, 39).

There is still another Greek word, *proserchomai*, which

means "to come forward" (see Matt. 24.1; 25.20, 22, 24).

Also the word *deute* (the plural imperative for *deuro*), which means "come here" or "come hither" (see Matt. 25.34).

And the word *heko*, which means "to be present" or "to come upon" (see Matt. 24.14, 50).

All these terms show how accurately the Bible chooses its words.

The Disciples' Third Question

Concerning the third question ("What shall be the sign . . . of the end of the world?"), two different Greek words are translated in the New Testament as the "world": (1) *kosmos*—the organized world, pertaining to the material part; and (2) *aion*—age, which points to time. When the Scriptures speak of that which is "of the world" (e.g., John 17.14), it means a being trapped by the things of the systematized world; when the Bible says "according to this age" (Rom. 12.2 mg.), it denotes a being caught by the current fashion of the time.

The Greek word used for the "world" here in verse 3 is *aion*. Therefore, what the disciples ask here is: "What shall be the sign . . . of the end of the age?" Now "the end of the age" is a specific term. It may also be called "the end" or "the consummation"—which refers particularly to the three and a half years comprising the Great Tribulation. This end of the age is the conclusion of the dispensation of Grace towards the Gentiles and the church. It begins with the rapture to the throne and terminates with the appearing of Christ and His saints from the air to the earth. Time-wise, "the end" coincides with *parousia;* but location-wise, they are widely different, for *parousia* is concerned with the things above while "the end" is concerned with the things on earth.

Let us again see when is to be the fulfillment of the first part of Matthew 24–25 (i.e., 24.4–31). Generally, there are two different interpretations: (1) that it was fulfilled in 70 A.D. when

Titus destroyed Jerusalem, since verse 2 has already been totally fulfilled; or (2) that it is yet to be fulfilled because the subject of Matthew 24 is the Great Tribulation. Among those who hold the first view is C. I. Scofield, and among those who advocate the second is J. N. Darby.

Seven arguments can be brought against the first view: (a) Though there were people who claimed to be Christ, yet none of them performed any wonder (24.24)—(b) "The abomination of desolation" (an idol is to be put in the temple) has not been fulfilled: the first school argues that this was fulfilled when the Roman flag was raised in the holy place—but when this happened, no Jew could flee anymore; yet 24.16 reads, "then let them that are in Judea flee unto the mountains"—(c) The Lord orders the Jews, upon witnessing the idol placed in the temple, to flee, that is to say, to flee in a hurry; but no such need to hasten was evident at the time in 70 A.D.—(d) The destruction of Jerusalem will affect the whole world, yet during the time of Titus such an aftermath did not happen—(e) In those days there was also no disturbance in celestial phenomena (24.29)—(f) The Lord will appear after the destruction, yet He did not appear after the destruction of Jerusalem in 70 A.D.—(g) This part from 24.4–31 is parallel to what is found in Revelation 6. The book of Revelation was written in or about 96 A.D. and the historical event involving Titus occurred in 70 A.D. Had this first part been completely fulfilled at the time of Titus, why should this old event which happened some 26 years earlier be gone over again by John in his prophetic writing?

The destruction of the temple (besides that by the Babylonians which took place around 586 B.C.) is to occur two times more. "The people of the prince that shall come shall destroy the city and the sanctuary," prophesied Daniel (9.26). Time-wise, this will come with the last of the sevens after the passing of 62 sevens. And the term "the end" is used repeatedly in Daniel 9 and Matthew 24 to show that this will be the second destruction (the first of these two having been that of Titus in 70 A.D.).

By comparing other Scripture passages, such as in Revelation, we will be able to understand more clearly this second destruction of the holy temple: "The court which is without the temple leave without, and measure it not; for it hath been given unto the nations: and the holy city shall they tread under foot forty and two months" (11.2).

By way of conclusion, then, we may say that in the first part of Matthew 24 and 25 (24.4–31), verses 4–6 of chapter 24 have already been fulfilled, verses 7–14 have not been entirely fulfilled since they are still in the process of being so, and verses 15–31 are yet to be fulfilled.

A Comparison of the Three Gospels

Mark 13 and Luke 21 also record the same general subject matter found here in Matthew 24 and 25, but there are differences from Matthew's account. All three Gospels have the first question: yet in the answer recorded, Mark and Luke give more details than does Matthew. And they differ from Matthew in the second question, and are even reversed in their emphasis with respect to the third question. Let us now note these differences as they pertain to all three questions.

Concerning the first question, Mark and Luke, as was indicated, are more detailed in the reply than Matthew. They give all which Matthew presents except for the statement that "this gospel of the kingdom shall be preached in the whole world for a testimony unto all the nations" (Matt. 24.14). Note, too, that Matthew's focus is more on the holy temple, whereas Luke has the holy city more in view ("But when ye see Jerusalem compassed with armies, then know that her desolation is at hand"— Luke 21.20): for the question in Luke is what shall be the sign for the destruction of the temple, the answer to which is given in terms of what will happen to Jerusalem. In Matthew, however, the parallel question involving a sign relates to the inquiry as to what shall be the sign of the end of the world.

Luke does not mention "false Christs" specifically, whereas both Mark and Matthew do mention them by that term (Matt. 24.23–24, Mark 13.21–22). This is probably due to the fact that Luke has already described them in general terms in 17.22–23.

The characteristic of Matthew is *parousia* which is covered by the disciples' second question recorded ("What shall be the sign of thy *parousia* and of the end of the world?"). How well, indeed, do the disciples ask this question, for *parousia* and "the end" occur simultaneously. This shows that the disciples have already attained to a certain understanding. Since Mark and Luke lay no emphasis on *parousia,* they do not record certain parables in Jesus' reply such as the days of Noah, the servants, the virgins, and the distribution of talents. These parables are very pertinent to the matter of *parousia.*

There is another point upon which all three Gospels do agree, which is, that all three speak to the church as well as to the Jews: Mark 13.5–27 is addressed to the Jews, 28–37 to the church; Luke 21.8–28 is addressed to the Jews, 29–36 to the church (notice that in both these Gospels, as in Matthew 24, the parable of the fig tree is spoken to the church).

With regard to the third question, that concerning the end, Mark and Luke seem to be in reverse of Matthew. For this question ("the end of the age") is related to the Jews as well as to the church. Matthew 24.20 says, "Pray ye that your flight be not in the winter, neither on a sabbath"—and no doubt this is addressed to the Jews. Luke, though, says this: "But watch ye at every season, making supplication, that ye may prevail to escape all these things that shall come to pass, and to stand before the Son of man" (21.36). Such prayer and exhortation is moral in nature, and is therefore directed towards the church. And the same is true of Mark 13.33–37.

Furthermore, neither Mark nor Luke includes the promise of Noah because the question of *parousia* is not recorded as having been raised by the disciples in their accounts (though of course it is in Matthew). The "days of Noah" phrase is especially related to *parousia*—to rapture (cf. Matt. 24.37–39a with 39b ff.).

In the second part of Matthew 24, there are two signs: (a) the days of Noah—the sign of *parousia;* and (b) the fig tree—the sign of the end of this age.

Mark and Luke do not have the parable of the sheep and goats, for they deal with the imminent arrival of the end, not the end of this age itself. The above parable depicts the end itself.

The fig tree should not be interpreted literally for it is a parable. It points to the restoration of the Jewish nation. The words "her branch is now become tender, and putteth forth its leaves" (Matt. 24.32) describe life in the nation. Due to the oppression by Hitler, 120,000 Jews recently returned to Palestine.* And even the rain, which had not fallen for about 2,000 years, is now beginning to fall.

Jesus' End-Time Prophecy, Part One:
Concerning the Jews, 24.4–31

v.4 The disciples have just asked about the destruction of the temple. This is a matter which deeply arrests their attention. In answering them, the Lord first warns them to be careful lest they be misled. For anyone studying prophecy, the preeminent safeguard which Jesus pronounces here is to "take heed that no man lead you astray"; yet how sad that many believers fall into errors because they do not pay attention to prophecy: "We have the word of prophecy . . . as unto a lamp shining in a dark place" (2 Peter 1.19). Not to be led astray exhibits that kind of spiritual discernment which will not take yea for nay, or nay for yea.

vv.5–6 By whom will they be in danger of being led

---

* Again, the reader should be aware that the author gave these studies in the early 1930's.—*Translator*

astray? (1) By false Christs. In his *Wars of the Jews*, the renowned Jewish historian Josephus recorded how false Christs and false prophets deceived the Jews by promising them miraculous deliverance. These false Christs were able to deceive the Jews because they had refused to believe in the real Christ. (2) By wars and rumors of wars. After the death of Christ, rumors of wars did spread abroad like wildfire.

"See that ye be not troubled: . . . the end is not yet"—The disciples asked when the temple would be destroyed, and the Lord answers with two signs: false Christs and wars. But do not mistake these phenomena as signifying *the end*. When these two signs are fulfilled, it only means that the holy temple shall thence be destroyed. And hence, do not be troubled by such signs, since all these phenomena must indeed come to pass—but the end is still not yet.

vv.7–8 Verses 7–14 deal with things that are "the beginning" while verses 15–31 deal with things at the end of this age. Hence verses 7–8 depict the conditions of the world through the twenty centuries of world history since the time of Christ. After "famines" there will be "pestilences" (AV). As the end approaches, such events will become more prominent and be greatly increased. We can therefore say that the world is now in the beginning of the end, since these phenomena have indeed intensified.

During the [first] World War ten million people lost their lives, and the loss of property was beyond calculation. Since that time, the aggregate of those who have died in numberless smaller wars has surpassed the number of dead lost in the World War. Since that time, the world has not known a single day of peace or rest: five million people have starved to death in Russia; 80 million Chinese died of starvation after the great flood. At one time six million people died of pestilence within a twelve-week period in South America; and five million people died in India. In 1923 a great earthquake in Japan destroyed much of the area in the cities of Tokyo, Kobe and Osaka in a few hours; and the death toll took over 150,000 lives. In 1927 the great earthquake that occurred in Kansu province in China took two lives out of every thousand people. On the average, there are three or four earthquakes each day. From a spiritual standpoint, peace on earth is the wonder, whereas the phenomenon of war is nothing to be surprised at. Formerly there was more the occurrence of nation rising up against nation (international war), but now there is more the incidence of people rising up against their own people (civil war).

Matthew 24.7–8 appears quite similar to the events surrounding the seals cited in the book of Revelation. The white horse of the first seal in Revelation 6.2 probably points to a fake Christ (cf. Matt. 24.5). The red horse of the second seal (6.4) is the war spoken of in Matthew, for red is the color of blood, and a sword obviously takes away peace. And without a doubt the red horse is now on earth. The black horse of the third seal (6.5–6) denotes famine, for people who are starved usually exhibit a black color on the face (cf. Lam. 5.10). The "balance" mentioned in 6.5 would seem to indicate that food is so expensive that every single milligram counts. A "shilling" is a day's wages (see Matt. 20.2). "A measure of wheat for a shilling" shows that what a man earns is not sufficient to support a family. "The oil and the wine" are luxuries, therefore they must not be wasted. The pale (or pale green) horse of the fourth seal (6.7–8) speaks of pestilence, since the faces of those who die of the plague usually look pale green. "Hades" is where the dead will go, hence it follows suit. Hades gathers up the dead through pestilence as a dustpan receives dust from the broom. The fifth seal has to do with the saints of God. The great earthquake of the sixth seal coincides with "earthquakes in divers places" spoken of in Matthew 24.7 (Revelation *mentions* an earthquake in five different places in the book, yet it actually *occurs* but three times, with the locale for all three being in the same vicinity—that of Jerusalem).

To sum up, there are altogether four plagues: war, famine, pestilence and earthquake. These four plagues are "the beginning of travail" (Matt. 24.8). She who travails in birth suffers pains and then experiences rejoicing. Before the Jews can experience the joy of the kingdom they must first pass through travail. Upon witnessing these various things, people may conclude that the end has come—not knowing, however, that they are but the beginning of travail. In Psalm 48.6 and 1 Thessalonians 5.3 the travail mentioned in both places refers to Gentile experience. When the world says "peace and safety" then travail suddenly comes upon them (1 Thess. 5.3).

Though these four plagues are travail, they are only the beginning of tribulation. The more severe tribulations are yet to come.

v.9 Here begins the real tribulation. Verses 9–13 form a small section which deals with persecution.

"You" here refers to the Jewish disciples. Recently such Jewish believers have been discovered in the northern part of Europe: they keep the commandments and the Sabbath, and also believe in the Lord Jesus as their Messiah. The "you" here are also the prophets mentioned in Matthew 23.34. These prophets and wise men will be persecuted, even killed (see James 5.6). Both Mark and Luke record this in greater detail. These Jews will be delivered up to synagogues and councils, but the Holy Spirit will guide them as to what to say and will speak through them. Mark 13, Luke 21 and Matthew 24 all speak of Jewish believers who are similar to the disciples sent "to the house of Israel" (see Matthew 10.6). But Luke 22.35–38 refers to the sending of the disciples to the Gentiles, for the dispensation of salvation had by that time already begun, and therefore those who were to go out now needed to take purse and wallet. Hence there is similarity between the prophecy here on the Mount of Olives and what is recorded in Matthew 10.5–6.

Then, too, let us compare: (1) Matthew 23.34 with Matthew 10.17–18; (2) Luke 21.14–15 with Matthew 10.19–20; (3) Matthew 24.9–10 and Luke 21.16–17 with Matthew 10.21–22; and (4) Matthew 24.13 with Matthew 10.22. The above all speak of the Jewish believers. The words "synagogues" and "councils" and so forth show a Jewish color. Since "all the nations" denote the unbelieving Gentile world, the "you" must refer to Jewish believers. According to Isaiah 49.9–10 the Jews will in the future be very zealous for the Lord in preaching the gospel. At the opening of the fifth seal in Revelation when the souls who were slain ask for vengeance, they are comforted by the Lord in His bidding them to rest for a little time until the number of all who are slain be fulfilled. These brethren mentioned in Revelation 6.11 who will be slain are the Jewish believers spoken of here in Matthew 24.9.

v.10 "Stumble"— "deliver"—"hate": These are words which describe the inevitable consequences of persecution (see also John 16.1–2, Matt. 10.36, Mark 13.12–13, and Luke 21.16).

v.11 "False prophets"— There are false prophets among the Jews (Hosea 9.7–17) as well as in the church (1 Tim. 4.1, 2 Tim. 3.13, 2 Peter 2.1,12). The purpose of these false prophets is to lead people astray.

v.12 The results of their enticement: (a) iniquity shall be multiplied, and (b) love shall wax cold. Such an environment creates the atmosphere for the coming of the Antichrist (see also Dan. 8.11–12,23, 11.30–31; Is. 65.11–15, 66.3–4; 2 Thess. 2.11–12).

v.13 "Endureth to the end"—Always waiting, always

looking for the Lord. The word "saved" here is different in meaning from a being saved in order to receive eternal life.

      v.14 "This gospel of the kingdom" is a phrase used three times in Matthew: 4.23, 9.35, and here in 24.14. In the original the word "heaven" is not attached to it. And hence it is the gospel of the kingdom. Paul states in the Letter to the Galatians that there is only one gospel (Gal. 1.6–7).

      Whatever description is attached to the term "gospel" here, the gospel is still one. Many think that "the gospel of the grace of God" mentioned in Acts 20.24 is different from the gospel of the kingdom. But this is not so. The gospel remains the same, though it is viewed from different perspectives and hence is called by different appellations. The gospel of the kingdom is the gospel which our Lord himself proclaimed while on earth. When the kingdom comes, the Lord shall reign. Its proclamation is accompanied by the healing of the sick and the casting out of demons as evidence. The gospel of grace stresses the question of sin and God's way of redemption, whereas the gospel of the kingdom emphasizes the sovereignty of the Lord. This kind of gospel will be preached throughout the world before the end shall come. Those who preach this gospel of the kingdom will be Jews, not the church. For if it is the church that thus preaches, the wording here would be differently formulated as signifying a testimony "unto all sinners" and not as "unto all the nations" as is the case here in verse 14.

      The Biblical proofs that the Jews shall be the ones who will bear such a testimony to the nations are as follows:

      Isaiah 40.5–9 The term "all flesh" includes the Gentiles.

      Isaiah 42.10 "Ye that go down to the sea, and all that is therein, the isles, and the inhabitants thereof"—These are the nations. Now the one who says this is Jacob (see 41.8, 42.1), who is also Israel.

Isaiah 44.8 Jacob shall indeed witness and testify: but what will Jacob testify? See the Psalms: 145.10–13; 96.3–4,10; and 68.9,11.

The purpose of preaching the gospel of the kingdom is to testify to the nations—for not necessarily will all the Gentiles repent and be saved. According to Revelation 3.10 the Great Tribulation is to come upon the entire world. Consequently, an opportunity is given to the world's inhabitants to escape.

"Then shall the end come"—Verses 15–31 to follow relate the things at the end. Today we are yet in the situation described in verses 7 and 8 above. Before we see the end, we hear and observe its coming. How long the period is before the circumstances described in verse 15ff., nobody knows; yet we do know this—that the length of time covered by verses 13–31 will amount to three and a half years.

v.15 "The holy place" may mean the land of Judea, Jerusalem, the temple, or the holy of holies.

"The abomination of desolation" refers to an idol. In the future when Antichrist shall come, he will place his image in the temple. This will mark the beginning of the Great Tribulation (for notice the words "then" and "those days" in verses 16,19 and 21.) For the end of the Great Tribulation, see verses 29 and 30. Soon after the Tribulation is over the Lord shall appear. Thus the Tribulation commences with the placing of an idol in the temple and ends with the appearing of Christ on earth. How long is the Great Tribulation? Forty-two months (Rev. 11.2), or 1260 days (Rev. 11.3, 12.6), or a time and times and half a time which is three and a half years (Rev. 12.14). What Matthew speaks concerning the destruction of the holy temple is the same as that to which Revelation 11.2 refers as the treading under foot of the holy city. By reading Luke 21.20,23 and Matthew 24.15–21 together, we know that the holy city and the holy temple will be destroyed at the same time. So the end, which is the Great Tribulation, lasts for 42 months from the time of the placing of an idol in the temple to the moment of the appearing of the Lord.

PROPHECIES CONCERNING "THE END" AS FOUND IN THE OLD TESTAMENT:

"What do ye devise against Jehovah? he will make a full end; affliction shall not rise up the second time" (Nahum 1.9).

"Our end is near, our days are fulfilled; for our end is come" (Lam. 4.18b). The end is come, so flee.

"An end: the end is come upon the four corners of the land. Now is the end upon thee . . ." (Ez. 7.2b-3).

". . . for the vision belongeth to the time of the end . . .; for it belongeth to the appointed time of the end" (Dan. 8.17,19).

". . . the end shall be at the time appointed . . . because it is yet for the time appointed. . . . And at the time of the end . . ." (Dan. 11.27,35,40).

". . . seal the book, even to the time of the end . . . for the words are shut up and sealed till the time of the end. . . . How long shall it be to the end of these wonders? . . . It shall be for a time, times, and a half; and when they have made an end of breaking in pieces the power of the holy people, all these things shall be finished" (Dan. 12.4,9,6,7).

"Abomination" is a Jewish saying for an idol (see Deut. 29.17; 1 Kings 11.5-7; 2 Kings 23.13; Jer. 4.1, 13.27).

"Of desolation" has a double meaning: (1) If there is an idol, God will certainly bring in destruction. An idol causes destruction, therefore it is called an abomination of desolation. (2) Antichrist is also called "one that maketh desolate" (Dan. 9.27). Hence he is that abomination who works destruction. "Apollyon" (Rev. 9.11), which in Greek means Destroyer, is the Antichrist who is also the Destroyer.

As to how Antichrist makes desolate, the book of Daniel gives a detailed picture. See Daniel 11.30-31, where "the holy covenant" is none other than the Ten Commandments which God had covenanted with the children of Israel, and where the phrase "them that forsake the holy covenant" points to the rebellious Jews. "Upon the wings of abominations shall come one that maketh desolate" (Dan. 9.27) are words which mean that he who makes desolate shall come swiftly. "From the time that the continual burnt-offering shall be taken away, and the abomination that maketh desolate set up, there shall be a thousand two hundred and ninety days" (Dan. 12.11): this is a month more than the 1260 days of Revelation 11.3 This additional month may be the period that will be used for the judgment of the sheep and the goats after the Great Tribulation.

In the New Testament, 2 Thessalonians 2.3–4 mentions the revealing of the Antichrist, and verse 9 speaks of his working lying wonders. Revelation 13.1–6 and 11–15 describe two beasts, which represent the Antichrist and the false prophet. "Sea" (in Rev. 13.1) signifies the nations, while "earth" or "land" (in Rev. 13.11) signifies the Jews. After the resuscitation of the Antichrist, the false prophet will make for him an image and cause the people in the world to worship it. This is the image which will be placed in the holy temple. "Let him that readeth understand" (Matt. 24.15b): the Holy Spirit has this word inserted in this passage because this matter of the Antichrist having "the abomination of desolation . . . standing in the holy place" is most easily misunderstood and that therefore the study of Matthew 24 must be done by making comparison with Daniel and the other prophets.

Many maintain that Matthew 24.15 refers to the condition of the church, but this is impossible; for the Lord mentions Daniel here, and none of the Old Testament prophets ever prophesied about the church. Some suggest that the Lord is aiming here at the destruction of Jerusalem in 70 A.D., but this too is inaccurate since the prophecies of Daniel about the resurrection of the dead, the purifying of the holy temple, the knowing of the wise, and so forth were not fulfilled at that time.

Matthew 24.15–31 is not yet fulfilled. Though the narrative in Luke 21.20–28 seems quite similar to that which is described here, most of what is in Luke has already been fulfilled in the war of Titus. For let us see that the objectives of Luke and Matthew are not the same. Luke emphasizes the destruction of Jerusalem whereas Matthew stresses the destruction of the holy temple. What Daniel stresses is also the destruction of the holy temple, and consequently Matthew quotes from him. Luke lays no special emphasis on the things at the end; he merely cautions that these things are aproaching; and hence what he records has mostly been fulfilled in Titus, though some elements are still left to be fulfilled in the future. Prophecies in the Bible often follow this principle, namely, that there is a partial fulfillment at the first, to be followed later on by a complete fulfillment. At the time of Titus, the believers fled only from Jerusalem to Pella.

"They shall fall by the edge of the sword" and "shall be led captive into all the nations" (Luke 21.24a) are things which have been fulfilled. "Jerusalem shall be trodden down of the Gentiles, until the times of the Gentiles be fulfilled" (v.24b): down to our present day this has been the case, for even today* the land of Judea, including Jerusalem, is yet in the hand of the Gentiles.** Without a doubt Luke 21.25 still refers to some future time.

Concerning the end, there are two explanations: (a) the Great Tribulation, and (b) the great trial. The former pertains to the Jews (see Dan. 12.1, Matt. 24.21—Daniel plainly speaks

---

*Again it should be noted that the author gave these studies in the early 1930's. —*Translator*

**Some students of prophecy are now suggesting that because Jerusalem came into the hands of the Jews (following the Six Days War in 1967), the "times of the Gentiles" has been fulfilled. This event may indeed have marked such a fulfillment.—*Translator*

to the Jews); the latter to the Gentiles (see Rev. 3.10). The following diagram may be of help here:

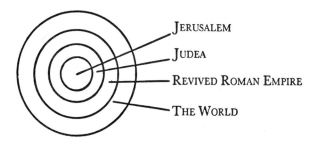

So far as *the Great Tribulation* is concerned, the center is Jerusalem and the circumference is Judea. So far as *the great trial* is concerned, the center is Rome and the circumference is the world. The throne of the beast and his kingdom cited in Revelation 16.10 refers to revived Rome. During the period of the end, the Great Tribulation and the great trial run together. The centers are Jerusalem and the revived Roman Empire, and the respective circumferences are the nation of Judah and the whole world.

In studying Matthew 24 special attention needs to be paid to Matthew 23.38: "Behold, your house is left unto you desolate": here the Lord openly declares His rejection of the Jews *as a nation* (individually, of course, they can still be received). So that Matthew 24 deals with the things concerning them, though not speaking directly to them. When the Lord delivers these prophecies to the disciples, the latter do not represent the Jewish nation but represent, in a double capacity: (1) the Jewish remnant who are faithful to the Messiah and who believe in the Lord Jesus as the Messiah; and (2) the church, for they are the pillars of the church. Verse 31, however, is the dividing line, since what follows that verse is related to the church.

Consider once more the questions asked by the disciples: (1) When shall these things be? (2) What shall be the sign of Jesus' coming? and (3) What shall be the sign of the end of the world? What exactly are "the coming" and "the end" about which the disciples ask? Their understanding is quite different from ours. In their mind, they have no conception of the church. Even at the ascension of the Lord they were still asking this question: "Lord, dost thou at this time restore the kingdom of Israel?" (Acts 1.6) Then, too, after the descent of the Holy Spirit on Pentecost, these disciples were most reluctant to leave Jerusalem. At first Peter was not willing to go to the house of Cornelius; but even after he went, his brethren quarreled with him. Hence "the end" in their thinking constantly harked back to the concept of "the end" in the Old Testament sense: after the end, the Messiah will reign. So that the end to them is that age or period just prior to the kingdom. Though the disciples asked in ignorance, the Lord will not *answer* them wrongly because they have *asked* wrongly. Ignorance cannot and will not hinder our Lord from giving the right answer. The Olivet prophecy in Matthew 24 has therefore much to do with the church.

Let us now return to verse 15 of Matthew 24. We earlier learned that the period from the setting up of the image to the appearing of Christ will be three and a half years. Soon after the image is placed in the holy temple, the latter's destruction will not be far away. The Destroyer will first *defile* the temple before he *destroys* it (see Ps. 74.3–7, Is. 64.10–11, Lam. 4.1, Dan. 8.11). Why will God allow the temple to be defiled and destroyed? Because the Jews have already defiled it (see Jer. 32.34, Ez. 8.5–15).

v.16 "Flee"—This is similar to the fleeing of the woman into the wilderness cited in Revelation 12.6. The dragon tries to swallow the woman, that is to say, Satan will persecute the Jews. Consequently, the woman must flee. "Water as a river" (Rev. 12.15) may mean armies, but the earth will open her mouth and swallow the armies. If the Jews will listen to the command in the prophecy and flee, they will be nourished for 1260 days. Fleeing is to their advantage.

v.17 "On the house-top"—A Jewish house has a flat top with stairs both inside and outside by which to reach it.

"Not go down to take out the things that are in his house" — which means that he is not to come down via the inside stairs nor to enter into his house and take things from it, but to flee by the outside stairs.

v.18 "In the field"—He who works in the field should flee quickly. He must not go back to his house "to take his cloak": he ought not treasure material things because tribulation will swiftly come: if he delays, he will be hurt.

v.19 "Them that are with child and to them that give suck"—Woe to them, for fleeing is inconvenient and highly unsuitable to such ones, for they cannot flee quickly.

v.20 "Winter"—People can neither flee speedily nor spend the night in the open. The temperature on the mountains is much cooler than that in the plains. And there is no food or water.

"Sabbath"—This word proves beyond doubt that verses 4–31 are related to the Jews. On the sabbath, the Jews are not permitted to walk more than 4854 feet (see Acts 1.12).

v.21 "Great tribulation"—Such a great tribulation is definitely coming, but through grace and prayer it has been delayed (see Ex. 32.30–34; see also Is. 6.7, Deut. 4.30–31, Jer. 30.6–7, Dan. 12.1; and also Rev. 12 where it is told that Michael chases away the dragon). God's disciplinary whip may be slowed down, but remember, it is neither canceled nor locked up. It may fall suddenly at any moment. The case of Nebuchadnezzar should serve as a good example of this.

v.22 Other passages which record the Great Tribulation to come are Isaiah 13.9–11 and 26.14,21. How terrible those days must be! The Lord will consequently shorten the days to only three and a half years, for otherwise no flesh would be able to stand it.

vv.23–24 The purpose of these verses is to show that the *parousia* of the Lord is not secretive towards the Jews, rather is it to be an open affair. He will not manifest himself only after being on the earth for some time. No, the Lord shall come in the clouds and appear on the earth. Hence this section serves as a warning to the Jews lest they be deceived by the Antichrist. The Lord's coming will be neither "here" nor "there"—but it will quite clearly come out of heaven. Christian believers have no such problem, but the Jews do. Because they have rejected Jesus, they are still waiting for a Messiah who will dwell in their midst. Here or there means anywhere. Yet Christ shall come from heaven as lightning comes forth (see v.27). Therefore, all who claim to be Christs manifested on earth are false Christs.

False Christs and false prophets are in plural number, thus indicating that there shall be more than one. Great signs and wonders will be performed during the three and a half years. And why? For the simple reason that the dragon will give his power to the first and the second beasts. Both 2 Thessalonians 2 and Revelation 13 record the wonders performed by these big three. Such wonders are not mere tricks or magic; nevertheless, the intention behind these wonders will be to cause people to believe in lies. They are the very opposite of the wonders of the Lord, which aim at leading people to believe the truth. The more we observe how evil spirits work wonders even in our own day, the more we are convinced that the lies of Satan are very real. Christians who live in the end time need to be especially careful. We receive the truth not because of seeing wonders, but because of trusting in the word of God. Take note that wonders will be greatly increased in the last days.

"So as to lead astray, if possible, even the elect"—The elect point to the Jews (Is. 45.4, 65.9; Deut. 7.6), though so far as the applicability of this verse's teaching goes, we Christians are not completely excluded. We also have the possibility of being deceived. He who thinks he stands should take heed lest he fall.

v.25 "Behold, I have told you beforehand"—How precious are these words, because the Lord foretells to us the things at the end. Is it not great to know future things? We may thus escape the unexpected. Unfortunately, saints fail to treasure these words. Whenever the Scriptures use the term "Behold" it suggests that something important will follow. Accordingly, we know the significance here of this Olivet prophecy. The word of prophecy, we are told, is likened to a lamp shining in a dark place (2 Peter 1.19). Neglecting it, one may easily fall into darkness. Many nowadays look upon society, nation, or the world with great expectation and hope. How misplaced is such hope. And this is because they lack the shining lamp. The Lord has told us beforehand. If we suffer at the end, we ourselves will be held responsible.

v.26 False Christs (and false prophets) have already been mentioned or alluded to several times (see verses 5,11,23,24). Here they are again alluded to in order to show how serious the situation is. "The wilderness" speaks of any place that is separated from the general intercourse with the world. While John the Baptist was in the wilderness he was asked if he were the Christ. "Inner chambers" denote a secret place, that which is not open to the public. Human psychology is such that it attaches great power and attraction to anything secretive. Yet the moment something becomes open, it loses its power. Did not the Corinthian believers, for example, despise Paul, saying that "his bodily presence is weak, and his speech of no account" (2 Cor. 10.10)?

v.27 "Lightning" flashes in the sky and everybody sees it,

whereas by contrast "the wilderness" is hidden from many eyes. The Lord's appearing is absolutely open. He shall come in the cloud. If anyone suggests that the Lord will come to the earth stealthily, do not believe him. Nevertheless, the *first* rapture does happen secretly, and the Lord's coming from the throne to the air is also in secret. Just as the lightning is first hidden in the clouds until the time of its flashing in the sky, so Christ will hide himself in the cloud until the right moment for His appearing (see Rev. 1.7, Acts 1.11). According to the record of the book of Acts, at His ascension the Lord was first taken up without any cloud, and only then was He received by a cloud. Even so shall be His coming again, except the order will at that time be reversed. First, He will be hidden by the cloud (which will include the rapture), and next will He appear publicly (by that time all the saints will have been raptured before His appearing). So that what we are waiting for in *parousia* is not the *coming* but the *going*.

v.28 "Carcase" and "eagles"—The word "carcase" is commonly interpreted as representing "Christ" and the term "eagles" as symbolizing Christians. According to this interpretation, this has reference to the breaking of bread, in that after the death of Christ the Christians eat His flesh. But such interpretation is not only untrustworthy, it is also absurd; it even borders on blasphemy. For the Scriptures speak of the life of the Lord as well as the death of the Lord. The One in whom we believe is the Lord who was dead and has been resurrected: for "if Christ hath not been raised," says Paul, "then is our preaching vain, your faith also is vain" (1 Cor. 15.14). Furthermore, a "carcase" (or corpse) decays and stinks (see John 11.39). Thus this word cannot point to Christ.

How, then, should this word be explained? (a) A corpse plus life equals a living person; a living person minus life equals a corpse—so that "carcase" here represents that which has no life, which in other words stands for all who are in Adam (see 1

Cor. 15.22). Believers are no longer in Adam; having received new life, they cannot be called by this term "carcase": instead, they are called the body of Christ. When they break the bread, they are not dividing up the Lord's corpse; for the Lord says, "This is my body" (and where there is life, such is not a corpse). (b) A corpse stinks as it decays (John 11.39 mg.; 1 Cor. 15.50,53). That is why a man is buried after he dies (see Gen. 23.4). Hence "carcase" here also signifies the decay of those dead in Adam.

The word "eagles" has several applications in the Bible: (a) The people of God. See Isaiah 40.31 and Deuteronomy 32.11. These two passages lay stress on the flying of the eagles. (b) In Leviticus, an eagle is classified as an abomination among the birds (11.13), for it devours dead flesh (see Rev. 19.17–18, 21b). The devouring of corpses by eagles ("all the birds that fly in mid heaven") as told in Revelation signifies God's judgment; so too is it here in Matthew. Wherever the corruption of the dead in Adam is, there also is the judgment of God. (Both the words "eagles" and "carcase" are interpreted spiritually here because the word "lightning" in the preceding verse is used in parabolic fashion too).

v.29 The words "immediately after" are most important in fixing the time. The sun and the moon and the stars should be taken literally. Some try to explain them symbolically as kings, princes and chief captains being shaken; but such an interpretation is unacceptable; because were this the case, the sun and moon and stars would have had to have been shaken before the appearing of the Lord.

The distress mentioned here in Matthew 24.29 is the same as that spoken of in Revelation 6.12–13—except that the time is different. In Revelation we notice that all seven seals (of which these celestial phenomena are the consequences of the sixth seal) are broken at the *beginning* of the Tribulation, with the seals then followed by further and greater trials in the trumpets and bowls; but here these same celestial things occur *after* the Tribulation: "But immediately after the tribulation of those days"; hence at the beginning of the Great Tribulation there is a change in these celestial bodies, and likewise at the end of the Tribulation there is still another celestial catastrophe. What we find stated in Joel 2.31 is the same as the sixth seal in Revelation 6, for Joel plainly mentions that these things will occur "before the great and terrible day of Jehovah cometh" (2.31b). Matthew, though, clearly states that such phenomena will take place "immediately after the tribulation of those days" (24.29). These changes in celestial bodies must therefore happen twice.

v.30 "Then" is the time after what is described in verse 29 has happened. We do not know what will be this sign of the Son of man. The familiar views are: (a) the Lord himself— but this is unacceptable since the Lord declares explicitly "the sign of the Son of man" and not the Son of man himself; and (b) the cross—with this being based on the sign of Jonah which the Lord gave to the scribes and the Pharisees as noted in Matthew 12. Although this is a definite possibility, we do not have a full conviction that it is so. Consequently, we will reserve our judgment on this view. One thing we do know, however, is that this sign must be something supernatural and mysterious.

"In heaven"—Since the sign appears in heaven, all the tribes of the earth shall see it. "All the tribes of the earth" refers to the twelve tribes of Israel. They shall mourn and weep (see Zech. 12.10–14).

With power and great glory"—At His first coming, the Lord manifested both great *authority* (in that He cast out demons and healed the sick) and glory. At His second coming, He will manifest *power* and glory. At His first coming, people marveled at His teaching and authority (Matt. 7.28). The Pharisees questioned Him as to the source of His authority (Matt. 21.23). A centurion believed in His authority (Matt. 8.8–9). But at His second coming, He will not only manifest authority but also power. He will not ride on a colt (as the Prince of Peace) but will ride instead on a white horse. Power is used in executing the judgment of God. In the future Satan will greatly increase his lawless works; so the Lord will destroy him with power. The difference between power and authority may be illustrated by the driving of a car (power) in contrast to the directing given by a policeman (authority). At His first coming our Lord healed the sick, cast out demons, and calmed the storm— all these being demonstrations of authority. Even when He overturned tables and drove out sheep and oxen with a scourge of cords, He did not use the whip on men. Only at His second coming will He exercise such power.

v.31 This verse is the fulfillment of Matthew 23.39: "Ye shall not see me henceforth, till ye shall say, Blessed is he that cometh in the name of the Lord"—After the Great Tribulation, the Lord will "gather together His elect": the "elect" or "chosen" are the Jews who are scattered among the nations. "From the four winds, from one end of heaven to the other"— This does not denote rapture, for here it is the idea of *erchomai*, not *parousia*. Here is a gathering together (see Deut. 30.3–5). After the destruction of Jerusalem, the Jews were either killed or captured. They were scattered to the nations. Now, the Lord begins to call them back (see Is. 43.5–7). They shall return from the east, the west, the north, and the south. Some shall even come from the land of Sinim (Is. 49.9–13). Now Sinim means China, and in Hunan province there is a large number of Jews, who, incidentally, take the family name of Tsan. See also Isaiah 49.22–26, 51.11, 56.8, 60.4, 62.10–12, 27.13; Ezekiel 34.13, 37.21, 28.25. "From the four winds"— Wind is moving all the time: the Jews have no settled place in which to live but wander all over the world.

The gathering spoken of here is not the rapture of the church, because (1) *parousia* has already passed, and rapture is within the scope of *parousia;* (2) this is a gathering together, and hence it has no connection with *parousia;* (3) if it were indeed *parousia* it would be totally foreign to the meaning of the preceding passage; (4) by it pointing to the Jews it agrees with Matthew 23.37; (5) at the trump of God, the Lord would come to the air; and (6) the context proves to be concerning the Jews.

Jesus' End-Time Prophecy, Part Two:
Concerning the Church 24.32–25.30

A. LESSONS FROM THE FIG TREE AND THE DAYS OF NOAH, 24.32–42

v.32 The word "now" marks the beginning of the second part. Since the Lord gives this part of His prophecy on the Mount of Olives—a place where there are many fig trees —He quite naturally could use the fig tree as an illustration. "When her branch is now become tender"—This speaks of the return of life. "And putteth forth its leaves"—This means the manifestation of life. The fig tree represents the Jews (Jer. 24.2,5,8). Earlier the Lord had cursed the fig tree which possessed only leaves but had no fruit. In reality the curse was upon the Jews who possessed the outward rituals but had no reality. "Summer" is the season of growth as winter is the season of withering and death. In the summer, life shows its greatest vigor, the air is warm, and the days are bright. It is a golden season, and therefore it stands for the kingdom. The Jews today are in the winter time. Winter points to tribulation, particularly the Great Tribulation. Spring speaks of rapture (see S.S. 2.10–14); summer speaks of the kingdom (see Luke 21.30–31). In Luke 21.29–30 we have the words "and all the trees"— which phrase represents the nations (see Daniel 4.10–17 and Judges 9.8–15). When "all the trees ... now shoot forth" (Luke 21.29–30), this is a signifying that nationalism will have been greatly developed among many peoples and nations.

v.33 Let us understand that the preceding verses 4–31 form a part and are not a break with what follows; and hence the thoughts in the earlier part are continuous into the next. The major difference between 24.4–31 and 24.32–25.46 lies in this: that the one part speaks about the Jews while the other part speaks about the church.

"All these things"—Such words should be connected with 23.36 ("All these things shall come upon this generation"), with 24.6 ("these things"), and with 24.8 ("all these things"). "All these things" have reference to the beginning of tribulation, as reflected in such things as false Christs, wars, famines, pestilences, earthquakes, and so forth.

"He is nigh"—"It is nigh" (mg.) is the more accurate rendering of this phrase in the Greek text. The "it" points to the kingdom. The kingdom is near, "even at the doors": this agrees with Luke—"Even so ye also, when ye see these things coming to pass, know ye that the kingdom of God is nigh" (21.31).

v.34 "This generation"—The Greek text is *genea*, not *aion*. The Chinese deem 30 years to be a generation; the West reckons 40 years as such. Neither calculation is applicable here, for had it been either case, all these things would have had to have been fulfilled in the lifetime of those living at the time of Matthew and thus all would have become past history. On the basis of such an interpretation (that is, that the meaning of "generation" is in terms of a given period of years) the historians maintain that Matthew 24 is already past: they argue that Titus destroyed Jerusalem exactly 40 years after the Lord had spoken these words recorded here in verse 34 and that therefore the word "generation" is here used in its most general sense.

Some try to avoid the problem by changing "generation" into "race" —the race of the Jewish people. But this is unlikely because (1) Matthew 1.17 says, "So all the generations from Abraham unto David are fourteen generations"; (2) we must not alter a word simply because of a difficulty, and (3) had this word been "race" in its translation, then such an explanation would mean that the Jewish race has the possibility of being destroyed since the Lord in fact declares that "this generation shall not pass away *till* all these things be accomplished" (v.34).

How, then, should *genea* be explained? We should try to find the clue from the Old Testament:

"Thou wilt keep them, O Jehovah, thou wilt preserve them from this generation for ever" (Ps. 12.7). This is a generation not in terms of a physical, but a moral, relationship.

"They are a perverse and crooked generation" (Deut. 32.5). The *genea* (Hebrew, *dor*) here is not 30 or 40 years or even a lifetime. As long as perversity and crookedness last, just so is the duration of that generation.

"For they are a very perverse generation, children in whom is no faithfulness" (Deut. 32.20). The generation continues as long as unfaithfulness persists.

"There is a generation that curse their father, and bless not their mother. There is a generation that are pure in their own eyes, and yet are not washed from their filthiness. There is a generation, oh how lofty are their eyes! And their eyelids are lifted up. There is a generation whose teeth are as swords, and their jaw teeth as knives, to devour the poor from off the earth, and the needy from among men" (Prov. 30.11-14). Obviously, such a generation is not limited to a few decades or a lifetime; rather, it points to a period marked by certain immoral characteristics.

We may receive further light from the Gospel of Matthew itself:

"But whereunto shall I liken this generation...?" (11.16-19).

"An evil and adulterous generation seeketh after a sign; and there shall no sign be given to it but the sign of Jonah the prophet . . . The men of Nineveh shall stand up in the judgment with this generation, and shall condemn it: for they repented at the preaching of Jonah; and behold, a greater than Jonah is here" (12.39,41).

"The queen of the south shall rise in the judgment with this generation . . . Even so shall it be also unto this evil generation" (12.42,45).

"All these things shall come upon this generation" (23.36).

This evil generation will last just as long as evil and adultery remain. Hence the meaning of *genea* in 24.34 is a period of time characterized by evil, adultery, perverseness, and crookedness. Such a period has not yet passed away, and will pass away only after all these things are accomplished.

"This generation" includes three classes of people: (1) the Gentiles who worship idols and reject God; (2) those Jews who reject Christ; and (3) the apostates—the so-called modernists. Before all these people pass away, all these things will be accomplished. The Lord will come and destroy them. Before the coming of the kingdom, all these things shall be fulfilled.

We should thus see the distinction among these three Greek words used in the Bible: *kosmos* is the world, *aion* is the age, and *genea* is the generation.

v.35 "Heaven and earth shall pass away"—The word of our Lord outlasts the heaven and the earth. Before the heaven and the earth pass away, all His words shall be fulfilled. The word "heaven" in the Scriptures has a double use: when it is cast in the singular, it is heaven in contrast to earth; when it appears in the plural, it means the kingdom, the one which God rules. Here it is singular in number.

v.36 Verses 36–42 form a small section which is not difficult to explain.

"That day and hour"—Day is longer, hour is shorter. The Lord seems to gather up all the future things into that day and hour. The disciples ask about the sign of *parousia* and of the end of the age. In reply the Lord uses the fig tree as the sign of the end, and rapture as the sign of *parousia*. The Jewish fig tree becomes the sign to us, and our *parousia* becomes the sign to the Jews. In spite of these signs being given, no one knows the day and the hour. The Lord says plainly: "knoweth no one"; unfortunately, though, people still try to compute the day and hour, and if not the day and hour, at least the year and month. This is an ungodly attempt. Mrs. White of the Seventh Day Adventists calculated 1844 as being the year of His coming, and Russell of the Watchtower Society considered some 1900 odd years after the year of our Lord as constituting the Lord's coming again. Both have failed. Many many attempts have been made to fix the time, yet all have failed.

"Not even the angels of heaven, neither the Son"—This last phrase may sound most strange in view of these words: "Jehovah saith unto my Lord, Sit thou at my right hand, until I make thine enemies thy footstool" (Ps. 110.1). Though the Father, the Son, and the Holy Spirit are one, yet the Son is content to wait and not be anxious about knowing. It is not because He cannot know. Furthermore, the word "knoweth" in "no one knoweth" is cast in the present tense, which means that the Lord does not know *today*. It cannot mean that He will never know.

vv.37–42 Four things are mentioned: (a) Human conditions at the end are quite similar to those in the days of Noah. At that time people knew about the flood through the preaching of Noah; nonetheless, they were careless in that as usual they were eating, drinking, marrying, and giving in marriage. (b) Just as God kept Noah and his household safely through the flood, so God will preserve a Jewish remnant through the Great Tribulation (this is that which is mentioned in Revelation 12.16: "And the earth helped the woman, and the earth opened her mouth and swallowed up the river which the dragon cast out of his mouth"). (c) The flood took all the people in the world away. (d) At the time when Noah entered the ark, the flood came; even so, in the time of rapture, one will be taken and one will be left.

v.37 How were the days of Noah? They were marked by seven things: (1) After the birth of Enosh men began to call upon the name of Jehovah (Gen. 4.26). This means that before Enosh, people worshiped God but not Jehovah. There is a difference here. Not worshiping Jehovah means not worshiping the Savior. Today people do the very same thing. They believe in God as Creator but not Christ as Savior.

(2) Genesis 4.19,22 gives the names of several women such as Adah (meaning pleasure), Zillah (screen), and Naamah (pleasant). These three names represent the conditions of women at that time. They were beautiful, vainglorious and frivolous. Look at women today. Their expenditures on dresses and cosmetics have skyrocketed to an unprecedented height. How many of them are also vain and flippant, an indication to believers that the days of Noah are here.

(3) Genesis 4.17 records the building of a city, while verses 20–22 speak of music, cattle raising, and forging of iron and brass. Today there are rapid developments in these areas. Metropolitan cities are being built everywhere, an example of which is our own Greater Shanghai. The cattle industry is prospering, and music is popularized through records and the radio. And iron in those days was made into spears and swords, whereas today it is made into guns and cannons.

(4) The fall of the church—Before the flood there were two lines of seed: (a) Cain (representing wordly people) and (b) Seth (representing the church). Of the seed of Seth, however, only one man—Enoch—was raptured, with the rest not walking with God but mingling with the world and thus being defeated. Today's church is likewise mixed with the world and is fallen.

Whoever cannot perceive the fallen condition of the church is himself fallen.

(5) Genesis 6.1 says, "when men began to multiply on the face of the ground"—Population explodes today. The rate of increase greatly surpasses that of even three years ago (1930). In that year the world population was 1.7 billion people. Today [1933] there are two billion. China alone has 500 million.

(6) Jude 14 and 15 tell how Enoch prophesied the coming of the Lord to execute judgment upon all, but his preaching was ignored by the world. The same happens nowadays. Since 1828* the second coming of our Lord has been widely preached, but few receive it with the heart.

(7) Genesis 6.1–2 "And it came to pass, when men began to multiply on the face of the ground, and daughters were born unto them, that the sons of God saw the daughters of men that they were fair; and they took them wives of all that they chose" —The sons of God are the angels; fallen angels had illicit intercourse with daughters of men. This is spiritualism, a form of which has become particularly rife even in our own day.

v.38 What does the story of Noah typify here—the rapture of the saints or believers' passing through the Great Tribulation? The rapture of the saints seems to be a more reasonable conclusion. People usually take Enoch as representing rapture and Noah as representing going through the Tribulation. But these interpretations are merely based on the histories given in Genesis. For in the Bible Noah typifies more than just one particular thing. As an example, we find that in 1 Peter 3.20–21 he stands for a being saved through baptism. What does the Lord want to signify here in Matthew 24.37? Doubtless, it is *parousia* (". . . so shall be the coming of the Son of man"). And hence the *parousia* in verse 37 is the entering of Noah into the ark cited in

---

*For the significance of this date, see footnote at 13.31-32 above.—*Translator*

verse 38. How Noah signifies rapture may be seen from the following observations:

(1) In taking male and female into the ark, Noah typifies the Lord's taking both men and women in the rapture of His *parousia*.

(2) As Noah shut the males and females in the ark, thereby out of sight, so Christ raptures us away so that we will no more be seen by the world.

(3) As Noah delivered them out of the flood, so our Lord keeps us out of the Great Tribulation (see Rev. 3.10). That animals in the Bible can represent human beings can be seen from what we learn in Peter's vision (Acts 10).

"They were eating and drinking, marrying and giving in marriage"—So are these activities greatly done today. How people are increasingly given over to the lusts of eating and drinking, and how much they engage in marriage and divorce.

v.39 "So shall be the coming of the Son of man"—As were the conditions in the days of Noah, so are they today. And just as the flood came suddenly upon them of old, so shall the Son of man come upon people unexpectedly in the future day.

vv.40–41 "One is taken, and one is left"—Why do we have these two verses? We know that all who belonged to Noah entered the ark and were therefore saved from the impending flood. According to strict typology, then, is not this to be interpreted that all the saints will be raptured together? Let us see that the Lord purposely adds the words of these two verses here lest we greatly misunderstand. Although it is true that as the days of Noah were, so shall be the coming of the Son of man, there is nevertheless this one exception which our Lord tries to explain here.

There are three different views on the men or women mentioned in verses 40 and 41: (1) they all refer to the Jews at that time; (2) the ones taken point to the regenerated, while the ones left point to the unsaved; or (3) both the taken and the left are Christians.

Let us first examine closely interpretations (1) and (3): According to (1) we must assume that the ones taken are the Jews who will be punished while the ones left will be those Jews who will enjoy the blessing of the kingdom on earth. But according to (3), we need to postulate just the opposite—that the taken are the saved who will enjoy the blessing of glory while the left are the saved who will go through the Great Tribulation on earth. Before we can settle on view (1) or view (3), we should investigate the words "taken" and "left" as to their meaning. If "taken" means good, then view (3) is more applicable since the rapture of Christians is a blessed thing. On the other hand, if "taken" means bad, then view (1) is more likely because these Jews will not be left on earth to enjoy the blessing of the kingdom.

The word "taken" is *paralambano* in Greek. Besides being translated "to receive" as its·basic meaning, it can also denote the idea of "to take to (or with) oneself"—In the New Testament this word is used 52 times, most of which instances convey a good meaning. John 14.3 ("and will receive you unto myself") is the only instance wherein our Lord speaks directly on rapture. Three times He took Peter, John and James along with Him (see Mark 5.35–43, Matt. 17.1 and 26.37). There, "paralambano" on all three occasions connotes a good idea. In John 1.11 ("they that were his own received him not"), the meaning will be good if people receive the Lord. The word "received" in Colossians 2.6, "received" in 1 Thessalonians 4.1, "received" in 2.13, "receiving" in Hebrews 12.28, "take" and "took" in Matthew 2.13–14, "took" in Acts 15.39, "took" in 16.33, and "took" in 23.18—all are *paralambano* and all suggest something good. Even in the Old Testament, the equivalent Hebrew word for "took" *(laqach)* in Genesis 5.24 refers to rapture; and the same

Hebrew word for "fetched" *(laqach)* in 1 Samuel 10.23 means something good.

Though the word "left" has also its favorable implication such as in Genesis 32.8, Numbers 26.65 and Isaiah 24.6, yet it can be used in both the good and the bad sense. The question is decided by the identity of the one who leaves them behind. If they are left behind by the devil, nothing is better. But if they are left behind by the Lord, can anything be worse? It is woe to those who are taken by the devil, but blessed are those who are taken by the Lord.

However, the meaning of a word is not in itself decisive enough for making a judgment. We have to consider its context. According to Matthew 24.19, those who are left behind because they cannot flee are in bad trouble. Then, too, verses 42 and 43 tell us that the Lord shall come as a thief; what He steals away must therefore be the best. Even in the parable of the ten virgins in Matthew 25, the virgins who are taken inside are the wise, while the virgins who are left outside are the foolish.

Of course, whether taken or left, all the men and women spoken of here in 24.40–41 are saved—so that the ones left cannot be viewed as being unsaved because of the following reasons:

(1) "Watch therefore" (v.42). The word "therefore" connects with the preceding verses 40 and 41. Since you are saved and have life, you are expected to watch. Those who lack the Lord's life cannot watch. The determining factor in rapture is not a being saved or unsaved but is a case of one's works after regeneration. To say that all the regenerated will be raptured together is a serious mistake.

(2) "Your Lord cometh" (v.42). The unsaved do not have the relationship of servant and master with the Lord. Man may misuse this word, but the Lord never will. The unsaved person may consider himself to be a servant of the Lord, but the Lord will not carelessly use such a term as "your Lord" here.

(3) "The thief was coming" (v.43). If a thief comes to steal apples, he will take the ripe ones and leave the unripened ones

behind. Thus it is not a difference in kind but one of degree.

(4) The five foolish in the parable of the virgins told of in chapter 25 are not false virgins. They are real, except that they are not wise as are the five wise virgins. The wise ones spare no effort to carry oil in the vessels whereas the foolish are too lazy to make such a provision. Nevertheless, both the wise and the foolish are virgins, and they all go forth to meet the bridegroom.

(5) Judging from typology, those who are left can be the saved as well as those who are taken. Both Enoch (who was raptured) and Noah (who entered the ark) were saved. Yet both Abraham (the intercessor) and Lot (who passed through tribulation) were saved too. But Elijah (the taken) and Elisha (the left) were saved. The disciples whom the Lord in His ascension left behind were all saved ones. Both Philip (the one taken away) and the eunuch (the one left behind) were saved.

We conclude, therefore, that the "taken" and the "left" in verses 40 and 41 are all saved.

v.42 Joining verses 40 and 41 with verse 42, one may readily see that the real issue lies in "watch" or "not watch"; otherwise the Lord cannot employ the word "therefore" nor can He exhort us to be watchful. If the condition for early rapture is regeneration and not watchfulness and proper works after regeneration, then there would be no reason for the Lord to enjoin us to watch. For in this verse He merely charges us to be watchful, with nothing being said about repentance, faith, or regeneration. Thus, both the taken and the left mentioned in verses 40–42 are saved ones. Surely our Lord will not advise the unregenerated to watch.

What is the significance of the word "watch"? Some people have suggested that this matter of watching concerns only the Jews, while we Christians need only to wait. Yet we know that the Jews will themselves have to pass through "Jacob's trouble": there is no way for them to escape the wrath of God. And hence they cannot avoid the Great Tribulation simply because they are watchful. But with the church, watchfulness is most useful. The meaning of watching is not to be careless. How prone Christians are to be overly self-confident. Watchfulness is the very opposite of carelessness. He who sleeps must be so confident in himself that he reckons nothing is going to happen, whereas the watchful person puts no trust in his flesh at all. The self-confident one is prone to fall, for to boast that "I am different from yesterday" opens the way to failure. Only the person who deeply senses his own inadequacy will be watchful. To watch is to be careful, guarding daily against the possibility of a fall. Whoever considers himself as unable to fall will not be vigilant.

We need to see from all this that if all believers were to be raptured together, what would be the need for our Lord to warn us to watch? Moreover, if we knew the time of His coming, we again would have no need to watch. But since the Lord has not told us the hour, let us ever be watchful and on guard.

B. Lessons from the Parable of the Master of the House, 24.43–44

v.43 This parable is used to illustrate further the *parousia* of the Lord. There are four factors in the parable—namely, (1) the house, (2) the master of the house, (3) the thief, and (4) the act of stealing.

(1) The house points to the work of the believer. Hebrews 3.6 speaks of the house of the believers and Mark 13.34 speaks of the house of the Lord. In both instances it is the house of faith. And Matthew 7.24 tells of how a believer builds the house.

(2) If the house refers to our works, then naturally the master of the house refers to us.

(3) The thief here typifies the Lord (see also 1 Thess. 5.2, 2 Peter 3.10, Rev. 3.3 and 16.15).

(4) The act of stealing. A regular thief steals to cause the

master of the house loss, but the Lord steals to give us greater blessing. An ordinary thief will come with no previous notice being given, but our Lord tells us beforehand that He is coming. A common thief will carry the things he has stolen back to his own place; even so, our Lord will bring us to His own place—the throne.

"And would not have suffered his house to be broken through"—Ordinarily, if the stealing is successful, the house will be broken through. If it is unsuccessful, the house will not be broken through. The thief will usually take away the precious things and leave the poor things behind, thus causing loss to the master of the house. But such a consequence will not be relevant with respect to the coming of the Lord. The main reason for using such a parable is to reinforce the concept of the unpredictability of the time of His coming. We have to leave the minute details in the parable unexplained. The only plausible explanation is to interpret it according to 1 Thessalonians 5.4–10.

The most lamentable situation today is that many Christians are prepared to be left behind. Does not 1 Thessalonians 5.4–10 inform us that positionally we "are all sons of light"? We should therefore not allow the Lord to come to us as a thief in the night. Did not the Lord warn Sardis, saying, "If therefore thou shalt not watch, I will come as a thief, and thou shalt not know what hour I will come upon thee" (Rev. 3.3)? When the church is like the church at Thessalonica, the believers are sons of light. But when the church is like that at Sardis, which is dead, the Lord will come as a thief and she shall not know the hour when He will come by.

If the master of the house allows his house to be broken through, it is his own fault, since the master of every house knows that the thief will come; for have we not all been notified by the words of prophecy? Our position is therefore this: we know He is coming, though we do not know in which hour He comes. After the Lord had left the earth, this age became a long and dark night (that is to say, the age is morally and spiritually dark). We know the Lord will come again during this long and dark night, but we do not know at what hour. Yet our ignorance of the hour ought to serve as an incentive to our watching: we should supplement our lack of knowledge with an attitude of watchfulness. Hence the failure of the master of the house lies in his despising what he knows and not supplementing for what he does not know. How we need always to be on guard against the enemy, the world, and our own selves. As Jessie Penn-Lewis once said: "The life of a Christian is a careful watching from the first day onward"!

Rapture is therefore a sign to the Jews, but to the believers who are left behind it signals the arrival of the days of trial.

Parousia to the Jews is like the lightning (that comes after the Great Tribulation); to the church it is as a thief.

v.44 "The son of man"—Some people (such as C. I. Scofield) maintain that the Lord styles himself the Son of man here only in relation to the Jews; and therefore He never uses it in relation to the church. Yet we shall note that the Son of man is also the Lord's name in His kingdom, and hence is related to Christians. For example, Stephen, who is a member of the church, called the Lord the Son of man (Acts 7.56). Moreover, in Hebrews 2.6, which points to Christ's glory in the kingdom (see Heb. 2.9), the Lord is called the Son of man. Note too that John 5.27–29 speaks of the Lord's authority to execute judgment in the kingdom because He is the Son of man. Matthew 19.28 mentions the Son of man sitting on the throne of His glory. And Matthew 25.31 says that the Son of man shall come in His glory. Matthew 13.41 and 16.27–28 all refer to the Son of man in the kingdom. And John 6.53–54 makes clear that all who eat the flesh of the Son of man and drink His blood shall be raised at the last day and thus be in the kingdom. Hence the name, the Son of man, is the Lord's name in the kingdom. He is King in the capacity of a man.

C. THE PARABLE OF THE FAITHFUL AND UNFAITHFUL SERVANTS, 24.45–51

In this passage we have still another parable—that of the two kinds of servants. The Lord mentions two different kinds of servants: one can either be a faithful and wise steward or be an evil steward.

vv.45–47 The parable of the *wise* servant or steward is presented in four steps: (1) the household, (2) the charge of the Lord, (3) the Lord's demands on the servant, and (4) the reward.

(1) The household. This is different from the house in the preceding parable. The former is personal and it speaks of the person himself, while this is corporate and it belongs to the Lord. It agrees with what is given in Hebrews 3.6 and Mark 13.34 where the house in question includes all the believers (cf. 1 Tim. 3.15). Therefore, the household here points to the church.

(2) The charge of the Lord.

(a) "Set over his household"—This represents authority.

(b) "Give them their food in due season"—This represents ministry.

Hence this is a keeping charge before God on the one hand and a serving men on the other. (Let us not misunderstand these words as signifying one servant ruling alone over the whole household. Such a misinterpretation unwarrantedly provides ground for the Pope to hold his position in the Roman Catholic Church. Nor does this verse suggest the idea of a pastor ruling over his pastorate, for note that this one servant has fellow servants being mentioned in verse 49. The Lord merely speaks of this one servant as an illustration.) The work is to govern. Each servant in the household of God has some authority. Every blood-bought bondservant of the Lord possesses a certain degree of authority to govern and to minister.

Some people advocate the concept that the church today should turn her face outward, which means she should preach the gospel with one accord to the near exclusion of any other work. But is not even the preaching of the gospel a gathering of materials for the building of the church (see Eph. 4.11–12)? To get people saved is a means, not an end. Whereas the end is to build up the church, which is distributing both material and spiritual food to the household in due season. Let us all do our best in serving our Lord by helping one another.

Distributing food in due season is our ministry. This is to serve people with the things of God as well as with the word of God. All who serve with the ministry of Christ are ministers. To preach God's word is distributing food, though it may not always be so. For unless people are really nourished and unless preaching leads to repentance and obedience, it is not a distributing of food. Let us therefore seek out those brethren who require various helps and distribute to them food according to their differing needs and measures. We need to see that we are all servants. We should distribute food in due season, and never assume a superior attitude lest people die of hunger.

(3) The Lord's demands. There are two conditions mentioned here: being faithful and being wise: being faithful towards the Lord and being wise towards the brethren. We, though, frequently reverse the order. On the one hand we become too faithful towards men by severely scolding them; and thus, although we are faithful, we nevertheless certainly lack wisdom because we do not know how to speak the truth in love. On the other hand, we are too unfaithful towards God by our using too much of our own wisdom in excusing and covering and consoling ourselves. (Let me hasten to say that unquestionably we should also be faithful to men. Only being wise towards men may turn us to clever maneuvering; yet only being faithful to them may likewise turn us to foolish loyalty. The correct solution is that we must be both faithful and wise towards the brethren.)

Being faithful is (a) not discounting anything: as much as

the Lord says, precisely that much is accepted; and (b) not considering one's own welfare: never becoming unfaithful due to any personal reason or consideration. Therefore, he who desires to be faithful must deny himself and take up the cross. He needs to forsake his own cleverness, because cleverness often comes from man whereas wisdom comes from God. Today those who are most faithful are at the same time generally the most foolish, most rude, most inconsiderate, and most independent. Hence, wisdom is greatly required. Many of God's works are spoiled by the faithful ones who are simultaneously without wisdom. Of course, it is better to be faithful though lacking in wisdom than to be wise though lacking in faithfulness. Nowadays, there are too many wise but unfaithful servants who widen the narrow gate. Such people are unfit to be God's stewards.

(4) Reward. "He will set him over all that he hath"—Verse 46 tells us blessed is he who faithfully keeps and wisely executes the command of the Lord. This blessing points to the reward in the kingdom. "Set him over"—This means to rule, to manage. To be busily occupied today is quite different from being busily occupied in the kingdom. There are many affairs in the kingdom which will require management. But today's tasks merely test whether one will be competent to be so occupied in the day to come. If a person is able to serve the brethren now, he will be used to serve then. Today God appoints him to do a little thing; in that day He will set him over all things. He who is selfish and lazy now has no chance to rule then.

vv.48–51 This section may also be divided into four parts: (1) whether the evil servant is a Christian, (2) what his faults are, (3) what the reason is for his faults, and (4) what the consequence is.

(1) Is the evil servant a Christian? He is indeed a Christian, a saved person. The reasons for this conclusion are as follows: (a) The evil servant is none other than the same servant spoken of in verse 45 whom the Lord has set over His household. The

Lord's appointment is not like human ordination, for the latter can be wrong. The Lord cannot appoint a wrong person; nevertheless, whether the servant is faithful or evil depends entirely on how that person performs. (b) The evil servant calls the Lord "my Lord"—thus proving his personal relationship with Him. And such confession is from "his heart" (to confess merely with the mouth may not be dependable). On this point see also Rom. 10.9–10 and 1 Corinthians 12.3 (c) The evil servant not only believes in the Lord but also waits for His return. His fault is in thinking his Lord will tarry. An unsaved person can never think such a thing in his heart.

In spite of the above three decisive reasons, there are still many people who hold the view that on the basis of (a) his conduct, (b) his judgment, and (c) his punishment, this evil servant is unsaved. Those who hold this interpretation argue these three points as follows: (a) If he is saved, how can he ever beat his fellow servants and eat and drink with the drunkards? In reply, let it be said that actually a saved Christian is still capable of committing all kinds of sins after regeneration. Let us recall that the person who committed the heinous sin of incest in 1 Corinthians 5 was a born-again believer! (b) The Lord appoints this evil servant's portion with the hypocrites. May we state in reply that this simply indicates that he as a believer is as hypocritical as are the unbelieving hypocrites. It is made even clearer in Luke 12: "Appoint his portion with the unfaithful [original, "unbelievers']" (v.46). He is therefore a believer who will share his portion with the unbelievers. (c) "Cut him asunder" is not a phrase to be taken literally, for how can the servant subsequently weep and gnash his teeth if he has physically been cut into two? What is probably signified here by such a phrase is most likely an action which will cause him to be separated temporarily from the Lord. Compare Matthew's account with that found in Luke 12.47–48 where we are told that the evil servant shall be beaten with many stripes. To be beaten is not to perish, for the Lord's sheep shall never perish (see John 10.27–28).

(2) What are the faults of the evil servant? Verse 49 discloses two sins: (a) he beats his fellow servants—an action taken towards believers, that is to say, towards those within the household, and (b) he eats and drinks with the drunkards—an action taken towards unbelievers, which is to say, towards those without the household. "Fellow-servants" are those who serve together. "Beat" is a word signifying the misuse of the authority which the Lord has given him. To "eat and drink" is to have fellowship with the world.

To "beat" someone is to consider oneself as possessing greater authority—and therefore as being higher—than others: forgetting, however, that the matter of discipline is in God's hand. The utmost a brother can do to another brother is to reprimand him. To "beat" another is to deprive God of His own authority to discipline. Whenever anyone deems himself to have special authority to rule over his fellow companions, he as it were is beating them. On this point, see Matthew 23: "All ye are brethren" (v.8).

To "beat" someone else is in addition a losing one's self-control. When one is in control of himself, he will not "beat" people. To "beat" others is not necessarily something that is done with a staff or whip. Spiritually and psychologically speaking, whatever causes people pain or inflicts a wound on them is sufficient to be termed a "beating" of others. One can hurt people with words, causing them untold sufferings by means of a sharp, biting tongue. His aim is to make people miserable for three or five days while he concomitantly is enjoying great pleasure. And such is in actuality a beating. We ought always to be healing wounds—and that with oil and wine—and not constantly to be operating on them by inflicting new cuts. God's children have enough wounds and pains. How can we ever think of adding more to them? All who are proud, independent, or ill-tempered tend to "beat" people.

The other sin is to be united with the world. A drunkard according to the Scriptures is a man who is ensnared by the world.

He who is blurred in vision through drink is undoubtedly intoxicated. Likewise, a person whose heart is overcharged with riches, fame, and so forth is dulled in his spiritual senses and can therefore also be reckoned as being drunk. The servant, being a believer, ought not communicate with the drunkards (this is the teaching of 2 Corinthians 6.14ff.), for eating and drinking, in the Scriptures, denote especially the idea of communication or fellowship. After Lot was separated from Abraham he moved to Sodom, which action signified his being joined to the world. Whenever any believer detests a brother but delights in the worldling, he is fallen.

The above two sins can easily be committed by any believer.

(3) What is the reason for his faults? It is given in verse 48, "My lord tarrieth"—He truly believes in the second coming of the Lord, except that in his estimation the Lord will come tardily. Whoever does not believe in the soon return of the Lord is an evil servant. What does the Lord say is the fault of this evil servant? Just this, that though he confesses with his mouth that the Lord shall indeed come, he nevertheless says in his heart that the Lord will delay. How precarious is such a position! Will a person watch if he has no idea that the Lord is coming soon?

Many people do not want the Lord to return soon lest His coming would destroy or terminate their plans. They are unable to pray with John: "Amen: come, Lord Jesus" (Rev. 22.20).

We must have both the attitude and the desire for the soon return of the Lord. Familiarity with prophecy alone is not enough, since the evil servant is also well-acquainted with prophecy.

(4) What is the consequence? The Lord returns earlier than the evil servant thinks. If any should speculate that the Lord will tarry, he will find his Lord coming quicker than he thinks. What is the penalty? The Lord will separate him and appoint his portion with the hypocrites. To be assigned a place with the hypocrites does not mean to receive precisely the same punishment, just as those who share the same place in jail do not

receive the same punishment. "The weeping and the gnashing of teeth" signifies deep regret and true repentance.

D. THE PARABLE OF THE TEN VIRGINS, 25.1–13

This parable may be divided into seven parts: (1) the ten virgins going forth to meet the bridegroom (v.1); (2) the two different classes of virgins (vv.2–4); (3) their history or process (vv. 5–7); (4) the discovery of a lack (vv. 8–9); (5) the distinction (v.10); (6) the request of the foolish (vv.11–12); and (7) the lesson (v.13).

v.1 "Then" refers to the time of *parousia*. "The kingdom of heaven" and not the church is in view here. The kingdom of heaven is the sphere of the righteousness of God, the realm in which God rules and reigns.

"Virgins" refer to Christians; and "bridegroom" to the Lord.

"Ten" in the Scriptures is a number which, as we shall see below, denotes the greater part of the whole. There are altogether four numbers in the Bible which represent perfection: "three" (the perfection of God); "seven" (the perfection of time, temporary perfection); "ten" (the perfection of man); and "twelve" (the perfection of the ages, eternal perfection). In Revelation 21 everything noted there is twelve—gates, pearls, the names of the apostles, the tribes of Israel, the precious stones, the height of the wall $[144 = (12^2)]$. Before this chapter 21, all is seven in the book of Revelation. But commencing with the new heaven and new earth (the subject of chapter 21), all is twelve. Three is the number of God and four is the number of man. Three *plus* four is seven (God's number plus man's number), which is yet separable and hence represents temporary perfection. Three *multiplied* by four is twelve (God's number multiplied by man's number), which is inseparable and therefore stands for eternal perfection. Ten is a little short of the perfect number of twelve. By adding two to it, the result will become the number of eternal perfection: in this connection let us see that in Matthew 24, the two women grinding at the mill represent the living believers; while in chapter 25 the ten virgins represent the dead believers ("they all slumbered and slept"—v.5).

In the Bible there is the usage of the number twelve in both Greek and Hebrew as often being ten plus two: ten being the majority number and two the residual number. For example: ten brothers and two brothers (Gen. 42.3–4); ten spies and Joshua with Caleb (Num. 14.37–38); the prophet Ahijah rent his new garment into twelve pieces and gave them away by distributing ten pieces and two pieces (1 Kings 11.29–31); and the controversy between the ten disciples and the two disciples (Matt. 20.24).

"Virgins"—In a parable, the matter of virginity cannot be taken literally. The virgins instead represent us who are re-created in Christ. They point more to the idea of our being hidden ones than to the idea of chastity, for married women may also be chaste. The term "virgins" cannot be applied to either the Jews or the unbelievers; only Christians can adopt this term. The one purpose of these virgins is to go forth with their lamps to meet the bridegroom.

"Lamp" in the Bible may mean several things: (1) the word of the Lord (Ps. 119.105); (2) the word of prophecy (2 Peter 1.19); and (3) the outward testimony of the Christian (Matt. 5.14–16). It does not say "candle" here since a candle burns its own wax to give light, whereas oil is poured into a lamp from the outside in order for it to shed light. So the outward declaration of the Christian ought to be a going forth to meet the bridegroom. Just as in the breaking of bread, we not only remember the finished work of the Lord but also remember that the day of His coming is near.

vv.2–4 Two classes of virgins. Many commentators take the five foolish virgins to be the unsaved, yet there are so many iron-clad evidences to overturn such an interpretation that we will mention only fifteen of them, which serve also as important proofs that these foolish virgins are saved ones:

(1) These five foolish ones are virgins. Even through verse 11, they are still termed virgins. Throughout the parable the Lord never called this matter into question; on the contrary, He continually recognized this as a fact.

(2) There are lights in their lamps (v.8). These lights sustained them up to midnight and the time of their lamps "going out" (not even that they had "gone out"), showing that the lights are not yet extinguished. And hence these virgins have "good works" and they "glorify [their] Father who is in heaven" (Matt. 5.16) due to the indwelling Holy Spirit in them, except that now their lights are going out.

(3) They all go forth to meet the bridegroom. The unsaved will never be able to go out to meet the bridegroom. Will bandits ever light their torches and go forth to meet the government troops?

(4) "But at midnight there is a cry, . . . Come ye forth to meet him"—The cry is to all the ten virgins. The archangel surely will not call mistakenly nor the Lord use any word incorrectly.

(5) Oil in their lamps, even though it is granted that there is no oil in the vessels. Oil signifies the Holy Spirit, and hence these foolish virgins must be saved ones.

(6) "Then all those virgins arose" (v.7). It refers to but one resurrection common to all ten. For note that a thousand years shall separate the resurrection of the saved from that of the unsaved.

(7) The five wise virgins go in with the bridegroom (v.10); afterward come also the foolish virgins (v.11). They all are raptured to the air, except that the latter five cannot attend the marriage feast.

(8) The difference between the five wise and five foolish virgins lies in their conduct, not in their nature—since all of them are virgins with no divergence of true or false, the only dis-

tinction being between being wise or foolish. To be foolish does not mean to not be saved.

(9) Due to the tarrying of the bridegroom (v.5), the lamps of the foolish are going out. If the bridegroom does not tarry, these may be just as qualified as the wise ones to enter.

(10) These five foolish are virgins from the beginning to the end (v.11).

(11) "Buy for yourselves" (v.9). To the unsaved, it cannot be a matter of "buying" but one of "asking" since grace is freely given. Only to the saved can the word be "buy"—which means paying a price.

(12) If the five foolish are unsaved, then according to this interpretation it would seem that they are being given another opportunity to be saved after they die, because the wise virgins counsel them to go and buy oil.

(13) If the five foolish are unsaved, would the five wise say, "Peradventure there will not be enough for us and you"? If these foolish are truly unsaved, these five wise cannot make any excuse but must pay any cost to help; for how can they stand by and do nothing for the perishing?

(14) "Watch therefore," says the Lord (v.13). To be watchful requires life. If the five foolish are not saved, they cannot be exhorted to watch but must be urged to repent.

(15) In contrast to the parable of the gospel feast told of in Matthew 22, which is directed towards the lost, this parable is spoken to the disciples. Matthew 22 is concerned with the question of being saved or perishing, but this is not the concern of Matthew 25. Whoever is bound and cast out in the parable of Matthew 22 is totally helpless, but the foolish virgins who are barred are still quite free. The earlier parable relates to the gain or loss of the king, while the latter story pertains to that of the virgins. The one refers to the glory of the king; the other reflects upon the welfare of the virgins.

In interpreting the Scriptures believers today devote themselves almost entirely to the problem of whether saved or unsaved, not realizing that there is the equally important question of the kingdom after once being saved.

The wise and the foolish differ not in nature, only in conduct. There is one place in the New Testament that can prove this point, and for this we must consult Matthew 7.24–26. The wise man is he who does the words of the Lord, while the foolish man is one who does not obey them. The rock stands for the words of the Lord, but the sand signifies the ideas of man. To build upon the rock is to do everything according to God's word; to build upon the sand is to do things according to one's own ideas. "The fear of Jehovah is the beginning of wisdom" (Prov. 9.10). It is therefore wise to be simple before God and foolish to rebel against Him. To say "perhaps" or "according to my own opinion" is really being foolish. To do what God says may look like utter foolishness to man but it is real wisdom to God.

Only in two points do the two classes of virgins differ: (1) the wise ones carry oil in their vessels while the foolish do not; and (2) the wise virgins go in to the marriage feast whereas the foolish ones are rejected. Their similarities are many, such as they *all* (1) are virgins, (2) have lamps (the appearance), (3) they bear light (the conduct which glorifies God), (4) have oil (the Holy Spirit), (5) go forth to meet the bridegroom (waiting), (6) sleep, (7) hear the midnight cry, (8) arise (resurrection), and (9) trim their lamps (prepare oil). Yet however numerous are their similarities and seemingly limited are their differences, the consequences for each group are far, far apart. What care must we therefore exercise! Whatever may be the cause, that will be the effect. Today's difference will produce tomorrow's divergence. The glory or shame in the age to come is decided today.

"Took no oil with them"—That is to say, the foolish prepared no oil apart from what was already in the lamp. The wise have extra oil in their vessels. Oil in the *lamp* speaks of the Holy Spirit who dwells in every regenerated person. A Christian, even a beginner, has the indwelling Holy Spirit (see Ez. 36.26–27,

Eph. 1.13). "The spirit of man is the lamp of Jehovah, searching all his innermost parts" (Prov. 20.27). "If any man hath not the Spirit of Christ, he is none of his" (Rom. 8.9). "Know ye not as to your own selves, that Jesus Christ is in you? unless indeed ye be reprobates" (2 Cor. 13.5). "Hereby we know that he abideth in us, by the Spirit which he gave us" (1 John 3.24). "Hereby we know that we abide in him and he in us, because he hath given us of his Spirit" (1 John 4.13). The Lord therefore dwells in us by His Spirit.

But oil in the *vessel* means more than the indwelling of the Holy Spirit; it speaks of being *filled* with the Holy Spirit. The indwelling Holy Spirit is received at the time of regeneration, but the filling of the Holy Spirit comes through continual seeking following the moment of regeneration. Each believer has the Holy Spirit, yet not all have the fullness of the Holy Spirit. A vessel is something other than the lamp. Yet this is not the emphasis here. Since oil is a liquid, it has to be contained in a vessel. God's will is for us to be filled to the full, not just having oil in the lamp. In order to realize this, neither trimming nor decorating the lamp will be a good way, for God looks for extra oil in the vessel. Yet the believer's attention is usually drawn to the outward appearance of the lamp. The less oil one has, the more assiduously he takes care of the appearance. Nevertheless, trimming can never be a substitute for the oil.

We imagine that receiving oil once is enough, but God desires us to receive it twice. The second time is different from the first, in that at the first instance God gives freely whereas at the second instance He demands a price to be paid. If anyone refuses to pay the price—denying himself and seeking earnestly—he will not be given the oil again. So let us be alert. People may not be able to detect whether or not we have the oil twice over; and we may indeed get by without any trouble today, but on that future day we will be found out. Are we willing to pay the price? To be filled with the Holy Spirit is the condition for rapture. Just as a balloon filled with helium will ascend heavenward, so will those who are filled with the Holy Spirit be caught up. Let us therefore pay the price in providing oil in the vessel, or else we will be those like the foolish virgins.

vv.5–7 These verses form the third part of the parable and narrate the history of these virgins. Spiritual foolishness may not be readily discerned in the world, but the tarrying of the Lord is the acid test. At the beginning, both the wise and the foolish receive the same light. And the latter may therefore ridicule the former for being cumbered about with carrying extra oil. Oh how many are fit to be raptured at first but render themselves unfit later on! This is due to the delay of the Lord. Indeed, it is the evil servant who thinks that the Lord will delay His return; just the opposite, though, is the foolish virgin who imagines that the Lord will come earlier! The parable of the evil servant teaches believers to be ready to meet the Lord today, while the parable of the ten virgins instructs us to be prepared for any unexpected delay of the Lord's return. Should the Lord tarry for 56 more years, will you still be ready to meet Him? Be careful lest your lamp can only burn till midnight but not after midnight. If you set your lamp to burn only till midnight, the Lord may tarry until after that hour. Do not despise the testing of the Lord. The usefulness of the oil in the vessel is revealed in the Lord's tarrying. So that what is being emphasized here is not the initial burning but whether there is extra oil in the vessel for longer burning.

The bridegroom, of course, is the Lord.

"Now while the bridegroom tarried, they all slumbered and slept"—Since this is a parable, it naturally should be interpreted spiritually. Sleep in the Scriptures may convey either one of two meanings: (1) a falling away spiritually (see Rom. 13.11–14, 1 Thess. 5.6); or (2) death (see 1 Thess. 4.13, John 11.11–14). It cannot mean a spiritual falling away because (a) the wise virgins fall asleep as well as the foolish; (b) the sleep here is unimportant since the wise are not evilly affected by it; (c) the Lord does not reprimand them for their sleep, instead He completely ignores the fact; and (d) we should notice the lesson to be gained from verse 13 wherein the Lord is found teaching His hearers to watch just as the wise virgins had done. In view of these observations, therefore, the sleep mentioned here cannot have reference to a spiritual falling away but instead signifies physical death.

"But at midnight there is a cry"—Some say this refers to the renewed interest in the study of prophecy and the preaching of the second coming which occurred at the beginning of the nineteenth century. This may sound attractive, but unfortunately in the parable none of the ten virgins awakens on her own accord. They do not awaken through any initiative of their own but must be awakened by the action of the bridegroom himself. Hence the sounding of the midnight cry must yet await its fulfillment at the time of the voice of the archangel and the sound of the trump of God as mentioned in 1 Thessalonians 4.16 and 1 Corinthians 15.52. The voice of the archangel is for the purpose of waking people up, and the sounding of the trumpet of God serves to gather people together. So that in the parable, those who hear (all ten virgins) stand for all the dead believers.

"Behold, the bridegroom! Come ye forth to meet him"— Since the two sides (that is, the bridegroom and the virgins) are both coming together, they will accordingly meet in the air.

"Then all those virgins arose"—This proves that all dead Christians are resurrected together. Here the virgins seem to have time to talk things over; but according to 1 Corinthians 15.52 the event all happens in a moment—in the twinkling of an eye—so that there is no opportunity left to make conversation. Let us understand that what we have here is a parable, and there frequently is portrayed in parables an element of time which actually does not exist. For example, in the parable of the laborers in the vineyard (Matt. 20.1–16), a contention is mentioned as arising between the Lord and those who labor earliest but are paid last. Such contending with the Lord is in fact impossible. The same thing happens in the parable of the marriage feast as told in Matthew 22.1–14. Consequently, when we study parables we should concentrate on their teachings and not so much on the details.

vv.8–9 The fourth part of this parable is the discovery of lack in the five foolish ones. They discover their lack of oil because of the tarrying of the bridegroom (v.5a). His tarrying is for the purpose of testing the wise and the foolish. The foolish virgins no doubt deemed the five wise ones to have encumbered themselves unnecessarily in carrying oil in vessels, but now they too find the need for oil, and so they ask the wise virgins for it. The *gift* of the Holy Spirit may be imparted (see Acts 8.17, 19.6; 1 Tim. 4.14; 2 Tim. 1.6), but the *fullness* of the Holy Spirit cannot be transferred. It is not enough simply to ask for the gift of the Holy Spirit. There is absolutely no way to share other people's oil, not even with parents, brothers and sisters, or close relations. One's spiritual fullness can come only from paying the price himself. Counterfeit spirituality may pass for real today, but it cannot pass the test on *that* day. To be filled with the Holy Spirit requires fellowship with the Lord and costly pursuit of Him. No matter how long we may be in company with spiritual people, we will not automatically share in their oil. *Light* may be borrowed, but *oil* cannot.

"Peradventure there will not be enough for us and you"—In other words, there can be no help since help in *this* situation is impossible. The Lord does permit a certain kind of holy selfishness here. Although we should always be sympathetic toward others, can *we* afford to be foolish because *others* are? Should we not rather keep a definite amount of sacred holiness for the Lord? "There will not be enough for us and you"—It will mean loss to both; and moreover, the other party will not be helped at all.

"And buy for yourselves"—This injunction signifies a great deal of truth:

(1) At least there is still the possibility and the opportunity

to buy oil at that time. Yet please notice that this does not refer to one more opportunity being given to the resurrected dead to be saved, because the resurrection of the unsaved does not occur at that time.

(2) This injunction does suggest, however, that the oil of the wise ones was originally secured with a price. The indolent will not be filled with the Holy Spirit.

(3) To be filled with the Holy Spirit requires paying a price. It has to be bought, not to be begged for. Also, one needs to know what to buy. Who would go to a department store to buy, and when asked what he wants would not know what to buy? Nevertheless, a great number of Christians are like that because (a) they do not realize the necessity for buying oil, (b) they do not know the price, and (c) they do not wish to pay the price.

Believers today do not understand how essential it is to be filled with the Holy Spirit. The oil in the lamp is not sufficient to burn after midnight; only the oil in the vessel is sufficient enough. Most Christians, having received the New Covenant, know only new desires but not new power. It is most painful to have a new desire without the power to fulfill it. This proves the need to be filled with the Holy Spirit. Since there is need, there is reason for paying the price. Before one builds a tower he should first sit down and count the cost, and before he goes to war he should first take counsel as to how many soldiers he would commit to the fight (see Luke 14.25–35).

Many are frightened away by the heavy cost, not considering how essential is the oil. The price each pays will vary. Some may have to forsake something. One thing is certain, which is, that oil cannot be bought without paying a price. It is not freely obtained, neither is it obtained for personal interest but for the glory of God and for His work. How many there are who like to adorn themselves with gifts and power, yet God does not give these to exalt men. People may know what price they have to pay, but they ought to know that a price must be paid. Obviously, dealing with sin is a prerequisite. If sin is not dealt with, who can talk about paying a price? Yet to confess sin is not the paying of any price since this is minimally what one and all ought to do anyway; for let us understand that even the five foolish virgins have dealt with sin too.

(4) Pay the price—a matter of paying the right price for the right merchandise. The measure of the price paid will determine the amount of oil obtained. Let us see that the cross and the Holy Spirit are inseparable. Let the slaying of Jesus be manifested in your body (see 2 Cor. 4.8–11), for the cross will create in you an empty space for the power of the New Covenant to fill. The fullness according to the New Covenant is a fact more than it is a matter of consciousness—just as the heartbeat is a fact, although it may not always be felt. God's only begotten Son is freely given, but the oil in the vessel must be bought.

There are four things cited in the Bible which must be bought:

(a) "Buy the truth" (Prov. 23.23). In order to know the truth, one must be determined to practice the truth and to seek earnestly after it.

(b) "Buy . . . gold refined by fire" (Rev. 3.18). Such buying of refined gold and white garments and eye-salve is not action for the unsaved to take, because God cannot ask the unsaved to buy. Laodicea is, after all, a church. "Gold refined by fire" signifies that faith which has gone through trial and has been proven undefeated. It is the faith which overcomes environment (see 1 Peter 1.7). God allows you to go through a trial in order to show His love to you, and also for him to be glorified before Satan (such as in the case of Job).

(c) "Buy . . . white garments" (Rev. 3.18)—There are two kinds of white garments spoken of in the book of Revelation: (1) those white garments we received before God, which garments are the Lord Jesus himself. We are clothed with Christ, and thus are we cleansed. Whoever does not have this white garment is not saved. (2) those white garments we wear before God, which represent the righteousnesses of the saints (Rev.

19.8 Darby) that are the result of the operation of the Spirit of the Lord within us. Whoever does not have this white garment is naked before God and will not be rewarded.

(d) "Buy ... eyesalve" (Rev. 3.18)—This is the revelation of the Holy Spirit, without which no one really sees.

(5) Such an injunction here in verse 9 hints at the fact that oil must be bought. To be filled with the Holy Spirit is not something you can decide. Sooner or later you must be filled with the Holy Spirit. Do not think that those who are like the five wise have gone to an extreme. One day God will force you to go to such an "extreme": for Ephesians 5.18 *is* a command.

(6) "Go ye rather to them that sell"—Where will they be able to buy this oil? We can only take it as signifying that they must pay a price for obtaining their extra oil.

(7) The injunction in verse 9 touches upon this question too: How can there be suffering after resurrection? Such notion that there is no suffering after resurrection is erroneous. For all who shall suffer in the lake of fire will have themselves been resurrected too. Some people are resurrected to enjoy life, while others are resurrected to suffer eternal death. If a person has not been able to control his temper while living, his death will not automatically change him. For let us realize that the lusts, pride, and selfishness of the rich man spoken of in Luke's parable remain with him in Hades (16.19–31). Therefore, after the virgins arise they all are found trimming their lamps. Yet the statement —"Our lamps are going out"—made by the five foolish virgins (v.8) indicates that the lamps will not be completely extinguished. God gives us life that is once and forever. Although in the Christian's experience of the Holy Spirit there are many times when it looks as if his lamp is going out, nevertheless the Holy Spirit will never leaves us: He will not leave, even in the face of our unfaithfulness.

v.10 The fifth part of the parable deals with the separation. "And while they went away to buy"—Oil these foolish ones must have; but while they go away to buy, the Lord arrives; and only those who are ready go in with Him to the marriage feast. Hence the whole problem is whether one is ready. Yet they do not cease to be virgins because they are not ready; for many are true Christians, but few are ready ones.

"Went in with him to the marriage feast" (see also Rev. 19.7,9). The bride is the New Jerusalem, which includes all who are chosen to be united with God—both those of the Old Testament time and of the New Testament dispensation. The bride mentioned in Revelation 19 emerges *before* the millennial kingdom, whereas the bride spoken of in Revelation 21 appears *after* the kingdom. There is thus a gap of a thousand years. Since one becomes a bride but once, it is evident that the marriage feast extends over a period of a thousand years.

"Marriage feast"—This means to be with the bridegroom and to rejoice together. Such joy is very special, and therefore Revelation 19 says how "blessed are they that are bidden to the marriage supper of the Lamb" (v.9). The "blessed" mentioned in Revelation 20.6, though, has relationship to the matter of reigning and appears to be the same supping and reigning as is described in Revelation 3.20-21. Altogether, there are seven times in Revelation when the word "blessed" is proclaimed.

Why does Matthew 25 not speak of the bride? For the simple reason that the bride is corporate, whereas the virgins here in the parable are seen as individuals. The bride cannot be viewed as five and five.

"And the door was shut"—It is the door of the kingdom, the entrance into the joy of feasting with the bridegroom.

vv.11–12 The request of the foolish virgins forms the sixth part of the parable. Now they have come back from buying oil. Keep in mind that both the five wise and the five foolish are virgins, all ten having oil in their lamps, all going out to meet the bridegroom, all falling asleep while waiting, and all rising and trimming their lamps after having heard the cry, Behold, the bridegroom! Now, both parties have oil in their vessels, with the only difference being one of time. Recall how once the Lord had chided the two disciples on the road to Emmaus, saying, "O foolish men, and slow of heart to believe in all that the prophets have spoken!" (Luke 24.25) Recall also how He had likewise admonished Thomas, saying, "Because thou hast seen me, thou hast believed; blessed are they that have not seen, and yet have believed" (John 20.29). The matter of quickness or slowness is of great importance. Do we not know that all who will suffer in the lake of fire will have to believe sometime, only they have believed too late? "Look therefore carefully how ye walk, not as unwise, but as wise; redeeming the time, because the days are evil" (Eph. 5.15–16). The foolish do not redeem the time, but the wise ones do. The latter are filled with the Holy Spirit. Let us realize that we must all some day be filled with the Holy Spirit. Then why not now? Why have this experience come afterwards?

"I know you not"—Will the Lord ever say to the saved that He does not know them? However, we need to examine this answer of our Lord's very carefully:

(1) "But he answered and said"—The word "but" shows that the answer is unusual and out of all expectation. In Luke 15.22 the same word indicates how totally unthought-of, unhoped-for, and unexpected by the prodigal son were the father's words to his servants. The word "but" here proves that the "know not" is not an ordinary not knowing.

(2) The Lord knows all who are saved (2 Tim. 2.19, Gal. 4.9, John 10.14). Two Greek words are used for "know" in the New Testament: *ginosko* and *oida*. The former signifies an objective knowledge while the latter signifies a subjective and deeper knowledge. Now *oida* is the Greek word employed here by the Lord.

(3) How is *oida* used in the Scriptures? It is recognizably employed to mean approve, commend, endorse, or applaud.

What follows are a few examples from the New Testament which illustrate the use of this Greek word. In each example, the verb "to know" or "to not know" is *oida* or its variant. "In the midst of you standeth one whom ye know not" (John 1.26). In this situation, of course, the Jews know *(ginosko)* the Lord, but they do not really know *(oida)* Him because they do not love Him. "I knew him not" (John 1.31). Since John and the Lord Jesus are cousins, the Baptist certainly knows Jesus objectively *(ginosko)* but not subjectively *(oida)*—that is to say, John does not know Him deeply. "Ye know neither me, nor my Father" (John 8.19). Though the Jews know *(ginosko)* the Lord quite well externally, they do not approve of Him nor do they receive Him. "I know you not whence ye are" (spoken twice in Luke 13.22–30). Here the Lord speaks of the situation in the kingdom. Some who have eaten and drunk with the Lord and have also heard Him teaching in their streets doubtless know objectively *(ginosko)* the Lord well, yet they are referred to. by the Lord as "workers of iniquity"—a phrase which in the original is worded as "workers of unrighteousness"—that is to say, those who do not walk according to rule. "Ye know the house of Stephanas" (1 Cor. 16.15). The Corinthian believers know deeply *(oida)* and not just know objectively *(ginosko)* the house of Stephanas. Hence from all these examples we learn that *oida* is subjective knowing of a person, which implies a sense of trust.

(4) "Whosoever shall deny me before men, him will I also deny before my Father who is in heaven" (Matt. 10.33; cf. also Luke 12.9). These two instances of the word "deny" have reference to things in the kingdom. Secret Christians will not perish, yet neither will they be approved by the Lord in the kingdom. "Deny" *(arneomai)* is to not know (in the *oida* sense of not knowing) (see Matt. 26.70). It is to contradict, refute, or overturn.

(5) There are similar examples of this matter of knowing and not knowing in the Old Testament, as for instance in 1 Sam-

uel 3.7 ("Now Samuel did not yet know Jehovah") wherein Samuel had indeed *objectively* known Jehovah, but he had yet to know the Lord in a subjective way.

(6) The reward of the kingdom is based purely on righteousness. For the Lord to deny has about it the flavor of righteousness. Just as a judge must ask the name of the offender even if the latter is his own son, so the denial here in Matthew 25.12 ("I know you not") refers to the action and not to the person. It means the Lord cannot accept or approve.

v.13 The lesson in this final part of the parable is "watch"—The Lord commands us to be watchful; He does not urge us here to be regenerated and be saved. The "they that were ready" in verse 10 are those who have watched. Thus, "ready" and "watch" are joined into one. To be "ready" means that there is no unfinished business, and one is therefore ready to be reckoned with daily. To "watch" means to so live as to be always ready for the coming of the Lord. We believers should daily be prepared for reckoning. The Lord may come at any time. The five foolish virgins were ready and watching at the beginning, but alas, they did not continue on. The word "ready" here is concerned with self as to whether or not there is anything left undone. The word "watch" on the other hand has its direction towards the Lord; it signifies a waiting to meet Him at any time. To be ready and watchful and waiting, we need the fullness of the Holy Spirit. It will not do if we depend on ourselves, for very soon we will be weakened and become foolish. But if we are filled with the Holy Spirit we will spontaneously bear fruit to the glory to God.

He who is truly watchful often feels he is not yet entirely ready. He does not trust in his own self. This is true humility.

Yet what does it avail if we have such prophecy but are not watchful? Will it not be tragic if we have prophetic knowledge and still suffer loss in the future? Be ready, for the Lord only looks into our lamp and light. Be watchful, because we do not know the day nor the hour. For if we knew, we would have no need to be watchful.

In chapters 24 and 25, five times we are told that no one knows the day of the coming of the Lord. Such intense repetition signifies extreme importance. How unreliable is the concept of our all being raptured after the Great Tribulation; for if that were indeed the case, we would be able to compute most accurately the day of His coming: we would need only to count three years and a half after the image of the beast has been placed in the temple. Yet the reason why the Lord does not inform us of the date is because He wants us to be watchful.

E. The Parable of the Talents, 25.14–30

This parable is divided into four parts: (a) the householder delivers his goods (vv.14–15); (b) the way the servants handle the talents (vv.16–18); (c) the judgment of both the first and the second servant (vv.19–23); and (d) the judgment of the third servant (vv.24–30).

In order more accurately to study this parable, we must first know the difference between our reconcilation with God and our relationship to the Lord. Otherwise, we shall not be able to understand clearly the Scriptures but will find difficulties and conflicts in this passage and in many other places in the Bible.

Let us see that before the Father we are children, but before the Lord we are servants (or bondslaves). Through faith we become children; by works we become servants. On the principle of grace we come to be children; on the principle of responsibility we come to be servants. We become children through the blessed Son; we become servants by the Holy Spirit.

This passage speaks of the relationship between the servants and the Lord, not of the relationship between the children and the father. Commencing from Matthew 14, the relationship between children and the Father is no longer mentioned (such relationship being eternal); only that between servants and the Lord is thereafter presented (such relationship lasting only until after the millennium). The relationship we have to the Father pertains to salvation and eternity, whereas the relationship we have to the Son pertains to overcoming and kingdom reward. The parable of the talents is related to reward and not to eternity, since the problem of eternity has already been solved.

There is a basic difference between the Old and New Covenants. The Old demands works before life, which means being servants before becoming children. The New Covenant, though, gives life before works, that is to say, being born again before becoming servants. And why? Because God does not want believers to serve Him by their flesh.

v.14 "For it is as when a man, going into another country"—This man is the Lord. He is truly going into another country, for His country is not of the world and is totally different from the nations on earth. Our citizenship belongs to that country (see Phil. 3.20). The phrase "going into another country" points to the ascension of the Lord (see Heb. 9.11, 1 Peter 3.22).

"Called his own servants"—These are His bondslaves; hence they are neither Jews who are not His bondslaves, nor are they the unsaved, but they are those who have been bought by Him with a price.

Formerly Abraham performed circumcision on the slaves whom he had bought, as well as on his own sons, because of the covenant which God made with him. Now our position is that of slaves (being bought with His blood) as well as children (being born again). The Lord wants us to serve Him as slaves. In the church today there are two schools of extremes: one stresses works but not faith, while the other emphasizes faith but no works.

"And delivered unto them his goods"—The Lord delivers His goods to them because He is going to another country. This will be a test to the servants, because the servants may be faithful in the presence of the Lord, but true faithfulness will be seen only when the Lord is absent. The Lord delivers His goods to them for them to manage His property. The same is true with us today. The Lord has delivered His goods to us, and we are now serving the Lord whom we do not see.

This parable is different from that in Luke, for in Luke's account we have our Lord adding this statement: "Trade ye herewith till I come" (19.13). Here in Matthew's account the Lord is recorded as not instructing these servants what to do with His goods. He wants us to seek His will and do accordingly. Whoever knows the Lord's will and does it is fit to be rewarded. Not telling the servants what to do is a real test.

v.15 "To each according to his several ability"—What is meant by the word "talent"? Most people will say that the talent represents property, position, influence, time, life, personal character, keen mind, health, church position, and so forth. But we maintain that it speaks of gift, not ability. For (1) a talent is something which Christians have but which the Gentiles do not have, because the Lord delivers it to His *own* slaves and not to anybody else's; (2) a talent is given according to each person's ability and not given casually or indiscriminately; (3) a talent may be increased through earning; (4) it can be taken back; and (5) it is not something which *God* ordinarily gives to men; rather is it something given by *the Lord* after His ascension. On the basis of these five points we conclude that "talent" cannot refer to property, position, and so forth as is usually understood.

Talent, therefore, is the gift of the Holy Spirit. For the gift of the Holy Spirit (1) is something which the Lord possesses exclusively (Acts 2.38); (2) is that which can be distributed (Acts 19.6); (3) is that which can also be increased (1 Cor. 14.12–13); (4) is given according to the ability of each person, such as Peter who being a fisherman is given the gift of fishing for men while John who was found mending nets is given the gift of mending the broken net of the church; (5) is given at the ascension of the Lord on the day of Pentecost (John 7.39, 16.7); and (6) is something which can be laid aside unused—and hence Paul exhorts Timothy with these words: "I put thee in remembrance that thou stir up the gift of God, which is in thee through the laying on of my hands" (2 Tim. 1.6). Without any doubt, therefore, "talent" speaks of the gift of the Holy Spirit.

"And unto one he gave five talents, to another two, to another one"—The Lord mentions only three servants, yet the number "three" can represent all the believers, just as the number "seven" in the counting of the seven churches mentioned in Revelation 2 and 3 can represent all the churches (for note that the city and church at Colossae is also in Asia, but the Lord does not name this local church since she is included in the seven mentioned). The number "three" also stands for three *classes* of servants; otherwise, the Lord would have but three individual servants. Remember that this is a parable; it therefore cannot be literally interpreted. All servants (or believers) have the gift of the Holy Spirit. Each of them has at least one talent; so that no one can excuse himself by saying that he has no gift.

Please do not plead that you have no gift. You are not a child of God if you have none. Having the gift of the Holy Spirit, you will be reckoned with one day.

"To each according to his several ability"—The Lord gives to each according to his ability. Today people regard ability too highly, but ability cannot be a substitute for "talent": for ability without capital (talent) cannot accomplish anything. Yet we cannot despise ability, either, because it is that which turns the capital into profit: ability manages the talent. Even so, we cannot dictate to the Lord as to what talent(s) He must give simply on the basis of our ability; the giving of the talents is something that must be strictly left to the Lord to determine. Hence there is no ground for pride and satisfaction to the ones who receive five and two talents, respectively; nor, on the other hand, is there any reason for shame and envy by the one who only receives one talent. How believers in the church today esteem the more and despise the less! All this is the activity of the flesh. Just keep in mind that gifts are distributed by God for us to trade with. Let all of us trade according to the gifts given by God. This will greatly reduce many strifes and much confusion in the church: for abilities are different, and gifts, too, are diverse.

Notice how the Lord divides His goods himself. He has not asked someone else to divide and distribute for Him. For this reason no church can ordain a pastor, nor can a seminary confer a gift. Whatever gift one has is given by God, not by man.

Notice also that reward is not dispensed according to the amount of talent given. Both the five talent person and the two talent person received the same reward. And if the one talent servant had gained one talent, he too would have received the same reward.

"And he went on his journey"—This speaks of the Lord's ascension.

vv.16–18 These verses cover the second part of the parable—the way the servants handle their talents.

The servants go ahead and trade with the talents because they know this is the will of the Lord. They know their Lord does not wish His talents to lie idle but would like to see them increased. They have the same mind as does the Lord. Therefore, in the future they will share in the joy of the Lord. Now doubtless trading is not at all easy: it involves difficulty, anxiety, risk, and hardship.

The focus of this parable, however, is on the third servant. More verses are devoted to him than to the others. He who receives but one talent has the greatest temptation. He tends to bury his gift and grow lazy. He is ashamed of the little he has been given; he is also conscious of how little he can earn from it by trading. So that he simply buries his gift in the earth. People often say it is better to have none than to have little, but the Lord says it is better to have little than to have none. Please understand that the issue here is not over the amount given and received; rather, it is over the way the talent or gift is used. He who receives five talents has the responsibility for those five talents while he who receives two is responsible for those two. How discontented today's believers are towards the gift of God. If, before anyone will begin to serve, he looks to receive from God a gift such as a certain other brother or sister has, he looks in vain, for God will never give it to him.

Hence the emphasis of this parable is on the one who receives one talent. Though he cannot preach a great sermon and save several hundred people at one time, though he is unable to do such spectacular work, he still can do a little something for the Lord. Digging in the earth and burying the talent shows the lack of courage to do anything. May we be willing to do a little work if God is willing to give a little gift.

Do note, by the way, that the talent is not put in a chest in the attic but is buried in the earth. The earth can easily bury the gift of God. Intimacy with the world quickly buries God's talent in the earth so that the gift of God becomes inaccessible. How, for example, can a believer stand up before men and speak the truth if just beforehand he has uttered some coarse jest or some unclean words? He has lost his testimony. For this reason, let us stand firmly on our ground and exercise the gift which we have received. Do not be intimate with the world lest your gift be buried. Always remember that the flesh will make you despise the gift of God, and the world will cause you to lose the testimony of God.

"To trade" means to circulate or to be actively engaged in. May God make us channels of His blessings.

If we do not learn to exercise our gifts today, how can we render a positive account at the reckoning in the future? Most certainly will we be less likely to exercise gifts in the coming kingdom.

A comparison of the parable of the talents with the parable of the virgins tells us that the first stresses the importance of exercising the gifts of the Holy Spirit while the second stresses the importance of being filled with the Holy Spirit. Talent is for the Lord but oil is for oneself. All who are gifted by God are used by the Lord to build up His church, not to build up themselves. God never gives a gift which is only for self. (Even though speaking in tongues, for example, does build up a person, it is nevertheless for the church as well.) Hence when a person buries his gift, the Lord suffers loss. Oil is for life just as talent is for service. Having oil—that is to say, being filled with the Holy Spirit—enables one to use gifts wisely.

Ability alone is useless, because nothing can be accomplished if there is no capital, no talent, no gift. How believers need the gift of the Holy Spirit!

Gift must be accomplished by the fullness of the Holy Spirit. A talent or gift without oil is most dangerous. And this is precisely why the parable of the virgins precedes the parable of the talents. The church at Corinth was full of confusion because the Corinthian believers had an abundance of talents yet a scarcity of oil. Nevertheless oil without talent or gift may result in good life but no good works, even as talent or gift without oil produces good works but not a good life.

The parable of the virgins touches on rapture, but the parable of the talents speaks of the judgment seat of Christ and His kingdom. The condition for the rapture of the virgins is to be filled with oil—which is to say, to live according to the Holy Spirit. The condition for the servants to enjoy the joy of the kingdom is to trade with the talents—which means to serve the Lord faithfully. These two are closely linked.

As a matter of fact, work today is not meant to solve the matter of reward in the kingdom. Today's work simply prepares us for the position in the kingdom. Our works today can actually be likened to "kindergarten works"; but in the future our works will be greatly increased in both number and substance. Yet what we learn now will be something that can be used then.

Let us notice that the lord in the parable did not order his servants to trade; nevertheless, the good and faithful servants in the parable knew the mind of their lord. The same is true of the good and faithful servants of our Lord Jesus. But how sad that many of us frequently wait for people to ask us, even to appoint us, before we will exercise our gifts. And if otherwise, we will rather bury our talents than use them.

vv.19-23 The third part of this parable is the judgment of the first and second servants.

"After a long time"—The testing period must be long. It covers the entire period of the church (almost 2,000 years). It is very easy during such a long period to forget the Lord's charge. How apt we are to be zealous at the beginning, but as the time wears on we gradually grow cold—thus losing the first love. Yet it is only after a long period that the time of judgment arrives.

"The lord of those servants cometh, and maketh a reckoning with them"—The coming again of our Lord is a most certain fact. People may say the Lord is *delayed,* but they cannot mock and say that He is *not coming.* Even in the case of the evil servant, he can only say that the Lord tarries (see Matt. 24.48).

"Reckoning"—The failure of the church today is revealed in her ignorance that the Lord will come and settle accounts with His own. From the time we believe in the Lord, whatever we do or do not do will all await a time of reckoning. Reckoning here has nothing to do with salvation. Our walk (see 1 Cor. 3.10–15), speech, and even thoughts will all be presented at the judgment seat. Unlike the great white throne where judgment is meted out according to books, we give our own accounts at the judgment seat of Christ (see Rom. 14.12). If our faults are under the blood, they have already been judged and will therefore not be recalled. But if they are not repented of and have not been put under the blood, there will have to be an accounting of them. Accordingly, let us learn to judge ourselves. We will have to answer for everything which today has not been judged by the blood of Christ. God will prosecute all that is not under the blood. The grace and love of God are manifested in the blood of the Lamb, but on the other hand His righteousness and holiness are revealed at the judgment seat of Christ. He will not overlook our unholiness.

At the judgment seat of Christ, not only what was done will be judged but also what was not done will be too. That which was done blindly will be judged and that which was not done by quenching the Holy Spirit will also be judged.

Please notice the word "cometh" in verse 19 and the word "came" in verse 20. The Lord comes, but so also come the servants. They shall meet in the air (see 1 Thess. 4.17). The "cometh" in verse 19 refers to the coming of the Lord to the air, and the "came" in verse 20 points to the rapture of believers to the air.

"And he that received the five talents came and brought other five talents"—The other five talents are extra to the five talents originally received. At that time some people will appreciate the preciousness of earning another five talents as well as others will become anxious over *not* earning another five talents. Whether a person is or is not to receive a reward is not decided at the judgment seat; rather, it is determined today. The key to this matter is how one handles the God-given gift today. Hence believers should not despise the gift of the Holy Spirit, whether great or small. Earning is not done at the judgment seat; it is accomplished on earth now. Today if we hear the word of the Holy Spirit, let us not harden our hearts. Both the five talents given and five talents earned are brought to the Lord, thus indicating that works are for Him and not for ourselves. Stealing secretly from the Lord shows one to be an evil servant. We must instead give all the glory to God.

"Well done, good and faithful servant"—By reading verse 20 alone we might think that reward is dispensed on the basis of earning; but verse 21 clearly shows us that reward is according to being good and faithful. The five talent servant, the two talent servant, and the one talent servant can all be good and faithful.

"Good and faithful"—Not good Christians but good and

faithful servants. The extra five talents earned does not represent success, it instead represents the goodness and faithfulness of the servant. By outward appearance Stephen might have seemed to have been a failure, yet in spiritual reality he had done a good and faithful work. So if a cup of cold water is given for Christ's sake (this is faithfulness), it shall be rewarded. To be faithful means to do it for the Lord. For whom do we really work? Oftentimes we seek for success, not realizing that if success is not for the Lord it is but wood, hay, and stubble. The Lord looks for our faithfulness.

"Well done"—This is the Lord's commendation. We seek for the Lord's commendation only. The reason for the patient endurance of the saints is to receive a "Well done" from the Lord. The world's praise has no value whatsoever because it is most inaccurate, since it cannot discern in us what is really good or bad.

"Thou hast been faithful over a few things"—The "few things" here refer to the works done today. Even the works done with five talents are deemed but a few things when compared with what will be done in the kingdom.

"I will set thee over many things"—The "many things" point to the things to be done in the kingdom. How often we mistakenly consider the things of *today* as exceedingly great.

The church is like a school in which we learn. After graduation we are sent to the kingdom to practice what we have learned. This is why we may foretaste the powers of the age to come (Heb. 6.5).

"Enter thou into the joy of the lord"—See also Hebrews 12 which says: "Looking unto Jesus the author and perfecter of our faith, who for the joy that was set before him endured the cross, despising the shame, and hath sat down at the right hand of the throne of God" (v.2). Why is "joy" mentioned but not "kingdom"? Because the recompense of faithfulness is an inward satisfaction, not an outward position. The greatest reward is to rejoice with the Lord. This exceeds kingdom, glory, and position.

For we are satisfied with just the Lord himself.

"Set thee over"—This is a matter of authority. Today is the time to be faithful; the future will be the time to reign. He who is anxious to rule today must be the evil servant of Matthew 24. God cannot give authority to one who loves to rule; He gives authority only to the obedient.

Yes indeed, for us to reign does happen in the kingdom. We shall rejoice on the one hand and reign on the other. The Lord will give joy to compensate for sufferings on earth, and authority He will give to recompense for loss incurred in the world. All who are faithful must be willing to suffer loss. We cannot be the rich man in life and Lazarus in death.

vv.22–23 The words spoken to the servant with the two talents are exactly the same as the words spoken to the servant with five talents. Why are they repeated? To show that what the Lord looks for is neither success nor amount but faithfulness. What He requires of the five talents is five more talents and what He requires of the two talents is two more talents. The amount of gift has nothing to do with reward. Faithful service is what really counts. Trading in gift will never incur loss. What the Lord holds us responsible for is faithfulness. Do not admire the great gift that another has and despise the little gift you have. Gift—whether great or small—is the prerogative of the Giver, the Lord himself.

Of him who is given more, more is required. Of him who is given less, less is required. The Lord rewards the five talent servant not because he has gained five talents more, but because he is faithful. According to the calculation of the world, the difference between the first and the second servants at the time of reckoning amounts to six talents. But according to spiritual arithmetic, five beyond five and two beyond two are equal. Each and every believer may receive reward. Though we do not have gifts comparable to Paul's, yet we may receive the same reward because the opportunity for faithful service is the same.

The servant with the two talents should give us great consolation. We may have less gift, but our faithfulness must not be behind that of anybody else.

vv.24–30 We now come to the fourth and final part of the parable of the talents—the judgment of the third servant with one talent.

v.24 Is the one who receives but one talent saved? Of course he is. The reasons are as follows:

(1) If this man is not saved, then it means that all the saved will be rewarded.

(2) If this man is not saved, it is as if the Lord were telling us that however a Christian may fail he will not be disciplined.

(3) This man is the Lord's own servant, having been redeemed through His blood; for the Lord will not choose anyone who is unsaved to be His "servant"—the Holy Spirit, incidentally, never uses incorrect terminology.

(4) How can the Lord give His goods to an unsaved person?

(5) When he is sentenced this one talent person is still called a "servant" by the Lord: an "unprofitable" one, yes—but not a false servant.

(6) He is judged for his works and not judged for believing or not believing. If he is not saved, how can the Lord ever judge him for works? He should be judged for despising the precious blood. Moreover, if earning another talent will *save,* then salvation will not be by faith.

(7) With whom is he judged? He is judged together with the saved who receive reward. Will the unsaved be judged with the saved? Before the judgment seat of Christ only the saved are going to be judged.

(8) If the person is unsaved, can the Lord ever blame him for unfaithfulness, for not trading with the gift? Can, for example, the Lord be unhappy with the unsaved for not preaching the gospel? He would much rather not have him preaching the gospel.

(9) At the coming of the Lord, His servants shall come to Him, which means that they shall be raptured to the air. Can an unsaved person be raptured?

(10) The Lord has not ordered the servant to be brought in; instead the servant comes himself because he is the Lord's. An unsaved soul will not dare to see the Lord; he would rather summon the rocks to fall upon him in order to hide himself from the face of God and of the Lamb. Yet we must notice that this servant has not lost even the one talent which the Lord gave him: he ate his own food and carefully kept the talent for the Lord. He thinks he has done well and has done nothing wrong.

(11) This parable agrees with the one in Luke 19.11–27 where the wicked servant (saved, v.22) and the unsaved ("these mine enemies"—v.27) are clearly distinguished and definitely not to be mixed up.

Nonetheless, people will ask why the evil servant is cast into outer darkness. Is not this hell? they ask. Yet if it is hell, then it should be termed the lake of fire which will appear only *after* the millennium. Yet this parable speaks of what is to take place *before* the millennium.

vv.24–25 No one really dares to utter these words; the Lord is only revealing here what is in the heart of man.

"Hard" means strict. This makes the servant afraid. His failure lies in not really knowing the Lord, not knowing His grace. He imagines that the Lord is overly strict; and thus he obviously is still under the fear of Mt. Sinai (see Ex. 20.18–21). Are we not now in the dispensation of Grace and not of Law? We therefore need not be afraid. The Lord is responsible for our success; we are only responsible for being faithful.

v.26 If our Lord reaps where he sowed not and gathers where He scattered not (and yet we know He *has* actually sown and scattered) He will not require something from us. At the judgment seat, there is no ground for argument. This servant's poor showing is attributed in the parable entirely to his laziness. D. L. Moody once said that it is hard for a lazy person to be saved. We can at least say here that no lazy person will receive a reward. Let us not allow our gift to remain idle because it is small. Let us not wait for a more convenient or more promising time to serve.

v.27 "Thou oughtest therefore to have put my money to the bankers"—Gift may be distributed to others for trading. We should contact one or more people. We should never bury the gift so as not to pass it on to another's hand. However little our gift may be, it must not go unused. Whether or not we succeed is not, as we have said, our responsibility; but why not at least *put it to use* to save one soul, help one life, or comfort one person? How very sad if we have not led anyone to Christ.

v.28 "Take ye away therefore the talent from him, and give it unto him that hath the ten talents"—This third servant receives double punishment—a taking away from him and a casting him out, just as the faithful servants had received a double reward —joy and authority. And incidentally, the giving of the one talent to the servant with the ten talents proves that the Lord is not "a hard man" since He keeps nothing for himself.

v.29 This is a principle: He who has today shall have abundance in the future. He will be elevated to rule over many things. In the kingdom, gifts will be used even more extensively than today. But he who does not have today will not have in the future; for all who despise gifts now will have their gifts taken away then.

v.30 "And cast ye out the unprofitable servant into the outer darkness"—This is the second punishment. Outer darkness is a relative, not an absolute, term. In order to understand this word "outer" we need first of all to know where the Lord will speak these words. As we have noted earlier, the Lord will come to the air, to where as well His saints are to be raptured. There they appear before His judgment seat where these words are spoken. And hence the "outer" spoken of here is "outer" in relation to the air. Never in the Scriptures, not even once, is hell called outer darkness. As a matter of fact, hell is not dark but has about it the element of fire! Let us see that when the Lord comes, He shall be surrounded by darkness, although there shall be glory within (see Ps. 18.9–11). And hence the "outer" mentioned in the parable is in relation to this darkness that shrouds the darkness of the Lord's glory at His coming.

"Weeping"—This term has reference to a repentance on the part of this servant as to his lost opportunity in using the talent properly.

"Gnashing of teeth"—Such a servant will murmur *against himself* for the loss incurred; for he loses out in the matter of joy and authority.

Three elements are closely related: the blood, the cross, and the judgment seat. Although there are no Bible verses plainly connecting these three, both life and experience bear witness to this undoubted link. The cross of Christ stands at the center of the three. Now whereas the judgment seat is yet to come, the blood and the cross have already been accomplished. Whatever the blood and the cross miss (that is, whatever sin or failure will not have been dealt with throughout our lives by the blood and the cross), will not be missed at the judgment seat. What the cross may have missed in our lives ought at least to have passed through the blood (in terms of forgiveness). If a believer anticipates nothing but grace at the judgment seat, then everything will have needed first to have passed through the blood and the cross. The blood of Christ is for washing and redeeming; it is something much more objective to us. The cross, on the other hand, is for crucifying death, sin, the old man, the world, and the old creation. To us this is far more subjective.

Our personal failures may affect two sides: God and self. If we sin and our fellowship with God is interrupted, we may be cleansed again and again by the blood and thus have our fellowship repeatedly restored. The blood deals with sins while the cross deals with the power of sin. Through the blood sins are forgiven, but the blood cannot give a guarantee to us never to sin again—nay, not even never to sin the *same* sin again. And hence the flesh and the world (the power centers of sin) must be dealt with by the cross. The blood forgives, but only the cross can deliver.

All failures and sins throughout our lives which have passed under the blood and been dealt with on the cross will not be judged at the judgment seat. Indeed, at this seat the Lord will only judge our undealt idle words, thoughts, and works. As penetrating as the light of the judgment seat may be, it can never uncover sins which are already under the blood. How then do we deal, for example, with the tongue which often delights to indulge in idle words? We need the cross. And the same is true with our unprofitable thoughts and works. They too need the cross. Let us therefore accept the cross by faith, reckon that this old man was crucified on the cross, and then the judgment seat can never search out for judgment those things in our lives that have already been dealt with by the cross.

Upon being cleansed by the blood with respect to any particular sin or failure, we must turn immediately to the cross; otherwise, there is the possibility of our sinning again and thus we shall have to be judged at the judgment seat.

Jesus' End-Time Prophecy, Part Three:
Concerning the Gentiles, 25.31–46

THE PARABLE OF THE SHEEP AND THE GOATS

This parable applies to the Gentile nations. According to the Scriptures the inhabited world is divided into three classes of people: the Jews, the church, and the nations. Both the Jews and the church have already been touched upon in chapters 24 and 25. Now in this remaining passage of chapter 25, Jesus' prophecy as to what will happen to the nations at the end time has been recorded.

However, two erroneous interpretations of this parable have been set forward. One of these propounds a universal judgment in the future; and the other has this parable signifying the judgment of the Christian. Let us examine each of them closely, making a number of observations about each interpretation.

(1) Universal judgment

(a) If the meaning of this parable has reference to a future universal judgment, such judgment must obviously include the Jews, the church, and the nations, both the living and the dead. In the first place, holding a view of there being one grand universal judgment is a serious misconception among some in the church today. For the Bible never teaches the concept of a universal judgment. On the contrary, its pages teach that judgment is dispensed severally—to the church, to the Jews, and also to the nations. Unfortunately, people use this parable as the basis for the idea that one cannot know for sure his salvation until the time of the judgment seat. Consequently, many hope that there will yet be opportunity for people to be saved after death. And thus the church today becomes a haven for many people who can only *hope* for salvation. For if the teaching of a universal judgment is true, then we do indeed have no way of knowing with any degree of certainty our salvation today.

(b) *Who* in this parable are the ones to be judged? It tells us that it is to be "all the nations" (v.32). This word "nations" is the same as is translated "the Gentiles" in Matthew 4.15; 6.32; 10.5,18; 12.18; and 20.19,25. It is a Greek word which in its meaning includes all the Gentiles.

(c) *When* is to be the judgment that is spoken of here in this parable? We are told by the Lord that it will be *before* the millennial kingdom (see v.34). Revelation 20.11–15 tells us that there will be the judgment of the great white throne *after* the millennium. And thus by these facts we know that no such concept as a universal judgment can be true.

(d) *Where* is the judgment in this parable held? The Son of man, we are told, shall sit on the throne of His glory. In Revelation 3.21 we see two thrones—the Father's and the Son's. Today our Lord sits on His Father's throne. In the future, though, He will sit on His own throne. The throne here in Matthew 25.31 is His own throne, that is to say, His throne *on earth* in the kingdom; for how can the nations be separated if they are in the air and not on earth, since it is only on earth that national boundaries exist? If they are in the air, then it would mean that the judged must be raptured—which would further mean that a part of the raptured are unsaved, a circumstance which we know cannot be true.

(e) The ones to be judged in this parable are living, none of them is dead. The Scriptures reveal that resurrection occurs twice, and these two are separated in time by a thousand years. Now we know that in the first resurrection, there is none unsaved. Yet here in the parable the goats are condemned to eternal fire, and hence this parable cannot be speaking of the first resurrection and therefore has nothing to do with Christians.

(f) At the time alluded to in this parable, Satan has not yet been cast into the lake of fire; for the word "prepared" in verse 41 proves that this action has not yet been taken. If the judgment here were the same as that of the great white throne, Satan would at this time now be cast into the lake of fire.

(g) The appellation "the Son of man" is a name used in connection with the kingdom. After the millennium, the Son "will deliver up the kingdom to God, even the Father" (1 Cor. 15.24).

(h) Prophecy must be interpreted with other prophecies. And by doing so, we shall easily see that the Bible speaks of several judgments.

(2) Church judgment. This parable of the sheep and the goats does not allude to a judgment of the church. People usually think of sheep as only referring to Christians (see John 10), but such is not the case here, for the following reasons:

(a) As we have seen, the "nations" mean the Gentiles.

(b) These people (both the sheep and the goats) have never known the Lord.

(c) They are judged not according to Mosaic law, nor according to faith, but according to works alone—thus distinguishing them from the Jews and the church.

(d) The church is chosen *before* the foundation of the world (see Eph. 1.4), while these sheep in the parable are chosen *from* the foundation of the world (Matt. 25.34).

(e) These sheep showed kindness to the least of the brethren of the Lord (see Matt. 25.40) without realizing they had done it to the Lord. If these were Christians, how could they fail to know? For surely, Christians deal kindly with the least of the Lord's brethren for the sake of the Lord himself; and even the Jews give alms for the sake of Jehovah; yet these people are totally ignorant. The church, which includes the lazy servant as well as the wicked servant (see Matt. 25.24 and 24.48), certainly knows the Lord.

(f) Our judgment as Christians is carried on in the air, not on the earth.

(g) The judgment in this parable is no related to the first resurrection because these people (both the sheep and the goats) are the unsaved.

(h) The judgment in view here results in either eternal life or eternal death, but believers have already had this matter in their lives settled.

(i) In the sight of God the saved and the unsaved are never mixed together.

(j) The least of the brethren (see Matt. 25.40) must of necessity be those who are distinct from the goats and the sheep. They are the believers who have already passed through judgment. They cannot be the Jews,* for the Lord has cut asunder such a relationship with the Jews (Matt. 12.46–50). And if the sheep are Christians, they are really mixed up with the goats.

(k) Christians well know that they must love God's children, but these people have no such knowledge.

(l) If these sheep represent Christians, then Christians are saved not by faith but by showing kindness to the least of the brethren.

(m) If people are saved by distributing food, showing hospitality, sending clothes, and visiting the sick and the imprisoned, then the least of the brethren would themselves have no chance to be saved: for how can the imprisoned perform such good deeds?

The parable of the sheep and the goats may be divided into four parts: (1) the gathering of the sheep and the goats (vv. 31–33); (2) the conversation with the sheep (vv.34–40); (3) the conversation with the goats (vv.41–45); and (4) the consequence (v.46).

vv.31–33 These verses form the first part of the parable—the gathering of the sheep and the goats.

v.31 "The Son of man"—All the names of the Lord given in chapter 25 are full of meaning: the name of bridegroom is significantly related to the virgins, the name of lord is characteristically related to the servants, and the name of the Son of man is appropriately related to the nations (as well as to the kingdom — see below). As the Son of man, the Lord Jesus has a relationship with all mankind in general. *Strictly* speaking, the passage in verses 31–46 of Matthew 25 is really no parable, for it does not begin with such words as "like" or "as" but is instead a rather

---

*But see the footnote on this at 25.34–40 (more specifically at vv.35–36) below.—*Translator*

factual account. The Son of man has the power to judge. As the Son of God the Lord raises people from the dead, and this is His relationship to the church; as the Son of man He executes judgment, and this is the Lord's relationship to the Gentiles (see John 5.25,27). The Son of man is also related to the kingdom (see Dan. 7.13–14). The Lord shall come to establish His kingdom, but He first must judge the world. Only those who pass through the judgment successfully are qualified to be people in the kingdom. Are we not to reign as kings with Christ? How then can we reign if there are no people? Where is there a kingdom which has no people?

"Shall come in his glory, and all the angels with him"—The glory of the Lord is manifold: the glory of the Godhead, His moral glory, the glory of being man, and the glory which God gives Him (Phil. 2.9–11). Here, it is His glory as the exalted Man. He receives this glory as the result of His becoming obedient even to death. The kingdom is God's reward to Him. This glory is therefore not His eternal glory which He only shares with His Father in eternity.

The scene here is similar to that of Matthew 24.30. And hence this judgment follows closely that of Matthew 24.30.

"All the angels with him"—This is in order to gather all the nations. These Gentiles have not followed the Antichrist in war. For the Gentiles who follow the Antichrist will all be slain by the sharp sword which proceeds out of the mouth of Christ (see Rev. 19.21). Hence we see that these people neither believe in the Lord nor follow the Antichrist.

"Then shall he sit on the throne of his glory"—Today it is the mercy seat on which the Lord sits and where we can receive seasonable helps (Heb. 4.16). But in that day it will be the throne of glory which is most holy and where judgment will be quickly executed: glory $\longrightarrow$ holy $\longrightarrow$ righteous $\longrightarrow$ judgment.

This throne is set on earth at Jerusalem. The throne of God is now in heaven (Matt. 25.31), and today the Son sits on His

Father's throne (Rev. 3.20). How do we know that this throne will be set in Jerusalem? The proofs are found in Psalm 122.3,5 and Luke 1.32–33. The throne of David is set in Jerusalem and we know that the throne of Christ is the throne of David. His glorious throne is already mentioned in Matthew 19.28.

The first "glory" in verse 31 is the glory with which He comes, while the second "glory" in the verse is that which shall continue on.

v.32 The phrase "all the nations" refers, as we have said, to all the Gentiles. Who are these Gentiles who are gathered? They are those who are still alive and who are to be judged. Let us understand that there are two classes of Gentiles: one class will be slain by the sharp sword which proceeds out of the mouth of the Lord because they follow the Antichrist; the other class, which will be the majority of the Gentiles, are those who do not follow the Antichrist. The judgment which comes upon those Gentiles who follow the Antichrist is described in Joel 3.12, Micah 4.11–13, Zephaniah 3.8, Zechariah 12.3, and Revelation 16.14 and 19.19,21. They are instigated by the Antichrist to go out and destroy the Jews, but they themselves shall be destroyed by the appearing of the Lord.

"Separate them one from another"—This action is likened to a shepherd who separates the sheep from the goats. This statement injects a little parable into this passage before us. From the Scriptures we can discern that the Lord seems to have three distinct kinds of sheep: (1) the believers in the church (see John 10); (2) the Jews (see Ps. 80.1, Jer. 23.1–4 and 31.10); and (3) the nations or Gentiles (see Ez. 34.20–22 and Ps. 100.1–3). And thus, sheep cannot be applied exclusively to Christians.

There is absolutely no possibility to perform this separation in heaven or in hell. Separation is only possible on earth.

First separate, then judge. It is not to be as n the case of the great white throne (where it will be first the books and then the execution), for to be precise it is a judgment not according to works but according to nature: because the sheep act naturally as sheep while the goats act naturally as goats.

v.33 "On his right side"—This phrase signifies the position of glory, since we know that the Lord ascended to the right side of the Father after He was glorified.

vv.34–40 This second part of the parable covers the conversation with the sheep.

"Then shall the King say unto them on his right hand"— "King" is injected as a new title here. The Lord is also King to the Gentiles. To the church He is her head as well as her bridegroom.

"Ye blessed of my Father"—It says "my" Father here and not "our" Father. The Bible rarely says "our Father"; but the Lord did say on one occasion, "my Father and your Father" (John 20.17). By the Lord only saying *"my* Father" in the parable here, it indicates that these people have no relationship with Him, thus proving that they are not Christians. Since they do not know the Lord, He obviously cannot say "our Father" or "your Father" as He had done elsewhere when speaking to those who know Him.

"Blessed"—This blessing is earthly ("inherit the kingdom"). The church, on the other hand, receives heavenly blessing.

In the future kingdom of the heavens, there will be three distinct realms: (a) the realm of earthly blessings such as God originally gave to Adam in having dominion over all things, with the earth yielding abundantly for man. These blessings which will be in the earthly kingdom were lost after man had fallen. Hence the Lord says, "from the foundation of the world" (v.34c). Today we are afraid of beasts lest they hurt us, but in that day there will be no need for such fear. (b) The kingdom of the Jews. Though its realm will be Canaan land or Palestine, yet its sphere of influence will be far-reaching. See Genesis 17: "She shall be a mother of nations; kings of people shall be of her" (v.16); Isaiah 60· "That nation and kingdom that will not serve thee shall perish; yea, those nations shall be utterly wasted" (v.12); and Deuteronomy 15: "Jehovah thy God will bless thee, as he promised thee: and thou shalt lend unto many nations, but thou shalt not borrow; and thou shalt rule over many nations, but they shall not rule over thee" (v.6). (c) The spiritual realm of the kingdom. See 1 Corinthians 15: "Now this I say, brethren, that flesh and blood cannot inherit the kingdom of God; neither doth corruption inherit incorruption. Behold, I tell you a mystery: we all shall not sleep, but we shall all be changed, . . . and the dead shall be raised incorruptible, and we shall be changed" (vv.50–52); and Romans 8: "If children, then heirs; heirs of God, and joint-heirs with Christ" (v.17). The kingdom in view in Matthew 25.34 points to that kingdom realm wherein neither asp nor lion will hurt anybody and into which the parable's first group of people (the sheep) is placed.

vv.35–36 Herein lies the difference between the sheep and the goats: Why is it that the sheep could "inherit the kingdom"? Because they distributed food, sent clothing, provided hospitality, and visited the sick and the jailed. Believers will be judged before the judgment seat of Christ according to faithfulness; the Jews will be judged as to whether or not they worship the beast; and the nations at the very end will be judged at the great white throne according to the book of life and the books. But the nations here are to be judged differently from the nations at the very end of this old heaven and earth. Since the people of these nations *are still alive* at the appearing of the Lord on earth, they will be judged according to their work, that is to say, according to how they treat the least of the brethren of the Lord (see v.40).

Who are the least of the brethren of the Lord? Our Lord has three distinct kinds of brethren: (1) the Jews, He and they being of the same race (see Acts 7.23–26, Rom. 9.3, and Deut. 17.15); (2) His own brethren according to flesh (see Matt. 12.46–48 and 13.55); and (3) the believers who are His brethren (see

Matt. 12.48–50). The least of the Lord's brethren spoken of in Matthew 25.40 do not refer to the first or second kinds (the Jews), since by the time of Matthew 12 the Lord had already deliberately severed such relationships.* Consequently, they must refer to those believers who shall have to pass through the Great Tribulation.* Since believers are joined to the Lord as one (1 Cor. 6.17), then whatever is done to them is done also to the Lord.

The overcomers have been raptured but the majority of believers are left to go through the Great Tribulation. They will be afflicted and persecuted. The sheep in this parable will have heard the eternal good tidings proclaimed by an angel warning people to "fear God, and give him glory; for the hour of his judgment is come: and worship him that made the heaven and the earth and sea and fountains of waters" (Rev. 14.6–7). They will be those who do not follow the crowd in persecuting the Christians, neither will they worship idols. These sheep are those who shall fear God and treat believers kindly. It will not be easy to perform these kind deeds during the Great Tribulation.

Since the judgment is to be based on deeds done in the flesh and not on spiritual things, these people cannot be Christians.

Please note finally that these righteous ones in the parable are astonished at what the Lord says, and the Lord accepts their astonishment, because He well knows that they have not done all these things for the sake of the Lord: they indeed are not Christians.

vv.41–45 This third part deals with the Lord's conversation with the goats. These wicked ones are condemned because

---

*In Mr. Nee's study on the book of Revelation entitled *"Come, Lord Jesus"* (New York, Christian Fellowship Publishers, 1976), the author puts forth the view on page 83 that the little brother spoken of in Matthew 25.40 ("one of these my brethren, even these least") points to the Jews or those Christians who yet remain on the earth. It is therefore an interpretation which is open to discussion.—*Translator*

they have not treated the Christians well during the Great Tribulation.

v.46 This is the fourth and final part: the consequence. The wicked shall go into eternal punishment while the righteous shall enter eternal life. Notice that the righteous enter "into" eternal life, they do not "have" eternal life. Believers enter in *with* life, but the righteous enter *into* life. The believers gain the kingdom because they are chosen by the Father *before* the foundation of the earth, whereas the righteous enter into the kindgom which God has promised Adam *from* the foundation of the earth.

The righteous regain the position of Adam. The Old Testament speaks of how the righteous shall inherit the earth (Ps. 37.10–11,22,26–29,34; and Gen. 27.28).

What is comforting most is the fact that even though believers may pass through the Great Tribulation, the Lord yet remembers them by sending an angel to proclaim the eternal good tidings.

The general lessons: (1) Deal kindly with suffering brethren. Do not be like Job's friends, but help those who suffer. And (2) The Lord is one with the believers. Though they may be put in jail, the Lord is still with them.

TITLES YOU
WILL WANT TO HAVE

By Watchman Nee

Basic Lesson Series
Volume 1 – A Living Sacrifice
Volume 2 – The Good Confession
Volume 3 – Assembling Together
Volume 4- Not I, But Christ
Volume 5 – Do All to the Glory of God
Volume 6 – Love One Another

The Church and the Work
Volume 1 – Assembly Life
Volume 2 – Rethinking the Work
Volume 3 – Church Affairs
Revive Thy Work
The Word of the Cross
The Communion of the Holy Spirit
The Finest of the Wheat – Volume 1
The Finest of the Wheat – Volume 2
Take Heed
Worship God
Interpreting Matthew
The Character of God's Workman
Gleanings in the Fields of Boaz
The Spirit of the Gospel
The life That Wins
From Glory to Glory
The Spirit of Judgment
From Faith to Faith
Back to the Cross
The Lord My Portion
Aids to "Revelation"
Grace for Grace
The Better Covenant
A Balanced Christian Life
The Mystery of Creation

The Messenger of the Cross
Full of Grace and Truth – Volume 1
Full of Grace and Truth – Volume 2
The Spirit of Wisdom and Revelation
Whom Shall I Send?
The Testimony of God
The Salvation of the Soul
The King and the Kingdom of Heaven
The Body of Christ: A Reality
Let Us Pray
God's Plan and the Overcomers
The Glory of His Life
"Come, Lord Jesus"
Practical Issues of This Life
Gospel Dialogue
God's Work
Ye Search the Scriptures
The Prayer Ministry of the Church
Christ the Sum of All Spiritual Things
Spiritual Knowledge
The Latent Power of the Soul
The Ministry of God's Word
Spiritual Reality or Obsession
The Spiritual Man
The Release of The Spirit
Spiritual Authority

By Stephen Kaung

Discipled to Christ
The Splendor of His Ways
Seeing the Lord's End in Job
The Songs of Degrees
Meditations on Fifteen Psalms

ORDER FROM:

Christian Fellowship Publishers, Inc.
11515 Allecingie Parkway
Richmond, Virginia 23235